MOUNTAIN MAN

Karl Bodmer (1809–1893). *Herds of Bisons and Elks on the Upper Missouri.* Aquatint and etching, ca. 1840–1844. *Courtesy of the Amon Carter Museum of American Art, Fort Worth, Texas. 1965.169.65.*

MOUNTAIN MAN

John Colter,
the Lewis & Clark Expedition,
and the Call of the American West

David Weston Marshall

THE COUNTRYMAN PRESS
A division of W. W. Norton & Company
Independent Publishers Since 1923

Manufacturing by LSC Communications, Harrisonburg
Book design by Lovedog Studio
Production manager: Devon Zahn

The Countryman Press
www.countrymanpress.com

A division of W. W. Norton & Company
500 Fifth Avenue, New York, NY 10110
www.wwnorton.com

978-1-68268-048-3

1 2 3 4 5 6 7 8 9 0

for Vicki

CONTENTS

PREFACE

In 1804, John Colter set out with Meriwether Lewis and William Clark on the first US expedition to traverse the North American continent. During the twenty-eight-month ordeal, Colter served as a hunter and scout, and honed his survival skills on the western frontier. As the expedition returned and his companions pushed eagerly homeward, he chose to remain in the northern plains and Rocky Mountains. Alone and on foot, Colter discovered unexplored regions, including the majestic Tetons and Yellowstone country.

As he trekked through dangerous and unfamiliar territory, he became a trusted friend to several Indian nations and a foe to another. Some tribes taught him native lore and helped him survive, while a rival tribe declared him a mortal enemy. The tales of his daring adventures and chilling escapes remain unsurpassed.

Colter was the first of the mountain men, acclaimed by the frontiersmen of his time as a living hero. After his death, he became a legend to the explorers, trappers, cavalrymen, and cowboys who followed in his wake. He was the prototype of the ideal Westerner—ruggedly independent, self-sufficient, and quietly confident in his abilities. Colter grabbed the American imagination in his own time and maintains his hold to this day.

AUTHOR'S NOTE

HISTORY IS A STORY—A NARRATIVE INTERPRETATION
of the past built upon a collection of verifiable facts. Some historical studies contain a substantial core of hard facts. Others have
fewer at their disposal and rely more on interpretation. The story of
John Colter fits the latter description. Information on the subject
is sparse, and Colter himself left no written records.

Accounts of his life exist in a handful of primary documents
bequeathed to us by those who knew him. These include the journals of the Corps of Discovery (the Lewis and Clark Expedition);
the writings of Thomas James, John Bradbury, Doctor Thomas,
and Henry Brackenridge; and a map drawn by William Clark that
marks Colter's route of 1807–8. Secondary writings based on these
accounts have appeared since Colter's time. Some have come from
authors of caliber like Washington Irving. Beyond these sources,
many aspects of Colter's life may be surmised from information
left by men like him who scouted and explored, trapped and traded,
traveled and survived in the same wilderness in the same era. These
primary and secondary accounts are liberally quoted in the follow-

ing text in order to provide the reader with original documentation and an authentic feel for frontier thought and expression.

In addition to written sources, information can be gained by retracing Colter's steps—seeing what he saw, hearing what he heard, and experiencing firsthand how he and his contemporaries survived in the wilderness—how they pitched a shelter, built a fire, followed a trail, and forded a stream. Chapter Four offers an interpretation of Colter's 1807–8 winter trek based on this kind of careful, on-site investigation of the entire route, in collaboration with cited historical, archaeological, and cartographic evidence.

Reconstructing Colter's movements based partially upon secondary evidence is acceptable in this context. Like scientific theory, such an endeavor involves using informed interpretation to prompt further investigation. The result is an accumulation of knowledge on the subject and a steady movement toward verification. In this case, it is important to refrain from claiming the final word on the subject. Further thought and study are encouraged. Substantial endnotes are provided for this purpose.

In addition to firsthand and secondary evidence, other information exists—apocryphal information that envelops every legendary person like a fog, obscuring the story. This makes the task of creating a valid interpretation all the more difficult—and important. While searching for every available scrap of useful information, the researcher must dismiss many sources. Those sources deemed valid and pertinent to the study of John Colter appear in Works Cited.

MOUNTAIN MAN

Colter's Travels, 1804–1808

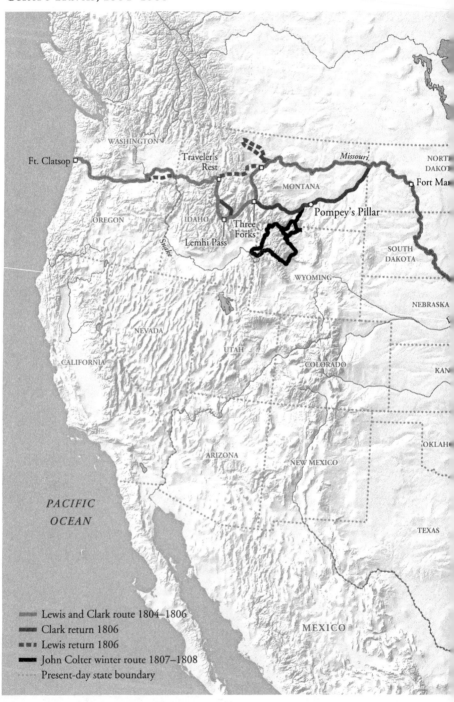

PACIFIC
OCEAN

Ft. Clatsop
WASHINGTON
Traveler's Rest
OREGON
IDAHO
Three Forks
Lemhi Pass
Snake
MONTANA
Missouri
NORTH DAKOTA
Fort Mar
Pompey's Pillar
SOUTH DAKOTA
WYOMING
NEBRASKA
NEVADA
UTAH
COLORADO
CALIFORNIA
KAN
ARIZONA
NEW MEXICO
OKLAH
TEXAS
MEXICO

    Lewis and Clark route 1804–1806
    Clark return 1806
    Lewis return 1806
    John Colter winter route 1807–1808
    Present-day state boundary

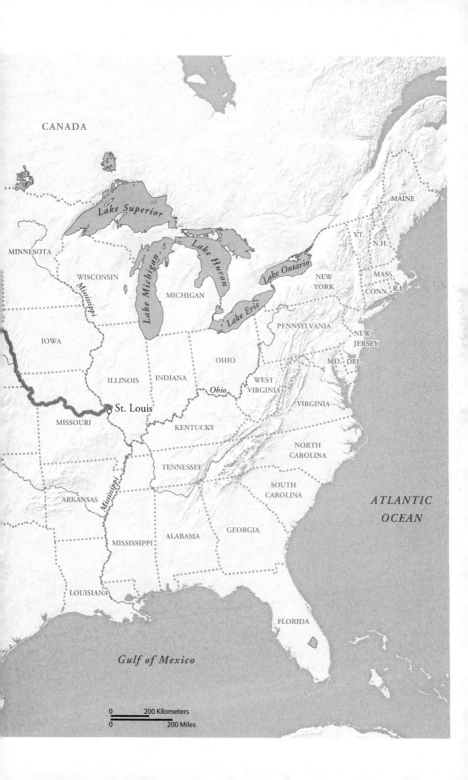

Colter's Winter Trek, 1807–1808

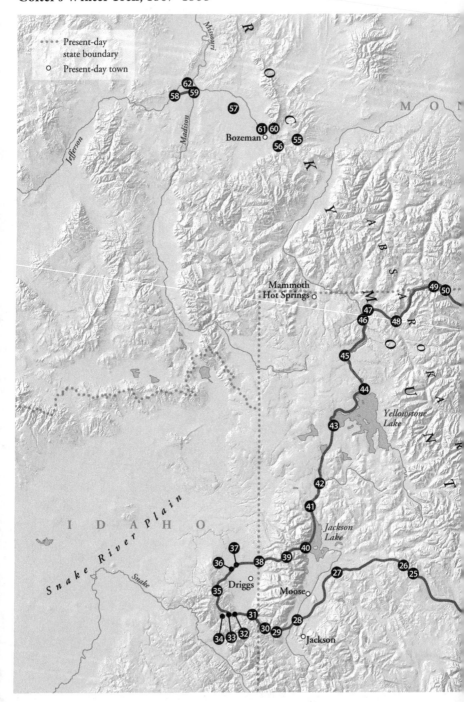

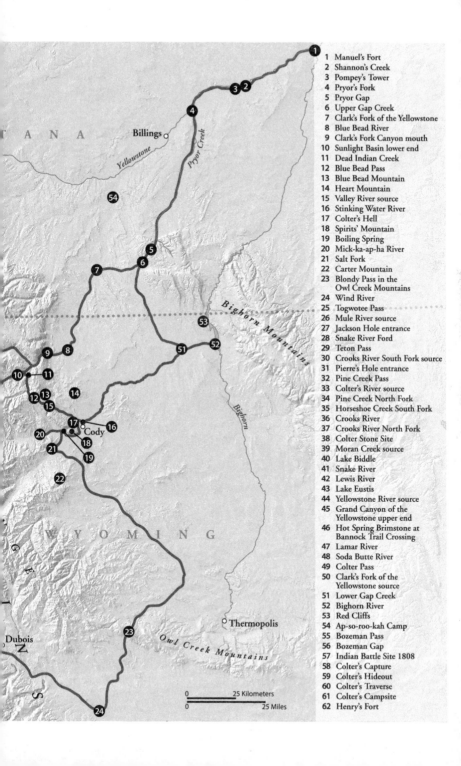

1   Manuel's Fort
2   Shannon's Creek
3   Pompey's Tower
4   Pryor's Fork
5   Pryor Gap
6   Upper Gap Creek
7   Clark's Fork of the Yellowstone
8   Blue Bead River
9   Clark's Fork Canyon mouth
10   Sunlight Basin lower end
11   Dead Indian Creek
12   Blue Bead Pass
13   Blue Bead Mountain
14   Heart Mountain
15   Valley River source
16   Stinking Water River
17   Colter's Hell
18   Spirits' Mountain
19   Boiling Spring
20   Mick-ka-ap-ha River
21   Salt Fork
22   Carter Mountain
23   Blondy Pass in the
        Owl Creek Mountains
24   Wind River
25   Togwotee Pass
26   Mule River source
27   Jackson Hole entrance
28   Snake River Ford
29   Teton Pass
30   Crooks River South Fork source
31   Pierre's Hole entrance
32   Pine Creek Pass
33   Colter's River source
34   Pine Creek North Fork
35   Horseshoe Creek South Fork
36   Crooks River
37   Crooks River North Fork
38   Colter Stone Site
39   Moran Creek source
40   Lake Biddle
41   Snake River
42   Lewis River
43   Lake Eustis
44   Yellowstone River source
45   Grand Canyon of the
        Yellowstone upper end
46   Hot Spring Brimstone at
        Bannock Trail Crossing
47   Lamar River
48   Soda Butte River
49   Colter Pass
50   Clark's Fork of the
        Yellowstone source
51   Lower Gap Creek
52   Bighorn River
53   Red Cliffs
54   Ap-so-roo-kah Camp
55   Bozeman Pass
56   Bozeman Gap
57   Indian Battle Site 1808
58   Colter's Capture
59   Colter's Hideout
60   Colter's Traverse
61   Colter's Campsite
62   Henry's Fort

Chapter One

DISCOVERY

THE MISSOURI RIVER MEANDERS THREE THOUSAND miles across the interior of North America. It begins as snowmelt in the lofty peaks of the Rocky Mountains and trickles into rivulets that converge to form the river. From there, the Missouri follows its ancient path through arid foothills and windswept prairies.

As the river flows eastward, the climate grows wetter and other streams join the course. At last it enters dark green stretches of humid forest. In the midst of this riparian lushness, only seventy-six miles from the end of its course, the Missouri passes a shady bluff on the south bank, upstream from a tiny village called La Charette.[1]

Before settlement arrived, nature had dominion over the surrounding woodlands. Wildlife ruled the forest floor and birds abounded in the leafy canopy. Interruptions to the serenity came only from an occasional clap of thunder or crash of a falling tree.

On an overcast day in May 1804, a strange sound rose from below the bluff. A party of men rounded the bend, struggling and cursing their way upstream against a current made heavy by snowmelt and spring showers—and made treacherous by driftwood and snags. They groaned aloud in English and French as they tugged on keelboat towlines and paddled their pirogues upriver.

These frontiersmen and voyageurs understood the contrary habits of waterways. They had received excellent educations along the river roads of the East. They could read ripples and rapids. They recognized woodland plants and animals. They knew how to hunt them for sustenance and shelter, and they kept a keen eye on the abundance around them.[2]

One man among them observed the land with more than passing interest. In the thick timbers and fertile bottomlands he saw a potential home. His companions called him Colter. Formal records gave his first name as John. Tradition says he was born about 1774 in the Shenandoah Valley of Virginia.[3]

Britain controlled the colonies then and prohibited settlement westward. But the frontier families, with their restless ways, felt confined by a boundary line impulsively scrawled on a map. Many chose to ignore the rules of a distant, disinterested monarch.

Some followed a man named Daniel Boone across the line to blaze the Wilderness Road. They hacked a route from the Holston River through Cumberland Gap to the Kentucky River to link those waterways. On the western end, on April 6, 1775, they began to chop stockade posts from the surrounding forest. Here they built Fort Boonesborough to protect themselves from the Shawnee whose hunting grounds they occupied.

Twelve days later, far to the east, British redcoats marched out of Boston to quell an American rebellion that was spreading through the colonies like a fever. In the darkness of night, the troops tramped toward Lexington and Concord. The bloodshed of the following day brought eight bitter years of revolution. In the end, the British Empire in America crumbled.

An infant nation, the United States, now emerged and claimed land that reached from the Atlantic coast far across the wilderness to the Mississippi River. Under the new government, prohibitions on moving westward vanished overnight. Hundreds of families now followed Boone's path through the mountains into the fertile lands of the Ohio River Valley.

Colter grew up in the shadow of war and in the glow of confidence that followed the American victory. Like the young nation, he turned his attention away from mother Europe and looked with longing toward the West.

Twenty years later he was in Kentucky, far beyond the Virginia border. Whether he followed the advancing frontier as a child in tow or as an adult is unknown. In Kentucky, on the Ohio River, Colter first appeared in the historical record on October 15, 1803, when he enrolled in the greatest adventure of his generation.

A Captain Lewis had arrived from the East to raise an expedition called the Corps of Discovery. With specific instructions from President Thomas Jefferson, Lewis began to stockpile supplies and fill enlistments. Jefferson envisioned an exploration of the continent's interior and beyond to the Pacific Ocean. He hoped to bring native tribes into trade and alliance. He hoped to discover water routes, flora and fauna, and fertile lands. And he hoped to claim territory unclaimed or uncontrolled by Europe.

Jefferson handed this daunting task to his personal secretary, Meriwether Lewis. Lewis in turn implored his friend, William Clark, to share the command. The two captains and just three other men constituted the Corps of Discovery when Colter stepped forward to join them. By the following year, there were thirty-two who would see the venture through.[4]

Lewis and Clark took nine long months to fill the ranks. They needed men who could withstand the physical and mental challenges of a hazardous trek across unknown wilderness.

The lives of all, including the captains, depended on the choices they made. Lewis was specific about qualifications. They must be "good hunters, stout, healthy, unmarried men, accustomed to the woods, and capable of bearing bodily fatigue in a pretty considerable degree."[5]

Colter met all the requirements. He was a skilled woodsman; he had traveled the Ohio and its tributaries and knew how to live off the land. At five feet ten, he was rather tall for the era and was hardened by a lifetime on the frontier. An acquaintance observed that "nature had formed him, like Boone, for hardy endurance of fatigue, privations, and perils."[6]

Colter was a solitary soul who had learned how to fend for himself. When he enlisted he did so alone, and he accomplished his greatest exploits all on his own. His best contribution to the Corps of Discovery was as a lone scout and hunter providing game.

Later he is known to have hunted alone in the rugged Absaroka Range—in a region no white man had seen. From there, he canoed downstream by himself—two thousand miles or so.[7] The following autumn, he returned upriver and set out alone for a thousand-mile trek in the dead of a Wyoming winter. Washington Irving was one of many who stood amazed at the feat. He called the ordeal Colter's "lonely wanderings."[8] Soon afterward, Colter returned to the wilderness and was wounded by Blackfoot Indians. He limped back "entirely alone and without assistance."[9] When his wounds healed, he returned again, by himself, to the same hostile country. Twice more he escaped certain death, alone.

Although Colter enjoyed his solitude, he was well liked and somewhat sociable. During his early days with the Corps of Discovery, his sergeant reported that Colter and his companions dipped too deeply into the whiskey barrel on New Year's Eve 1803. The following March, the captains confined him to camp along with several others who were caught visiting a neighboring whiskey shop when they were supposed to be hunting and tending to chores. For this, Colter asked forgiveness and promised to do better in the future.[10]

It seems he was true to his word. These infractions occurred before Lewis and Clark launched the expedition, and they stood as the first and last record of trouble with Colter. Apparently the independent-minded frontiersman adjusted to military discipline quickly enough. Soon afterward, the captains appointed him to serve on a court-martial to consider charges against two other men.[11] The officers quickly came to trust Colter's judgment. Their journals reveal that by the end of the expedition they held him in highest esteem.[12]

One reason for this was his reputation for honesty. A companion once remarked that he "wore an open, ingenuous, and pleasing countenance" and "his veracity was never questioned among us."[13] It stands to reason that a person who is committed to his duties and whose life is so packed with genuine adventure has no need to make up stories.

Colter soon proved that he was fully committed to the enterprise and had a personal interest in experiencing the western wilderness. On May 14, 1804, when the Corps of Discovery launched the expedition, Colter crossed the Mississippi River with his companions. This was his first time west of the river. No evidence suggests that he ever returned to the eastern shore.

Once the Corps reached the mouth of the Missouri, it turned to the task of struggling headlong upriver. In ten days, it moored at the hamlet of La Charette. Here a handful of French and English families wrested a living from the immense forest that surrounded them.

Nearby lived Boone, who five years earlier, at the age of sixty-four, had pushed westward once more, trying to escape the advance of civilization that followed every trail he blazed. The journals of the Corps of Discovery mention no meeting of Boone with Lewis, Clark, or Colter. But it is possible, even likely, that the young explorers made a point of visiting the famed frontiersman.

Upon casting off lines and leaving La Charette, the Corps of Discovery bid adieu to the last traces of civilization. Soon they passed the shady bluff on the south bank rising above the virgin woodland and set their sights upriver. Not for twenty-eight months would they come back this way and return to the comforts of St. Louis. But for Colter, the absence would last six years. Each time he turned eastward and descended the river, the Missouri headwaters and Rocky Mountains beckoned him back.

★   ★   ★   ★

THE DRUDGERY of dragging a keelboat and tons of supplies upstream against the heavy Missouri current was only the first of many tests for the men of the Corps of Discovery. Across a continent and back, through unknown prairies and mountains inhabited by dangerous predators, across the domains of unfamiliar and hostile Indian nations, the corps "suffered everything cold, hunger and fatigue could impart."[14]

Hardship often serves as the best teacher. It forces a person to learn to survive. By sharing hard times, the men of the Corps became close companions who learned to cooperate and contribute their unique talents to the enterprise. For twenty-eight months, they pooled their physical and mental resources and channeled their strengths toward the common goal of survival.

Within six weeks of the Corps' departure in May 1804, Colter found his niche. He proved more valuable with a flintlock in hand than with a towline or oar. He became proficient at bagging the pronghorn antelope that Meriwether Lewis and the others found so elusive, and he brought in the first mule deer that any of them had ever seen.[15]

Hunting for provisions became his preoccupation. He hunted whenever assigned. He even hunted when assigned something else. In August, when the captains sent Colter and another man to retrieve horses that had wandered from camp, the two men returned with the horses loaded with elk.[16] Later, Lewis sent Colter and Joseph Fields to search for stray horses and dispatched several others for hunting. The hunters returned unsuccessful. But late in the evening, wrote Lewis, "Colter and J. Fields joined us with the lost horses and brought with them a deer which they had killed. This furnished us with supper."[17]

In September, George Shannon, the youngest member of the Corps, wandered off to hunt and lost his way in the dense thickets along the river. The officers sent Colter, alone, to find him.[18] Shannon had gotten ahead of the keelboat and flotilla of men. But thinking he was behind, he pushed rapidly forward along the bank to catch them.

Eight days passed and Colter still had not found Shannon. But instead he had managed to procure "one buffalo, one elk, three deer, one wolf, five turkeys and one goose—one beaver also." The next day Colter's sergeant, John Ordway, noted in his journal that the Corps continued upriver and "took breakfast at one of Colter's camps where he had a scaffold of jerk."[19] It is no wonder, then, that it took thirteen days for Colter to locate Shannon.

The officers took all this in stride. They encouraged Colter to go with his strengths and continue to hunt. At any rate, he seemed determined to do so, and meat was in high demand.

Frontier travel created voracious appetites. A later explorer and botanist, F. A. Wislizenus, said, "Considering the absence of bread, and the traveler's life in the open air and daily exercise, it is not remarkable that the appetite makes unusual demands, and that people, who formerly were accustomed to eat scarcely a pound of meat daily, can consume eight and ten times as much of fresh buffalo meat."

Likewise, historian William Swagerty claims that a frontiersman's daily food consumption probably ranged upwards of five thousand calories, equivalent to about nine pounds of meat. According to mountain man Rufus Sage, this gave a person fortitude that allowed him to "shed rain like an otter, and stand [the] cold like a polar bear."

Western travelers and natives of the northern plains and mountains preferred fresh meat over every other means of sustenance. The men of the Corps of Discovery echoed this time and again, and later explorers agreed. Caleb Greenwood, an early trapper and later guide of settlers to California, complained about the emigrant fare of bacon, bread, and milk; he called it "mushy stuff." He preferred, instead, to hunt for good fresh meat such as grizzly bear and fat deer.

Meat preferences among frontiersmen followed a general order, with some variation according to the seasons when meat was in poor or prime condition. The bison cow was prized above all, followed by the bison bull, deer, elk, pronghorn, bighorn sheep, hare, beaver, prairie dog, badger, grizzly bear, fowl, fish, and eggs—in that order. The quantity of meat an animal provided also affected preference. A bison provided a thousand pounds of meat, an elk two hundred or three hundred pounds, and a deer sixty to one hundred pounds.

Bison was considered the "wholesomest and most palatable

meat." It tasted "much like beef, but of superior flavor, and remarkably easy of digestion." John Townsend, naturalist and explorer, said of bison cow meat that he "never had eaten anything so delicious. . . . We are feasting upon the best food in the world." He laughed at the greenhorn hunters who predictably pursued the largest bulls, while the meat of a bison cow was always preferred.

Trapper and adventurer Warren Ferris agreed, saying, "No other kind of meat can compare with that of the female bison, in good condition. With it we require no seasoning; we boil, roast, or fry it, as we please, and live upon it solely, without bread or vegetables of any kind, and what seems most singular, we never tire of or disrelish it."[20]

When game and edible plants became unavailable, men resorted to starvation foods and ate wolves, dogs, and horses. These animals ranked well below wild game in preference, partly because they often had wasted away or died of starvation themselves before being consumed. After devouring these meats, famished men had little choice but to chew on rawhide or cactus.

Sage reported that he and his starving party ate a straggling wolf for breakfast one morning. Later, they found an abandoned Indian camp where they "succeeded in gathering a few pieces of dry buffalo hide, that lay scattered about—so hard and tough the wolves had tried in vain to gnaw them; these, after being boiled some twelve or fourteen hours, afforded us a paltry substitute for something better."

David Thompson, a British fur trader, described his meager meal one wintry day on the northern plains: "We have no Meat, fortunately yesterday I picked up the Marrow Bone of a Buffaloe which had been pretty well Knawed by a Wolf—and this my day's allowance." Other starving men ate ants, crickets, grasshoppers, or leather moccasins "crisped . . . in the fire."[21]

Fortunately for the prairie traveler of the early nineteenth century, bison—the most flavorful and nourishing food—could often be found in abundance. Sage noted as late as 1841 that near the juncture of the North and South Platte Rivers, "the bottoms upon either side presented one dense, interminable band of buffalo, far as the eye could reach. The whole prairie pictured a living mass." William Swagerty has estimated that thirty million or more bison roamed the northern Great Plains alongside some twenty million pronghorn antelope and millions of elk and deer. This vast region has been aptly called the American Serengeti.[22]

Colter and the other hunters of the Corps of Discovery took advantage of this abundance of game and kept the men well fed during the tedious journey upriver. In November they reached the Mandan villages in present-day North Dakota and built a stockade, which they dubbed Fort Mandan. Here they shivered through a brutal winter while temperatures plunged to forty-five degrees below zero. In the bitter cold, normal tasks like hunting for food and standing guard became life-threatening duties.

By April 1805, the frozen Missouri River had thawed sufficiently for the Corps of Discovery to resume the upstream journey. From the Mandan villages, a hired French-Canadian trader named Toussaint Charbonneau and his young Shoshone wife, Sacagawea, accompanied them into the unknown lands to the west. Sacagawea had given birth to a son two months earlier. She carried the newborn the entire route to the Pacific Ocean and back.

In midsummer, the expedition took a grueling month to portage around a formidable series of cascades on the upper Missouri near present-day Great Falls, Montana. While the Corps rested above the falls on White Bear Island, one of the hunters came tearing toward camp no more than a step ahead of a large grizzly bear.

At forty yards out, the bear suddenly reeled and crashed a retreat through the brush.

William Clark quickly realized that the furious beast was headed toward the lower end of the island. There Colter was hunting alone, as usual. Clark and three others grabbed their guns and rushed to his assistance. At the lower end they found their comrade taking refuge in the river.

At their approach, the bear sullenly withdrew and headed for cover. Then Clark and his men "relieved the man in the water."[23] Colter returned to camp soaked to the skin. His companions must have teased him that night for taking an unexpected swim.

On the western plains and in the mountains, the grizzly bear reigned supreme. The men of the Corps now saw for themselves the difference in this huge, ill-tempered beast and the black bear they knew back east. Close calls with the bruins became so common that one has to wonder how every man in the expedition survived them.

Despite the narrow escape, Colter kept hunting alone in thickets and bottoms where grizzly bears roamed, and did so for years to come. Most men would have determined that their first grizzly encounter would be their last. But most men were not like John Colter.

His actions did not suggest a misplaced valor or a lack of the will to live. Colter simply had an unbounded curiosity and thirst for discovery that outweighed all concerns. A life like that was worth the risk. His intrepid nature made him the consummate explorer—a fearless adventurer who reached his prime in the most daring venture of his time.

From Great Falls, the Corps of Discovery pushed onward to Three Forks, where the streams named Jefferson, Madison, and

Gallatin converge into the Missouri River. Following the Jefferson upstream, they crossed the Continental Divide at Lemhi Pass in August. But progress was slow. Lewis became anxious to traverse the Rocky Mountains before the arrival of autumn snowfalls. He sent Clark ahead to search for a water passage through the maze of rugged peaks that lay before them.

Clark chose Colter and ten other men to join him in a descent by boat down the Salmon River—a water route to the Pacific. But treacherous rapids thwarted the plan. With time pressing hard, Clark sent Colter on a hurried mission to inform Lewis of the failed attempt. Clark might have remembered the hunter's slow progress in finding George Shannon the year before. This time, he "dispatched Colter on horseback with orders to lose no time."[24] The courier set out immediately and promptly delivered his message.[25]

The officers often appointed Colter to undertake similar missions. While searching for game, Colter also scouted routes in advance of the expedition and sometimes led the Corps over trails and fords that he had discovered.[26] Colter's hunting treks ahead of the men placed him in a position to make first contact with native people, and he gained a reputation for successful negotiation and diplomacy among them.

Such was the case at their next major campsite, called Traveler's Rest, where they arrived in September. Here, at the base of the Bitterroot Mountains, Lewis noted in his journal, "This evening one of our hunters returned accompanied by three men of the Flathead [Salish] nation, whom he had met in his excursion up Traveler's Rest Creek. On first meeting him, the Indians were alarmed and prepared for battle with their bows and arrows, but he soon relieved their fears by laying down his gun and advancing towards them."[27]

Clark confirmed that the hunter was Colter and that the first

encounter was indeed dangerous. The Flatheads were pursuing Shoshone enemies who had raided their village and stolen twenty-one
horses.[28] Colter had wandered unaware into the middle of a heated
situation. His cool reaction to the agitated warriors probably saved
his life—or theirs. The same calm demeanor also helped him escape
later scrapes.

Where diplomacy began, friendship followed. After allaying
their fears, Colter used sign language to invite the Flatheads to
camp.[29] Upon their arrival, the Indians responded in sign, lament-
ing the misfortune brought upon them by the Shoshone. Then, as
if in appreciation for a sympathetic audience, they offered a much-
needed description of the land that the Corps had yet to traverse.

Colter's regard for indigenous people showed forth on other
occasions. Two weeks out from Traveler's Rest, the expedition,
accompanied by a band of Nez Perce, struggled and starved their
way through the Bitterroot Mountains. Although game was scarce,
Colter brought in a deer, half of which he gave the Indians.[30]

As snowstorms descended upon the Corps of Discovery, the
food supply dwindled to nothing. With empty stomachs, they
pushed their way through deep drifts in the high elevations of
the frozen Rockies. In desperation, they resorted to eating their
candles to stave off starvation.

At last, in mid-autumn, the band staggered out of the mountains, fashioned dugout canoes, and descended the Snake and
Columbia Rivers toward the Pacific. But within reach of the ocean,
nasty weather pinned them down on an open bank exposed to the
surging sea and storm. Clark somehow found a dry moment to pen
in his journal a description of the tide as it "came in with great
swells, breaking against the rocks and drift trees with great fury."

In desperation, the captains called Colter, Shannon, and Wil-
lard forward. They sent them by canoe to "get around the point if

possible and examine the river, and the bay below for a good harbor" and a place to lie in safety. Despite huge waves that slapped the waters and tossed the boats, the three returned to report "a good canoe harbor and two camps of Indians at no great distance below."[31] From here the Corps pressed eagerly toward its foremost objective: to cross the continent and reach the Pacific waters.

"Ocean in view! O! the joy," Clark wrote, at last, in his November journal.[32] In elation, he made preparations to explore the shoreline. "I directed all the men who wished to see more of the ocean to get ready to set out with me on tomorrow daylight. The following men expressed a wish to accompany me," Clark wrote, listing two sergeants and only eight men—Colter among them. Clark explained, with tactful chagrin, that the others were "well contented with what part of the ocean and its curiosities which could be seen from the vicinity of the camp."[33] Colter always appeared among those ready for new discoveries.[34]

Although the Pacific Ocean had been reached, the late season allowed little time for celebration. Winter came quickly and weighed heavy with raging winds and soaking rains. Meriwether Lewis grew desperate to find a site to construct sturdy quarters. To help him, he picked Colter, Shannon, and three others. Together, the six launched a small canoe into choppy waters under threatening skies and surveyed the coast for potential sites.[35] Eight days passed before they found a spot to build a stockade and shelter. There, the men erected a few log huts for a winter home they called Fort Clatsop.

The weather remained foul, damp, and chill, and the food supply ran low. On a bitter day in mid-December, William Clark led several men into the forest in search of game. He complained in his journal, "Rained all the last night. We covered ourselves as well as we could with elk skins, and sat up the greater part of the night, all wet. I lay in the water very cold." Colter and four others suffered worse. Away from camp scouting for elk, they "stayed out all night without fire and in the rain." The next morning they staggered into camp half-frozen.[36]

After a wet and miserable four months at Fort Clatsop, the Corps of Discovery began their homeward trek up the Columbia River in late March 1806. But deep snowdrifts in the passes of the Rocky Mountains caused a delay, and game remained dangerously scarce. Other foods often had to suffice. John Ordway recalled a time when Colter sauntered into camp with one deer and eight duck eggs.[37] According to Clark, the other hunters killed nothing that day.[38]

Soon afterward, to stave off hunger, Colter and a companion "fixed two Indian gigs and went in search of fish in the creek." Meat was preferred, but fish could also satisfy the men's carnivorous diet. Frontiersmen favored those fish that swam the waters west of the Continental Divide, like salmon and trout. For travelers west of the divide, these fish often served as a substitute for the bison they had hunted east of the divide.

Fish could be speared, caught with a hook, or trapped in a woven-hemp fishnet or willow-branch basket. The men of the Corps of Discovery witnessed the indigenous technique of spearing fish with barbed tips, or gigs, fashioned from bone, antler, or thorn. In the salmon-rich Snake and Columbia Rivers, native fishermen would stand silent and still on a rock in a stream with a spear poised over the surface. Then, quick as lightning, they would thrust into the clear water and flip a wriggling fish to the bank.

Fur trader Robert Stuart later described how:

The fish begin to jump soon after sunrise, when the Indians in great numbers with their spears swim in, to near the center of the falls, where some placing themselves on rocks and others to their middle in water . . . assail the salmon. . . . Their spears are a small straight piece of elk's horn, out of which the pith is dug, deep enough to receive the end of a very long willow pole, and on the point an artificial beard [barb] is made fast by a preparation of twine and gum.

After their capture, the fish were dried on a rack, roasted over a fire, boiled in a basin, or even cooked in the hot waters of a thermal pool.[39]

Colter used the spearing technique. His first duty to the Corps was to find enough food for three dozen famished men. How he acquired it did not matter that much. Sometimes he even resorted to trade. Game and fish must have been scarce and the men extra hungry on the day that Lewis wrote, "Colter and Bratton were permitted to visit the Indian villages today for the purpose of trading for roots and bread. They were fortunate and made a good return."[40]

In June, with a supply of food in hand, the Corps of Discovery resumed its journey through mountain passes still perilously packed with snow.[41] As they pressed eagerly homeward, they tempted their fate on the icy slopes. On one precipitous path, Colter's horse stumbled off a ridge with its rider. Lewis recalled how Colter "and his horse were driven down the creek a considerable distance—rolling over each other among the rocks. He fortunately escaped without injury or the loss of his gun."[42] The next day, the indomitable Colter went fishing.

During two years of exploring the western lands, he had learned to take such hardships in stride. His focus seemed clear: to keep to the task at hand, to overcome obstacles, and to push resolutely forward.[43] This rugged and dangerous life became so commonplace that, in the eyes of later observers, Colter appeared unimpressed by his own endeavors.

That June, the Corps of Discovery returned to the previous year's campground at Traveler's Rest. Soon afterward, the company divided into smaller units in order to explore more country. Lewis led a small band north toward the present-day Canadian border. Clark's command, including Sacagawea and her family, descended the Yellowstone River. Colter accompanied Sgt. Ordway's squad as they paddled canoes down the Missouri. As luck would have it, they all reunited in August just upstream from the Mandan villages.

Soon after rejoining Capt. Lewis' command, Colter and John Collins were sent ashore for the usual hunt. Six days passed with no sign of the two. A worried Lewis wrote, "Colter and Collins have not yet overtaken us. I fear some misfortune has happened them, for their previous fidelity and orderly deportment induces me to believe that they would not thus intentionally delay."[44]

Assuming the boats were behind them, the two men had taken their time and gathered provisions—"6 buffalo, 13 deer, 5 elk and 31 beaver."[45] Already, Colter revealed a growing interest in trapping and trading for furs. He had become proficient at harvesting beaver pelts, and he happened to be standing in the heart of the best beaver country in the world.[46]

Several days passed before the two hunters realized that the flotilla had left them behind. To lighten their load, the two abandoned most of the larder and rushed to catch up with the expedition. At last, with relief, Lewis noted, "Colter and Collins . . . rejoined us. They were well no accident having happened."[47]

The Corps of Discovery was now a mere six weeks away from returning to St. Louis and completing the twenty-eight-month journey. The men had traversed the western expanse and crossed it back again. They had found their way eight thousand miles through unknown wilderness and somehow all survived, save one who died of appendicitis.

While Colter's companions longed for the journey's end, his mind remained fixed on sparkling headwaters and rugged mountains. While his comrades looked eagerly eastward toward home, Colter kept looking behind him. All he needed was an opportunity— an excuse to return to the West.

    ★   ★   ★   ★

ON THE DAY that Colter and Collins rejoined the party, they found two strangers in camp. Joseph Dickson and Forrest Hancock, trappers from Illinois, had worked their way up the Missouri beyond the Mandan villages. The two were eager to reach beaver country—more so after talking with Meriwether Lewis. The captain gave them "a short description of the Missouri, a list of distances to the most conspicuous streams and remarkable places on the river above, and pointed out to them the places where the beaver most abounded."[48]

To Dickson and Hancock, this was like a treasure map—giving them first claim to information obtained from the first expedition westward. Even Thomas Jefferson, who commissioned the venture, could not have hoped for so much. To sweeten the deal, the two men decided to enlist a member of the Corps who knew the lay of the land and would serve as their scout and partner. In return, they promised to furnish traps and a share of the profits.

No one was more qualified or more eager than Colter. This would be the first trapping party to reach the upper Missouri in the wake of Lewis and Clark's expedition. On August 15, 1806, after two years and ten months with the Corps of Discovery, Colter expressed a desire to join the two men.

As William Clark wrote, "His services could be dispensed with from this down, and as we were disposed to be of service to any one of our party who had performed their duty as well as Colter had done, we agreed to allow him the privilege." The captains only asked that no other man request similar leave.

To this they all agreed, and wished Colter every success. After the captains supplied him with powder and lead, the party also gave him several articles for use on the expedition.[49] Thus equipped, Colter prepared to return to the mountains. This time he carried knowledge and skills sharpened by more than two years in the western wilderness, along with Lewis' summary of the expedition's discoveries. With this and his subsequent travels, Colter would stand for a moment in history as the frontiersman most knowledgeable of the American West.

Two days later, at two o'clock in the afternoon, the men of the Corps of Discovery said farewell to Charbonneau, Sacagawea, and their toddler son at the Mandan villages, then launched their boats and drifted downriver toward St. Louis. At the same time, Dickson, Hancock, and Colter turned their canoe the opposite direction and paddled upstream against the current.[50] They followed the Missouri's main channel, then pushed up the Yellowstone River deep into the land of the Crow nation.

At the time, this indigenous group was known as the Bird People. Their name was described in Indian sign language by the flapping of arms to represent wings. They identified themselves with the name *Absaroka* or *Absarokee*, which some have defined as *Sparrowhawk*. Others have said the term meant *Children of the Large-Beaked Bird*, suggesting a raven or crow.[51]

Here, Colter first encountered the native people who would embrace him as ally and friend. The Crow were adept at stealing horses and often fought with their neighbors. But they typically befriended strangers who happened into their camps. To the hungry and far from home, they gave food and shelter—even when meat was scarce.[52]

Frontiersmen found most western tribes hospitable toward newcomers and ready to offer a warm place by the fire. The Flathead nation, in particular, had a reputation for natural friendliness, and other nations also showed acts of kindness. Rufus Sage—ragged, starving, with no weapon or possessions—once wandered into a Pawnee village. He reported being immediately taken in and fed by an old chief: "His benevolence was truly exemplary, as his conduct well attested. My moccasins, being much worn by long usage, exposed to the ground the bottoms of my feet. This was no sooner discovered by the noble-hearted old man, than he pulled off his own (a pair of new ones) and gave them to me! What white man would have done the like?"

Maximilian von Wied, a German naturalist and adventurer, claimed that even the warlike Blackfoot showed commendable kindness on occasion:

> In their camp and tents, these Indians, even the dangerous Blood Indians, are hospitable. White men, who visited them in the cold month of October, were immediately lodged in the tent of a chief, while the owner, with his whole family, slept in the open air; nobody dared to molest the guests. The horses were well taken care of, and there was no need to look after them, for, under these circumstances, they were perfectly safe, as well as all the effects of the strangers, which, in other cases, would certainly have been stolen.

Mountain man Daniel Potts commented similarly on the congenial nature of the Crow. He recalled that, when he lost two toes from frostbite, they "conducted me to their village, into the lodge of their Chief, who regularly twice a day divested himself of all his clothing except his breech clout, and dressed my wounds, until I left them." The Crow, unlike many Plains Indians, were also quick to adopt women and children captured from enemy tribes, rather than summarily executing or torturing them.

They were just as ready to adopt white strangers, as in the cases of Edward Rose, Jim Beckwourth, Thomas Leforge, and others. As for white men passing through their villages, the Crow proved willing to "feast them with the best they can procure" and "divide the last morsel of food with the hungry stranger, let their means be what it might for obtaining the next meal."

Canadian fur trader François Larocque said, "Any person of any nation going to their camp will be well treated and received, but when coming at night or seen skulking about need not expect mercy." Jim Beckwourth, a former slave turned mountain man who lived with the Crow for many years, agreed that a Crow might kill a man at random outside a village. But once he arrived peaceably in their midst, his life was sacred. In particular, a stranger was protected once invited into a lodge. At that point, to harm him would be reprehensible and to pilfer his possessions would be an outrage.

In his autobiography, *Memoirs of a White Crow Indian*, Leforge added that a person who came in peace, even from an enemy tribe, received safe passage and hospitality in a Crow village: "An open and announced approach in broad daylight and without the least appearance of stealth gave rise to a presumption of amicable intent. . . . It would be too easy to kill him, therefore it would be no honor to do so. Another idea influencing this conduct was that the visitor either was crazy or was sent by the Great Spirit."

The Crow typically offered newcomers a smoke, some minor

gifts, and a feast. They even vied with each other for the opportunity to provide hospitality. Sometimes they declared themselves brothers or sisters of the guests. They helped them with camp chores and invited them to stay in their lodges. Larocque said of the Crow that they appear "to be fond of us, treat us well and say they will shed tears when we leave them."[53]

Much has been said of contention and warfare between natives and whites, but cooperation and friendship more often prevailed during early encounters. Colter soon made himself at home and learned the life of the Crow.

Winter's approach brought the Crow bands together into large, sheltered encampments. On the bank of a river or creek surrounded by bluffs for protection, with grasslands for grazing and cottonwoods for fuel and fodder, the Crow passed the winters in relative comfort. They typically camped in areas of abundant game where they procured meat and tanned hides for covering lodges.

Western explorers were drawn to these villages and soon learned to establish their own winter quarters in similarly sheltered locations. George Catlin, frontier artist and ethnographer, described such quarters as "generally taken up in some heavy-timbered bottom, on the banks of some stream, deep embedded within the surrounding bluffs, which break off the winds, and make their long and tedious winter tolerable and supportable."

The ideal encampment had a thick stand of cottonwood trees that offered kindling for campfires and timber for shelters. Cottonwoods stood larger than other trees found along the watercourses of the plains, which made them the best providers of wood for these purposes. Indians and frontiersmen also used cottonwood branches for building forts when under threat of enemy attack. To help with defense, the smaller branches were easily carved into lightweight arrow shafts.

In addition, western travelers fashioned these trees into dugout canoes, paddles, masts, wagon wheels, benches, chairs, tables, and other furnishings. More important, the bark served as emergency winter fodder for horses. For this, the eastern cottonwood (*Populus deltoides*), also called sweet cottonwood, was favored over other cottonwood species.

Meriwether Lewis made special note of this tree and included a sample in his herbarium. Sweet cottonwood dominated the eastern woodlands and rivers of the plains. Like most frontiersmen, fur trader William Ashley was impressed by the readily available fodder and suggested that sweet cottonwood was almost as nutritious as timothy hay. Others considered it a fine substitute for corn or oats and suitable for fattening horses.

It certainly was preferred to other emergency forages such as sagebrush (*Artemisia tridentata*), saltbush (*Atriplex canescens*, also known as salt weed), and river rushes. In contrast to sweet cottonwood, narrow leaf cottonwood (*Populus angustifolia*) was "of the bitter kind." It grew in the mountains west of the main sweet cottonwood range and was not desirable for fodder. In fact, horses were very fond of sweet cottonwood, but sometimes starved to death rather than eat the narrow leaf species.

Horses often gnawed the bark off sweet cottonwood without assistance. Otherwise, men removed the bark and even thawed it for them in winter. When supplies of bark ran low, horses availed themselves of the branches. In times of dire necessity, Indian women sometimes climbed "fearlessly to the topmost branch of the highest tree" to chop the fodder and let it fall to the ground. On rare occasion, the entire tree was felled for the same purpose.

Sweet cottonwood not only offered forage for horses, but also for hungry bison whose grasslands were covered in snow. In fact, bison and horses often competed for cottonwood bark, which put horses and encampments at risk. Joe Meek, the famed mountain man, recalled: "In the large cotton-wood bottoms on the Yellowstone River, it sometimes became necessary to station a double guard to keep the buffalo out of camp, so numerous were they, when the severity of the cold drove them from the prairies to these cotton-wood thickets for subsistence." On the other hand, the intrusion of bison provided the encampment with plenty of meat.

Other useful trees could be found in abundance along western river courses. Sandbar willow (*Salix exigua*), peachleaf willow (*Salix amygdaloides*), and other species of willow were common in riparian areas of the Great Plains and Rocky Mountains. Their limber branches proved useful for making wigwams and baskets, their bark for fashioning cord and string, and their bark and leaves for medicinal purposes. Red osier dogwood (*Cornus sericea*) is similar to willow and was used for making frames for wigwams and barrel-vaulted huts. As an added bonus, its inner bark was prized as a substitute for tobacco.[54]

In autumn 1806, Colter, Dickson, and Hancock searched for a winter refuge among the cottonwoods and timbers near a large Crow encampment. Here they remained busy trapping, trading, and keeping camp. Some have suggested that Colter and his companions holed up for the winter in Clark's Fork Canyon, and that Colter hunted his way into Sunlight Basin.[55] But many beautiful, sheltered sites bedeck the Yellowstone tributaries, and any of these could have served as temporary quarters.

The men perhaps visited the pristine valley of Pryor's Fork, with its crystal stream gushing from a gap in the Pryor Mountains to join the Yellowstone River. Here the Crow enjoyed an abundant supply of water, food, and shelter.

A year earlier, the Crow had informed the French trader, Larocque, that "in winter they were always to be found at a park by the foot of the mountain" and that they often lit signal fires from its heights. They called this mountain *Amanchabe Chije* or *Amanchabe Clije*. The descriptions provided by Larocque, Leforge, and historian Burton Harris suggest that this is the present-day Pryor Mountains in southern Montana.

Leforge camped one summer with a Crow village on Pryor's Fork in the shadow of the Pryor Mountains. He reminisced of having "a glorious time, with plenty of buffalo ribs for roasting— the most delectable meat the Almighty ever made for mankind." Thickets of plum trees grew along the creek, providing a worthy supplement to the beef dinner. After the feast, "we jumped into the warm summer waters of Pryor Creek and played there. We gathered in a semicircle and smoked, talked, recounted coups, sang songs."

A sweat lodge was erected nearby for the rejuvenation of body and soul. Leforge recalled that "a favorite old-time place for the Crow Indians to go for devotional dreaming was on Pryor Mountain. While there was almost daily prayer and fasting and wailing by someone on some nearby hill, the pilgrimage to this lofty mountain resort was a special religious proceeding." In this mystical place, eagles screeched, lightning flashed, and thunder reverberated through the valleys, but "the mysteries of the environment were attractive rather than repellent to the Indians."

Pryor Gap provided a popular pathway through the Pryor Mountains, marked by a formation known as Medicine Rocks (now called Castle Rocks). One particular cliff in the gap "was held in special awe." In days of old, the Crow "often stood opposite the cliff and shot arrows across upon it, as sacrifices."

Leforge reported that Pryor Creek, which runs through the gap, was then known as *Shooting-at-the-Bank Creek*, and that "old arrowheads are plentiful there." Over the centuries, the Crow have called the cliff by other names as well—*Arrow Shot into Rock*, *Hits with the Arrows*, *They Shoot the Rock*, *Lots of Arrows*, *Where There Are Many Arrows*, and *Arrow Rock*.

Here the Crow launched arrows as an offering to the Little People—the legendary, elusive dwarfs thought to dwell in the gap in seclusion. The Crow considered them capable of conveying spiritual insight as well as material blessings.

The cliff was one of several holy sites in Pryor Gap, which also contained a number of cairns erected as shrines to commemorate fallen heroes of an ancient battle with the Arapaho.[56] To this day, the area is revered by the Crow.

If Colter, Dickson, and Hancock did not camp with the Crow on Pryor's Fork, they possibly ventured up Clark's Fork of the Yellowstone, which is the next watercourse west of Pryor's Fork. Marked by a swath of lush vegetation, it provided the Crow with a comparable cluster of favorite encampments. At a shady spot where Clark's Fork receives the waters of the Absaroka branch, evergreen plants offered ample winter fodder for horses. Bison, elk, and pronghorn also roamed the valley for forage. Here, the following year, the Crow had one hundred fifty lodges of dressed skins, suggesting an abundance of game and access to the bison range.[57]

In one of these bountiful valleys, the three men found shelter from winter storms. They spent their days setting and checking traps, skinning pelts, and hunting for food. They called on the Crow to talk of trade and smoke the pipe.

Colter understood enough sign language to make basic conversation. After a few years in the western wilderness, he knew how to convey peaceful intentions by holding up a hand palm forward, or by raising a blanket with both hands and laying it on the ground to indicate a parley. He understood that an offer of tobacco served as a symbol of friendship.

Indian sign language was readily learned by the novice. Before European contact, sign was disseminated through much of North America and was easily understood from one tribe to the next. In the nineteenth century, sign language continued to be in constant use by the Plains Indians. In turn, they transmitted it to western travelers who quickly became proficient in its use.

William Tomkins, a linguist and adopted member of the Sioux nation, described Indian sign language as "elemental, basic, logical." Warren Ferris wrote: "These signs are made with their hands or fingers, in different positions, with rapidity; and are so extremely simple, that a person entirely unacquainted with them, will readily conceive a great portion of what may be expressed by them." He added that Crow people worked patiently with strangers to communicate through sign, and that Indians in general seemed pleased by attempts to learn their language and culture.

François Larocque claimed that, although he did not understand their language, "They often told me long stories without hardly opening their lips and I understood very well."[58] No doubt, Colter, Dickson, and Hancock soon absorbed the fundamentals of sign and spoken language. This allowed them to learn additional native lore and partake of the lessons of how to survive in the northern plains and mountains passed through generations.

In their winter encampment of 1806–7, the days and months that the three men spent huddled around a fire in close company must have dragged by slowly. As soon as the icy rivers thawed, the restless Colter departed from Dickson and Hancock. Alone in a canoe, he rode the floodwaters downstream toward St. Louis. But again, as in the previous year, he never reached the lower Missouri.

An expedition under Manuel Lisa, a Spanish merchant from

New Orleans, had left St. Louis in April 1807 and headed upriver in search of trade with the native people. One member of the party recorded that, "At the river Platte, Lisa met one of Lewis and Clark's men, of the name of Coulter." Lisa immediately perceived that Colter's "knowledge of the country and nations rendered him an acquisition." He hired Colter on the spot.[59]

For the second time in two years Colter turned back toward the mountains. Perhaps his motive was money. The beaver hat was much in demand among aspiring gentlemen of America and Europe, before silk hats came into vogue. Prices for pelts stood at a premium—enough to entice men into dangerous mountains to wade icy streams to find beaver.

Perhaps Colter had other reasons. He might have disliked civil society with its unfair poverty and affluence; with its endless rules and demands. Colter probably typified the mountain men who followed his path. They loved the frontier for the sheer independence, the freedom of living in nature, the satisfaction of surviving in the wilderness, the exhilarating, even reckless adventure. Colter's days with Lewis and Clark suggest that he went west for more than just money. He loved the thrill of discovery.

Many of the men who followed in Colter's footsteps declared that profit was not the main reason for their western wanderings. Warren Ferris stated that most mountain men were not seeking money as much as they were responding to "the strong desire of seeing strange lands, of beholding nature in the savage grandeur of her primeval state." For western pathfinder Joseph Walker, "to explore unknown regions was his chief delight."

Jedediah Smith, the famous mountain man and cartographer, recalled, "I of course expected to find beaver, which with us hunters is a primary object, but I was also led on by the love of novelty common to all." The novelty of the western wilderness could be found in the pristine prairies and mountains, the amazing flora, the abundant game running free, and the natural lifestyle of the native inhabitants. The prospect was too intoxicating to resist.[60]

The wilderness also offered solitude. For those who had suffered rough usage in the East, this proved especially enticing. Moses "Black" Harris spent years carrying dispatches back and forth across the Rocky Mountains. Frontier artist Alfred Jacob Miller related how Harris' journeys

> *were made alone, and his plan was to ride all night, and cache or hide himself during the day; he carried with him a supply of dried meat so as to avoid making fires, which would have infallibly betrayed him [to hostile bands]. On being asked if he had not felt lonesome sometimes on these solitary excursions, he laughed as if it was a good joke—'never knew in his life what it was to feel lonesome.'*

When Rufus Sage launched out on a solitary hunting trip, he said:

> *I must confess, that after the first sensations of repulsive lone-liness had been overcome, I felt much attached to it. . . . There was something so forbidding in the idea . . . removed as I was far away from friendly aid, and in a dangerous country. . . . Still, in a little time I learned to forget all this, and roamed as freely by day, and slept as soundly by night, as though sur-rounded by friends. . . . There is a charm in the loneliness—an enchantment in the solitude.*

British adventurer George Ruxton, although far from his home and family, had this to say about solitude:

I must confess that the very happiest moments of my life have been spent in the wilderness of the Far West . . . with no friend near me more faithful than my rifle, and no companions more sociable than my good horse and mules, or the attendant cayeute [coyote] which nightly serenaded us. With a plentiful supply of dry pine-logs on the fire, and its cheerful blaze streaming far up into the sky . . . I would sit cross-legged, enjoying the genial warmth, and, pipe in mouth, watch the blue smoke as it curled upward, building castles in its vapory wreaths, and in the fantastic shapes it assumed, peopling the solitude with figures of those far away. Scarcely, however, did I ever wish to change such hours of freedom for all the luxuries of civilized life.

Ruxton was true to his sentiments. After living in the wilderness of North America, he traveled extensively in Africa, then back to America, always looking for a new frontier to explore.[61]

Camp life provided another irresistible attraction, with the stars above, the night sounds of the wilderness all about, and the aroma of wood smoke and roasting meat. William Anderson recalled one of the pleasures of being a mountain man: "Here I am, at a beautiful spring, my skewer in the ground, at a hot fire of buffalo dung, a set of good, sweet hump-ribs roasting before me, legs crossed, knife drawn, and mouth watering, waiting for the attack." At such a moment, he continued, life's other pleasures are forgotten—all except the ribs and perhaps a sweetheart back home. But first and foremost come the ribs.

"After the meal," Alfred Jacob Miller said, "we could then sit patiently and listen to some trapper relating reminiscences of his adventures—his huntings, and fightings with the Indians, and his loves with Indian beauties forming the principal ground work of his narrative." Finally, the weary frontiersman would wrap in a bison robe and stretch out on the ground with "his back to the earth; his feet to the fire," and fall fast asleep in perfect contentment.[62]

Travelers loved the solitude and serenity of the West, and also the independence and freedom the wilderness offered. The frontiersman, like the Indian, was conscious "of his self-reliant independence. . . . The Indian feels himself free, his wants are few, his resources lie within himself. This consciousness fills him with . . . contempt for all civilization." In like manner, "the mountaineer is his own manufacturer, tailor, shoemaker, and butcher; and, fully accoutered and supplied with ammunition in a good game country, he can always feed and clothe himself."

He "gradually learns to despise the restraints of civilization" because, in the mountains, he is "free as the pure air he breathes, and proudly conscious of his own independence." The mountain man is "a sovereign amid nature's loveliest works." Although the frontier life was devoid of elegance and luxury, it satisfied all one's basic needs and provided "room to wander without any man to call your steps in question."

Benjamin Bonneville, a US Army captain and explorer, told John Townsend and company that "he preferred the 'free and easy' life of a mountain hunter and trapper, to the comfortable and luxurious indolence of a dweller in civilized lands, and would not exchange his homely, but wholesome mountain fare, and his buffalo lodge, for the most piquant dishes of the French artiste, and the finest palace in the land."

George Catlin once conversed with a French free trapper named Ba'tiste who seemed contented with his rustic life although he made little money—only one dollar per beaver pelt. Catlin was shocked by the meager compensation, considering the hazardous work involved. He asked the trapper if he had ever been robbed by the Blackfoot.

Ba'tiste answered,

Oui, Monsr. rob, suppose, five time! I am been free trappare seven year, and I am rob five time—I am someting left not at all—he is take all; he is take all de horse—he is take my gun—he is take all my clothes—he is takee de castors [beavers]—et I am come back with foot. So in de Fort, some cloths is cost putty much monnair, et some whiskey is give sixteen dollares pour gall; so you see I am owe de Fur Comp 600 dollare, by Gar!

Catlin asked, "Well, Ba'tiste, this then is what you call being a free trapper is it?"

Ba'tiste responded, "Oui, Mons. 'free trapper,' free!"

Other frontiersmen also expressed the great value they placed on freedom rather than on money, comfort, and convenience. Alfred Jacob Miller recalled the scene of a trapper "sitting cross-legged in Indian fashion, with his hands over the expiring ashes" of a campfire "while a violent storm was raging and the rain pouring." The flashes of lightning revealed the man's facial features—"pinched with cold, and lank and thin," with "the rain streaming from his nose and prominent chin, and his hunting shirt hanging about him in a flabby and soaking embrace. Spite of such a situation which was anything but cheering, he was rapping out at the top of his voice a ditty: 'How happy am I! From care I'm free. Oh, why are not all contented like me?'"[63]

The Native American lifestyle that mountain men emulated differed sharply from that of civilization along the Eastern seaboard, with its frantic struggle for material gain and social status.

Jedediah Smith once sat a short distance from an Indian encampment, enjoying the sight of the painted lodges and

> *the children playing around in the intervals between them, the men going out or coming in from hunting, the horses feeding on the neighboring prairie, the dogs sleeping or playing in the sun or shade, the squaws at their several labors and the boys at their several sports. These, taken in connection with a beautiful mingling of prairie and woodland, or some undulation of the land, or some bend of the great river that brings them at once to view . . . would almost persuade a man to renounce the world, take the lodge, and live the careless, lazy life of an Indian.*

According to several observers, the Plains Indian male, unlike the female, enjoyed a life of relative leisure. He was able to procure sustenance and shelter with minimal effort, allowing abundant time for his greatest passions—the hunt, the raid, horse racing, target practice, and other favorite sports: "When at home, he attends only to his weapons and his horses, preparing the means of future exploit. Or he engages with his comrades in games of dexterity, agility, and strength; or in gambling games." It is small wonder that mountain men became attracted to the lifestyle.[64]

Colter had many reasons to be enamored with the frontier. These feelings must have welled forth anew in April 1807, when he saw old comrades returning upriver in the party of Manuel Lisa. There stood his hunting partner George Drouillard, his canoe mate John Potts, his scouting companion Peter Weiser, and other veterans of the Corps of Discovery.[65] Many who had traveled with

Lewis and Clark would be drawn back to the western frontier time and again.

No record exists of Colter's thoughts at the time. Perhaps he responded to the sight of Lisa's expedition in the manner of three fellow Kentuckians a few years later. The three men had been hunting, trapping, and struggling to survive in the Rocky Mountains. At last they had headed for home and were "in full career for St. Louis" when they too encountered an expedition heading upriver. According to Washington Irving,

> *The sight of a powerful party of traders, trappers, hunters, and voyageurs, well-armed and equipped, furnished at all points, in high health and spirits, and banqueting lustily on the green margin of the river, was a spectacle equally stimulating to these veteran backwoodsmen with the glorious array of a campaigning army to an old soldier; but when they learned the grand scope and extent of the enterprise in hand, it was irresistible.*[66]

Colter, like them, got swept up in the moment. He promptly joined the party and turned again toward the mountains.

In October, Lisa's expedition arrived at the mouth of the Bighorn River where it flows into the Yellowstone. A map drawn by George Drouillard marks this site and includes the inscription: ESTABLISHMENT MADE BY MANUEL LISA IN OCTOBER 1807. This puts to rest the question of Lisa's time of arrival at the Bighorn. Even so, an erroneous November date sometimes appears in historical studies.[67]

Here the men erected a trading post called Fort Raymond, or Manuel's Fort. The fort was located on the Bighorn's west bank at a strategic location at the juncture of two major rivers in prime beaver habitat. Nathaniel Wyeth, a frontier trader from New

England, later commented on the site in his journal: "Beaver sign all day. There is here the best trapping that I have ever found on so large a river."[68] Manuel's Fort stood opposite the location on the east bank where Clark and his men had camped fifteen months earlier, on July 26, 1806, during the Corps of Discovery's homeward journey.

Colter perhaps spent a few days helping with construction of Manuel's Fort. But Lisa quickly assigned him the task of visiting the neighboring Indian nations, including Colter's friends—the Crow. If he could spread word to them of the trading post on the river and show them some tempting trade items that fall and winter, native bands might bring beaver pelts and bison robes for exchange after the spring thaw.

Lisa was known for pushing his men to the primary tasks at hand. Three years later, he would send an expedition to Three Forks to construct a similar trading post. Within a few days, many of the men were assigned to start generating company profits by trapping beaver, while the others were left to complete the fort.[69] Lisa's primary task for Colter was to bring Indian nations to trade. It is likely, then, that Colter set out from Manuel's Fort within a few days of the expedition's arrival in October 1807.

In the days that followed, Lisa sent others abroad, including Edward Rose, who led a small party to open commerce with native encampments near Manuel's Fort. George Drouillard wandered more widely, up the Yellowstone and Clark's Fork to Spirits' Mountain, then back via Stinking Water River, Gap Creek, and Pryor's Fork.[70] A second journey took Drouillard up the Bighorn and Little Bighorn Rivers, and across the Tongue and Rosebud Rivers.

But neither man roamed as far into the unknown as Colter. Henry Brackenridge, a contemporary adventurer and author, reported that "shortly after" the expedition's arrival at the juncture of the Yellowstone and Bighorn Rivers, Lisa sent Colter "to bring some of the Indian nations to trade. This man, with a pack of thirty pounds weight, his gun and some ammunition, went upwards of five hundred miles to the Crow nation; gave them information, and proceeded from thence to several other tribes."

Surprisingly, a recent study has claimed that Colter departed a year earlier, in 1806, with the intention of visiting only the Crow nation. It claims that if Colter entered Yellowstone country, it was only to search out water sources so Clark could add them to his map. None of these claims are substantiated. In fact, they counter the major points made by Brackenridge—our only written source on the subject.

A more common misconception is that Colter traveled only five hundred miles. Brackenridge's statement refutes this, saying he traveled five hundred miles "and proceeded from thence to several other tribes." Afterward, Colter made the return trip to Manuel's Fort, probably arriving in spring 1808. William Clark's 1810 manuscript map includes landmarks that Colter described to him in person, along with dotted lines that mark Colter's route of about a thousand miles.[71]

Chapter Two

TRAVELING LIGHT

THE AMAZING TALE OF A MAN ALONE TRAVERSING this rugged country in winter has made for many a campfire story, from Colter's time to the present. Living for months from a pack weighing thirty pounds is in itself a feat. Colter, as a hunter and scout, knew that survival depended on mobility—the ability to carry everything necessary for procuring sustenance and shelter, and nothing more. The Corps of Discovery had learned a hard lesson when it had to cache or abandon tons of supplies along with the heavy keelboat and pirogues that carried it all upriver. In the end, the men had survived on what they could haul on their backs.

The problem of oversupply was not new. A generation earlier, Baron von Steuben, while training the Continental Army during the American Revolution, had urged the need for packing light. He frowned upon excess that slowed the march. So he issued a regulation: "It is expected, that for the future each officer will curtail his baggage as much as possible."[1]

Excess baggage continued to plague later frontiersmen. Expeditions often had to cache supplies in the ground, and they were frequently pilfered by native people or wolves, or ruined by seepage. Packing light was essential for individuals as well as expeditions. Ideally, one made do with items from nature, such as a piece of bark for a plate. After a heartbreaking abandonment of all her possessions during a passage through the mountains, Narcissa Whitman, a missionary to the Cayuse nation, wrote, "It would have been better for me not to have attempted to bring any baggage whatever, only what was necessary to use on the way. . . . The custom of the country is to possess nothing, and then you will lose nothing while traveling."[2]

Colter had learned the lesson well while fording icy rivers and traversing rugged mountains. The best way to determine an absolute necessity is to have to carry it on your back. Unneeded items are quickly discarded. Years of daily packing up and hiking out had forced him to define and redefine his load to perfection.

His clothing, like his pack, became tailored to the demands of the wilderness. Typical of the era and location, frontiersmen wore pants and shirts of linen, to be replaced by buckskin as clothes wore out and supplies of cloth became distant. A hunting shirt was the norm, with a shoulder cape to repel rain and snow, and fringe to wick moisture away. The length reached toward the knees. A wide leather belt and buckle held the shirt tight to the waist.[3]

Colter's moccasins likely followed the Crow pattern—similar to that of the Shoshone and Mandan. Each was fashioned from a single piece of deer or elk leather, or of bison hide in winter, with the hair turned inward for greater warmth. A single seam ran along the outside sole. This was a variation from the eastern woodland style with the seam on top, or the two-piece shoe of upper and sole found elsewhere on the plains.[4]

A second scrap of tough bison hide could be sewn to the bottom of the moccasin to fend against rocks and thorns. Meriwether Lewis complained of prickly pears that "pierce a double thickness of dressed deer's skin with ease." One night, he noted that William Clark "extracted seventeen of these briars from his feet this evening after he encamped by the light of the fire."[5]

Colter and the other men of the Corps suffered similarly and became adept at repairing and replacing moccasins and clothing. Rufus Sage declared that moccasin repair "is a business in which every mountaineer is necessarily a proficient, and rarely will he venture upon a long journey without the appurtenances of his profession." Randolph Marcy, an army officer and expert on frontier survival, added that "one of the most indispensable articles to the outfit of the prairie traveler is buckskin. . . . The awl and buckskin will be found in constant requisition."[6] Marcy also noted the advantage of native footwear, especially in frigid cold and deep snow where "moccasins are preferable to boots or shoes, as being more pliable, and allowing a freer circulation of the blood."[7]

For the upper body, a hooded capote—a watch-coat fashioned from a wool trade blanket—would have protected Colter from subzero weather. The same material, or pieces of fur, provided for gaiters that kept snow and slush out of moccasins and off the lower legs. Wool and fur were also used to make mittens and caps.

In addition to the clothing he wore and the thirty-pound pack on his back, Colter kept items of greatest urgency close at hand. In the arid western lands, a canteen remained by his side to be refilled at every chance. It might have been sewn from leather or made of gourd or gut in Indian fashion. Or perhaps he carried military issue—a metal container or a canteen of wood with staves like a barrel. Later frontiersmen fashioned makeshift water containers from buffalo paunches, deerskins, beaver pelts, and powder horns.[8]

Water was the precious commodity—the most basic of basic necessities. Its abundance or absence offered the quickest path to either life or death. Of all the hardships of hunger, pain, bitter cold, and brutal heat that frontiersmen endured, they complained that thirst was the worst. They had to know how to find scattered sources and how to carry and ration water while crossing the dry expanses.

Those who survived on the plains knew to watch for certain signs. Marcy noted that of the "many indications of water known to old campaigners . . . the most certain of them are deep green cottonwood or willow trees." With this in mind, at a distant glance one could locate a water source, whether on the surface or just beneath the sand.[9] Once underground water was found, a hole was dug as much as several feet deep to reach it.

The method of water procurement depended on the seasons. In winter, a tomahawk could be used to break river ice to reach water. Or snow could be melted in a hat or other makeshift container by dropping in rocks heated in a campfire.[10]

If Colter followed the example of his friends, the Crow, he seized every opportunity to drink all the water he could hold. The Crow believed water provided more than basic sustenance and held medicinal value as well. "Water is your body," a Crow proverb said. But it also was sacred—essential to mind and spirit. The best start to every morning, they believed, was a baptismal bath in a stream.[11]

Modern vanity demands that Indians, frontiersmen, and premodern people in general must have been relatively brutish and lacking in proper hygiene. But the opposite was often true. Western travelers took advantage of every watering hole. Upon finding one, they usually took a long drink followed by a bath or a swim.

The bath was often a cold one taken in a snowmelt stream, unless a man was fortunate enough to happen upon a thermal spring. If the water there was too hot, he simply moved farther downriver to a cooler place. Frontiersmen learned this technique by observing the indigenous people.

Warren Ferris recalled the Hot Springs in Pierre's Hole: "We passed in our route a well known hot spring, which bursts out from the prairie . . . and flows several hundred yards into Wisdom River." The water is scalding at the source, but cools as it descends. "The Indians have made a succession of little dams, from the upper end to the river; and one finds baths of every temperature, from boiling hot, to that of the river, which is too cold for bathing, at any season. Our Indians were almost constantly in one or other of these baths during our stay near the springs."[12]

Ferris added, "The Indians rise at day light invariably, when all go down to the stream they may happen to be encamped on, wash their hands and faces, and comb their long hair with their fingers. . . . Bathing is one of their favorite amusements, and when near a suitable place, if the weather be fair, some of them may at any time be seen in the water." Other observers said Indian children swam "like ducks."

Alfred Jacob Miller noted that native people are "remarkably fond" of swimming and bathing. "They bathe at every opportunity" and "make every effort to live cleanly." Various frontiersmen commented on the cleanliness of specific tribes with which they had contact, including the Crow, Flathead, Blackfoot, Mandan, and Oglala Sioux. Nor did winter weather deter them. Mountain man James Clyman said of the Crow Indians: "Many of them take a bath every morning, even when the hoar frost was flying thick in the air and it was necessary to cut holes in the ice to get at the water." Others witnessed the same.[13]

Another means of cleanliness and health involved the use of the sweat lodge. Thomas Leforge, who lived among the Crow, explained that a sweat was a means of "purifying our minds as well as our bodies." For this purpose, a wigwam or barrel-vault lodge was erected about six feet long with a tight covering of skins. Hot rocks were placed within and water poured over them to produce the steam. Some frontiersmen claimed that this form of treatment helped them overcome serious illnesses.[14]

Indians also had a reputation for keeping their clothing clean. Many used a specific white clay as a laundry soap to cleanse and whiten the dressed skins they wore.[15] Cleanliness of body and clothing was important for Native Americans because hygiene meant survival.

US Army routine also urged attention to health and cleanliness, and Lewis and Clark had insisted that the men of the Corps adhere to military standards. Evidence suggests that they followed the guidelines laid out by Baron von Steuben. His *Regulations for the Order and Discipline of the Troops of the United States* demanded proper hygiene. Officers were to see that their men "wash their hands and faces every day, and oftener when necessary. And when the river is nigh, and the season favorable, the men shall bathe themselves as frequently as possible."[16]

A clean camp was equally essential. Von Steuben ordered that

> *one officer of a company must every day visit the tents; see that they are kept clean, that every utensil belonging to them is in proper order; and that no bones or other filth be in or near them; and when the weather is fine, should order them to be struck about two hours at noon, and the straw and bedding well aired. The soldiers should not be permitted to eat in their tents, except in bad weather.*[17]

The first concern was for filth and disease. But Colter had a more urgent reason to keep a tidy campsite. A shelter that emitted smells ensured a rude awakening. Varmints enjoy nosing through odorous camps. Far worse, food and refuse broadcast to every neighboring grizzly that dinner is served.

Keeping a clean camp and body was fundamental if one hoped to survive, and every watering hole offered that opportunity. But the first order of business was to drink one's fill and top off a canteen for the long march ahead.

In addition to the indispensable canteen, the second essential that Colter kept close was a hunting knife. Typically, it had a sharpened edge for cutting and a fine point for stabbing. It could be wielded in the hand for defense or lashed to a pole as a spear. Jedediah Smith described how he and his men made spears for defense against an Indian attack: "We then fastened our butcher knives with cords to the end of light poles so as to form a tolerable lance."

More often, the knife served as a tool for grubbing roots and harvesting plants, killing and dressing game, slicing and chopping food, and skinning and scraping hides for cover and clothing. In addition, it frequently served as the only eating utensil. Considering its many uses, it is understandable that legendary frontiersman Hugh Glass said he "felt quite rich" when he found the knife, flint, and steel he thought he had lost.[18]

A typical hunting knife had a seven-inch blade of polished steel. A handle of wood, antler, or bone was held to the blade with a metal ferrule or a hilt to protect the hand.[19] With or without a scabbard, the knife remained nearby, tucked in the waist belt.

The knife represented a technological leap far beyond the sharpened flint that still was used in the lithic cultures of many indigenous people. Overnight, it became essential to the lifestyle of the Native American. The sight of Colter's hunting knife might have done more than anything else to entice the tribes to trade.

Colter probably carried a tomahawk beside his knife in usual woodsman fashion. This was standard equipment for riflemen of the American Revolution and for frontier hunters before and after. Like the knife, it doubled as weapon and tool—a portable ax and shovel, and a hammer when turned back to front. Colter's tomahawk was likely of the Kentuckian style, with a swept-down blade and an eighteen-inch hardwood handle.

Next in importance was the flintlock long rifle that Colter kept in his grip. The rifle was the frontiersman's constant companion. He slept with it, ate with it, and carried it always in hand. Various men referred to it as "my only companion" or "my trusty traveling companion." And they never allowed their guns "to remain empty for one moment."[20]

Colter probably relied on the Kentucky (also known as Pennsylvania) flintlock long rifle with an approximate forty-two-inch barrel. The new US flintlock rifle Model 1803 with a thirty-four-inch barrel was distributed to fifteen of the men of the Corps of Discovery. But those who were experienced hunters preferred their own longer-barreled rifles, with greater accuracy and better aim due to the distance between front and rear sights.

To improve accuracy further, an improvised barrel rest was often used, such as a rifle ramrod placed vertically under the barrel while firing from a kneeling position, or a felt hat used as a prop when shooting from a prone position. When a barrel rest was used, missing a target became almost inexcusable. William Anderson upbraided himself when he missed an elk and a pronghorn. He said, despite his good Kentucky rifle, a steady gun rest, and good powder, he missed the targets "at a distance that a Kentucky girl would have bored a squirrel's eye out."[21]

With flint in place and the pan always primed, Colter's rifle stood ready for instant use. In foul weather, the rifle lock remained covered with a leather frock to keep the powder dry. With this one weapon, the abundant game grazing just out of reach became an immediate supply of food, cover, and clothing.

More often than not, Colter could approach on foot within rifle range of bison, elk, and deer. In winter, with snowshoes strapped on, he could walk right up to bison floundering in deep snow. In summer, he could ambush them as they struggled in mud after fording a river. Or he could join the more honorable and dangerous native ritual of chasing the stampeding herd on horseback.[22]

Frontiersmen quickly learned the Indian methods of hunting bison. First, a hunter needed to find a herd that was grazing peacefully. If they had been recently disturbed, they would be scattered and skittish—ready to flee. When a quiet herd was located, the hunter determined wind direction. To do this, he tossed a feather or sand in the air. Then he approached from downwind in order to hide his scent.

If on foot, he often concealed himself with an animal skin or foliage. When close enough, he took a shot or waved a blanket to chase a herd into fallen timber or a deep snowbank. Or he could run them onto slippery river ice or off a ledge.[23]

On horseback, bison hunting became more efficient but riskier. Typically, a group of hunters chased a herd and fired at will, or ran the bison into a box canyon or off a cliff. These methods sometimes killed hundreds of animals—enough to feed an entire village. A slightly more subtle method involved riders surrounding a herd and tightening the circle until the bison were within easy rifle range. Jim Beckwourth lamented that white encroachments would one day result in the native people being taken by surround, like bison.[24]

The Indian method of shooting a bison with bow and arrow involved aiming for an area just behind the forelegs. After making a successful shot, the hunter patiently waited for the animal to bleed to death. White hunters with rifles preferred to aim behind the shoulder blades and the thick mane. A wound farther back often failed to stop the animal, while one in the head either glanced off or embedded in the surface of the skull.

As Rufus Sage said,

> *To shoot it in the head, is an inane effort. No rifle can project a ball with sufficient force to perforate the thick hair and hide to its brain, through the double scull-bone [sic] that protects it. A paunch shot is equally vain. The only sure points for the marksman are, the heart, lights [lungs], kidneys, or vertebrae; and even then the unyielding victim not unfrequently escapes. . . . I have witnessed their escape, even after the reception of fifteen bullet-wounds, and most of them at such points as would have proved fatal to almost any other animal.*[25]

To butcher a bison, the animal was turned right side up on its belly and an incision was made from the front of the hump to the rear. The skin on both sides was peeled down and laid on the ground, hair down, providing a place to set the cuts of meat. Then a tomahawk was used to sever the spine on each end of the hump ribs. These were removed along with the fatty fleece and side ribs.

Next, "the flesh was cut off in large masses from the rump, haunches, and shoulders." Native hunters often ate the liver raw, on the spot. But the favorite cuts were the hump ribs and tongue, followed by the fleece, side ribs, and bone marrow.[26]

Frontiersmen learned from the Indians how to proficiently hunt other game as well. Deer and elk could be stalked like bison or shot from ambush in wooded areas. Or they could be run into rivers or mud to slow them down. Deer were sometimes chased into brush-fence enclosures and shot or snared.

Pronghorn proved a much greater challenge. William Anderson quipped, "Today, I shot at four antelopes as they whizzed by me. I do not know whether my aim was twisted, or whether they outran my ball. Old traders and trappers tell marvelous things about their speed." Some men correctly noted that pronghorn could outrun hunting dogs with ease and leave them far behind. But pronghorn usually employed a more efficient method by simply keeping a great distance away from threats and far out of rifle range.

The best way to hunt them was to pique their curiosity by bleating like their young, which sounds "precisely like sheep." Or a hunter could hide behind a rise and raise a small flag to flutter in the breeze. Pronghorn are intensely curious and can be attracted to strange objects, to their doom.

Bighorn sheep were also difficult to hunt. After sheltering in lower elevations in winter, they ascended steep slopes as the weather grew warmer. In this way they kept pace with tender spring foliage as it emerged higher and higher up the mountainsides. In every situation they kept a wary eye for intruders and retreated up near-vertical cliffs at the first hint of danger.

Grizzly bears provided another meat source. Their flesh was poor in the spring after hibernation, but better in the summer and autumn. They and other large game could be caught in a pitfall—a simple hole covered with twigs and grass. The trappers then shot them at leisure.

Beaver meat also sufficed. A mountain man made his livelihood by trapping beaver and often had meat on hand for breakfast. In addition, frontiersmen learned from the natives how to hunt wild fowl without having to expend powder and lead. Grouse could be approached within several feet, allowing the hunter to hit them with a rock or stick.[27] But in most circumstances, the rifle remained the primary tool for hunting.

The use of a rifle required gunpowder, lead balls, and special equipment. These supplies and tools remained standard in the first decades of the nineteenth century. In 1803, Meriwether Lewis requested that the Corps of Discovery be supplied with powder, lead, gun worms, ball screws, extra lock parts, repair tools, and bullet molds. On the frontier, when supplies of ammunition ran low, a rifleman melted lead in an iron ladle or spoon and poured it into a bullet mold to form a round projectile.

In total, Lewis ordered two hundred pounds of gunpowder and four hundred pounds of lead in the typical weight ratio of 1:2. To waterproof the powder and carry it securely, Lewis had every four pounds of powder sealed inside a lead container weighing eight pounds. When a container was emptied, it could be melted to make lead balls and used with the next four pounds of powder.

Even with ample quantities of powder on hand, frontiersmen used it sparingly, and in most cases only fired at game when necessity dictated. They knew that surpluses of powder might be needed for defense or in case their expedition became delayed on the trail.[28]

Colter would carry rifle supplies in a leather hunting bag, or possibles bag, with a sturdy flap to resist the wind and "turn the severest weather."[29] Inside was wadding that had to stay dry because it was used to pack ball against powder. The typical bag also held extra rifle flints and a shot pouch containing a pound of lead balls. There was room to spare for dry tinder and flint and steel to spark a campfire.

On the frozen plains, the ability to strike a fire in all kinds of weather was essential to survival. Colter was expert at this after years of making his camp alone. Perhaps he fit the description given by Randolph Marcy decades later, after the sulfur match had come into common use: "I have seen an Indian start a fire with flint and steel after others had failed to do it with matches. This was during a heavy rain, when almost all available fuel had become wet. On such occasions dry fuel may generally be obtained under logs, rocks, or leaning trees. The inner bark of some dry trees, cedar for instance, is excellent to kindle a fire."[30]

A campfire was essential for cooking, warmth, and protection from predators. But first, one had to find fuel. This was not a problem in timber-rich river bottoms or evergreen-covered mountain slopes. But many places in the West are devoid of timber. Along barren watercourses, travelers gathered small willow branches and driftwood.

Otherwise, sagebrush sufficed. Western explorers and trappers learned its use from the native inhabitants. Sagebrush (*Artemisia tridentata*), sometimes called wormwood by early visitors, grew in the barren plains throughout the West and served its purpose adequately. One frontiersman said, "It burns well and retains fire as long as any fuel I ever used." The western bands of Shoshone carried a long rope of twisted sagebrush bark as a slow fuse from which to start fires whenever and wherever they pleased.[31]

The ubiquitous sagebrush served other purposes as well. It was a starvation food for bison, deer, and various game. Prairie chickens ate the buds and leaves, but western travelers complained that this tainted the flavor of the meat. Horses also grazed sagebrush out of dire necessity, and men sometimes used the leaves to concoct a bitter tea if they found local water sources unpalatable.

In addition, they learned from the Flatheads to use sage as a poultice to stop bleeding, treat open sores, and reduce swelling. Some Indians rubbed it on the body as a means of purification. Others mixed it with brains as a concoction for softening hides during the tanning process. The western bands of Shoshone even formed it into shelters—sometimes making a small hovel from a single plant. This is not surprising because sagebrush could grow to a height of ten feet with a five-inch-diameter trunk.[32]

Another emergency source of fuel was bison dung, or *bois de vache*, as the French voyageurs called it. Those who used it were pleasantly surprised that it made a fire hot enough for cooking meat. Narcissa Whitman claimed that it served "a very good purpose, similar to the kind of coal used in Pennsylvania." If timber, sagebrush, or bison dung was not available, an inferior fire could be made from river rushes. Bison fat or gunpowder was sometimes used to start a fire quickly or keep it from sputtering out.[33]

After a fire burned down to coals, Indians spitted meat on a stick and inclined it over the heat for roasting. Or they dug a hole, lined it with a skin, filled it with water and chunks of meat or roots, and then added rocks that had been heated in the fire. As the rocks cooled, the cook replaced them with more hot rocks until the food was sufficiently boiled. Indian sign language reflected this ancient method of using a hole in the ground as a basin. The sign for the word *kettle* or *basin* can be literally translated: *a hole scooped in the ground*.

To make bread, native people pounded available roots or seeds into flour. Then they formed cakes and baked them beside an open fire. Frontiersmen learned and used all these methods, but they preferred to carry a small kettle for boiling water and cooking.[34]

Colter's first action when pitching camp, before unpacking and making shelter, would be to find tinder and wood. A fire was then started and burned down to coals for cooking. For this purpose, he kept flint and steel handy, perhaps in the hunting bag alongside a carefully wrapped bundle of extra tinder.

In addition, the typical hunting bag held a whetstone for putting a quick edge on a knife or tomahawk. On top of the bag, most hunters carried their powder horn. The horn offered the best means of keeping a half-pound of powder dry and ready for immediate use.

All this gear was hung about the body within easy reach. In standard fashion, the knife and tomahawk remained strapped to the waist on the left, with a canteen slung close behind. The hunting bag hung on the right, with the powder horn resting on top. This allowed right-handed access to powder and shot while the rifle was cradled in the opposite arm.[35] Essential items like the canteen, weapons, and fire-making tools remained close at hand.

But other provisions could be packed away. The thirty-pound pack on Colter's back held supplies for camp and trade. The most essential component was the material that formed the pack: a single piece of hide, wool blanket, or oil cloth. In Colter's case it was probably heavy linen cloth, waterproofed or painted with linseed oil. With a length of about eight feet and a width of six or seven feet, it replicated the large bison hides that Native Americans had depended upon for thousands of years for packs, shelter, cloaks, and other uses.

Bison hides weighed around eighteen pounds. A waterproof cloth weighed seven pounds. In combination with a good wool blanket, cloth was a comparably effective cover and easier to tote. For this reason, oil cloth was often preferred over hides.[36]

But if the cloth wore out and could not be replaced, one could resort to the age-old method and make use of an animal hide in the indigenous manner. For use as a cloak, Indians draped a bison robe over the back and shoulders. From there it hung to the knees. As temperatures dropped they clasped the robe snugly beneath the chin, or they used a belt or rawhide strip to tie it about the waist.

In bitter cold they turned the hair in, then out as the days grew warmer. Skins of elk, deer, pronghorn, and bighorn sheep served the same purpose when bison were scarce. In warmer months, elk hides, with hair removed, provided a lighter robe or shawl.

A large bison hide offered all the basic shelter one needed—for cover and for clothing. Clothing, after all, is nothing more than tailored cover fashioned to fit the body. Meriwether Lewis observed that, for the native people, "this robe forms a garment in the day and constitutes their only covering at night."[37] As such, it was an essential possession.

The bison robe provided the standard attire of the Plains Indian adult. Children often wore smaller skins. William Anderson said of the Shoshone, "Each child, male or female, has its little blanket or rabbit-robe, in which it sits, stands or walks." Children, and sometimes adults, also wore ponchos made of deerskin or trade blankets.

For adult males, the bison robe was either worn by itself or with moccasins, leggings, and a breechcloth, while women added a dress. The robe was slung over the shoulders and held with the left hand. Perhaps this is why 85 percent of Indian sign language could be made with the right hand alone. Frontiersmen adopted the same use of the robe, or wore a blanket in similar manner, draped over the shoulders and kept in place with the same belt or sash that held their knife and tomahawk.

Native Americans relied on bison robes to shed water and freezing precipitation. They rarely wore hats, but pulled the robe over the head if necessary. Colter likely began his journeys with a low-crowned, broad-brimmed felt hat, but might have transitioned to a fur cap or simply used a bison robe for a hood.[38]

A green (untanned) bison hide, although heavy, could serve as an emergency blanket or shelter. Colter did not have to worry about using green hides or going to the trouble of tanning hides as long as he was in the vicinity of Indian villages. But elsewhere, circumstances might demand a freshly tanned hide.

Colter certainly knew the procedure, as described by F. A. Wislizenus:

They first stretch the fresh hide with pegs on the ground, clean it with sharp stones of all flesh, fat and skinny parts, and finally rub in fresh buffalo brains. . . . Hides that are to be tanned on both sides are boiled in a solution of brain. When the hair is removed, brain is again rubbed in; and finally the hides are smoked, which makes them very suitable for tents and clothing. In addition to the hide, the Indians never forget to take the strong sinews from the neck and back of the buffalo. They dry them, and use them, torn into threads, with aid of an awl, for sewing.

With this knowledge, and game nearby, a mountain man had all he required for shelter and clothing.[39]

Bison hides served a multitude of other purposes as well. They provided the primary material for bedding and for waterproof packs. They could be spread on the ground to catch rainfall when water supplies ran low. Hides also found use as boat sails and as a means of signaling from one hillock to another. In short, they served many fundamental purposes throughout a person's life, and when that person died, the bison hide became the burial shroud.[40]

Only in recent years had traders introduced wool blankets to the Plains Indians. These blankets were warm and light to carry, with a favorable ratio of weight to insulating value. Like hides, they could be used as robes or fashioned into clothing. They soon became popular among native tribes and assumed many of the functions of the bison robe. When a baby was born, it was wrapped in a blanket. A blanket later became its primary clothing, winter cloak, and bed-cover. The blanket could be used as a lodge door, a lean-to roof, or a sail. George Catlin "frequently witnessed . . . [Indians] sailing with the aid of their blankets. . . . When the wind is fair, [they] stand in the bow of the canoe and hold by two corners, with the other two under the foot or tied to the leg; while the women sit in the other end of the canoe, and steer it with their paddles."

In Colter's time, the Hudson's Bay point blanket was a common frontier possession. The point blanket had originated in sixteenth-century France and became a typical trade item in North America soon afterward. It was often distributed by French companies in Montreal. By the mid-eighteenth century, "four-point blankets were standard issue for the American colonial militiamen." With the defeat and withdrawal of the French after the French and Indian War, the British assumed control over all trade with the indigenous people of Canada and the upper Mississippi and Missouri Rivers. The British-controlled Hudson's Bay Company began dispersing point blankets as standard trade items in about 1780 to replace those that had been manufactured by Montreal-based companies.

The blankets were readily recognized with end-stripes, typically of blue or black on a background of natural white. Point markings appeared in the weaving on one side. The number of points roughly reflected the dimensions and weight of the wool. A three-point blanket measured about fifty-eight inches by seventy-two inches and weighed four pounds.[41] Lewis ordered fifteen three-point blankets for use by the Corps of Discovery. But a taller man, like Colter, would have preferred a four-point blanket at about seventy-two by ninety inches and a weight of six pounds. Tradition suggests he carried one of these.[42]

Wool blankets kept their owners warm, but they repelled water poorly. They were better used in combination with a heavy piece of oil cloth. A person of five-feet-ten inches in height could wrap in a seven-by-eight-foot oil cloth, with or without a blanket, and use it as a waterproof cloak. By forming a hood over the head and bunching the folds with a belt, an effective barrier could be made which repelled wind and weather. With a capote or blanket underneath, a person could stay warm and dry while on the march in the day or while curled up at night. The cloth could serve as a rain fly, ground cloth, or bedroll liner. It also formed various portable shelters: the barrel-vault tent, the half-face tent, the wigwam, the one-person tipi (tepee), and other makeshift huts.

Native Americans of the northern plains and mountains used several shelter types, but the best known kind was the tipi. This bison-hide tent varied in size to accommodate one to ten individuals. Its ingenious conical design allowed it to deflect the strong winds and shed the heavy snow of a brutal climate. A fire could be built within larger tipis because the smoke was able to escape by means of an adjustable flap at the top. The flap also served the purpose of letting in more sunlight on cold days and less on hot days. The bottom tipi fringe could be raised to allow a refreshing breeze to enter.

A small tipi could be quickly erected with four or more eight-foot poles. Randolph Marcy illustrated this type and encouraged its use among western travelers. He said: "We adopted this description of shelter in crossing the Rocky Mountains during the winter of 1857–8, and thus formed a very effectual protection against the bleak winds which sweep with great violence over those lofty and inhospitable sierras."[43]

In addition to tipis, people on the move erected small shelters in the manner described by F. A. Wislizenus: "In the summer the Indians find it often too cumbersome to carry their tents of skins with them, and so make at every place where they camp so-called summer tents. For this the squaws cut tree branches and wands, put them into the ground in semi-circle, and cover this little natural tent with a blanket or a hide."

Rufus Sage noted similar barrel-vault structures: *Shantees* were erected "by means of slender sticks, planted in parallel rows five or six feet apart, and interwoven at the tops, so as to form an arch of suitable height, over which was spread a roofage of robes or blankets." Alfred Jacob Miller's sketches indicate that these typically stood about five feet high and slightly less wide.

Sometimes, native people made comparable dwellings without cutting branches. Instead, they simply entered a willow thicket, pulled several tops together and bound them, and then stretched skins, blankets, or cloth above. Entire villages of lodges were sometimes erected in this fashion. An example appears in William Henry Jackson's 1871 photograph of a Shoshone family on the headwaters of Medicine Lodge Creek.

For a more temporary arrangement, a hide or blanket was simply draped over a few sticks, tree branches, or a bush to shield against rain or sun. A windbreak was made in similar fashion. Other shelters included pine branch hovels and snow caves. In the case of the latter, a hole was dug either into a snowdrift or into snow that was piled up for the purpose. Indians and frontiersmen also made use of natural stone caves or overhangs.[44]

Sgt. Patrick Gass described temporary huts contrived by the Corps of Discovery. "The party," he said, "were engaged in making places of shelter, to defend them from the stormy weather. Some had small sails to cover their little hovels, and others had to make frames and cover them with grass."[45]

Randolph Marcy, in his book titled *The Prairie Traveler*, illustrated the half-face tent—an oil cloth lean-to that Lewis and Clark had employed on their westward journey. The common tents of the Revolutionary era equaled two half-faces—two slopes of cloth at about seven-by-eight feet apiece.[46] Six men shared cramped quarters within. In comparison, one half-face, at seven-by-eight feet, would have accommodated Colter quite well.

Whether he used a hide or oil cloth to construct a half-face, a tipi, a wigwam, or a similar shelter, Colter was able to burrow down and ride out the roughest wind and weather. To keep off the cold, damp ground, he could form a padded sleeping area of willow boughs, evergreen branches, sagebrush, pine needles, grass, reeds, or leaves. A perimeter of logs, rocks, or bison bones prevented bedding material from scattering. Another option was to follow the example of the Crow, who lacked the low beds that other tribes used and had nothing more than a hide or blanket between them and the ground.

For many Indians and frontiersmen, a bison hide, wool blanket, or oil cloth served as the primary item of bedding and provided the only shelter. With no roof overhead, this bedroll sometimes became drenched by rain. In that case, the occupant wrung it out as best he could, wrapped himself in the damp bedding, and tried to get some sleep. In heavy snow, a person simply curled up tighter and let the snow cover his bedroll until morning.[47]

The oil cloth, like the bison hide, served many other purposes as well. Marcy noted that "a supply of drinking water may be obtained . . . by suspending a cloth or blanket by the four corners and hanging a small weight to the centre [of one edge], so as to allow all the rain to run toward one point, from whence it drops into a vessel beneath. . . . Painted canvas cloths answer a very good purpose for catching water."[48]

Oil cloth made a good boat cover to keep rain and river spray from collecting in the bottom of canoes, and it could be used as a sail in the manner of a hide or blanket. Or the cloth could serve as a float for crossing a river. By piling items in the middle of the cloth and tying it into a bundle, one could swim it across and keep the contents fairly dry. Sometimes leaves were bundled inside to form a makeshift raft.

Also, like the bison hide, an oil cloth was used for concealment while stalking or ambushing game. Conversely, the cloth was waved to cause panic and drive game toward traps or cliffs.

But the primary use, in addition to shelter, was as a simple pack cover. When spread upon the ground, a person's possessions could be carefully arranged and rolled into a bundle for transport. In this way, items stayed "perfectly protected from rain, and capable of being suspended from the shoulders and carried with comfort and ease during a march."[49]

To form a pack in this manner, the oil cloth is spread flat. The wool blanket rests on top, while the other items are bundled and centered at one end. The cloth is then folded inward from both sides. A six-foot strap of leather is laid crosswise, extending beyond the cloth on each side. Then the cloth is rolled and tied into a cylindrical pack. Finally, the strap is fastened into a loop to form a sling.[50]

The pack is now ready to be carried on the back in the ancient way, from a sling over the shoulder, or from a chest strap that crosses the upper arms and chest. Or the strap can serve as a tumpline across the upper forehead. A thirty-pound pack is easily carried by any of these methods. It also can be readily dropped to the ground and used as a rifle rest or as a cushion for quick naps between marches.

Inside the pack, Colter probably carried an additional two pounds of bar lead for rifle balls and an extra pound of powder for replenishing his powder horn.[51] A bullet mold allowed him to make lead balls either from a bar or from balls extracted from the game he had killed. His rifle cleaning and repair kit would include a vial of oil, spare lock parts, and small tools.

In the event that game proved scarce, frontiersmen kept food on hand. Colter was adept at jerking beef by slicing it thinly and hanging it on scaffolds in the sun to dry. To "make meat" was "a highly necessary precaution." It remained "sweet and sound" in the summer for ten or twelve days, and in the winter for months at a time. Rufus Sage claimed that "meat thus cured may be preserved for years without salt."

In order to expose the meat to wind and sun, it was laid on a frame, tied to wagon wheels, or spread out on bushes. If time was pressing, a small fire could be built under the jerky to hurry the process along. This also provided a pleasant, smoky flavor and kept the flies away.

Another means of preserving meat was to make pemmican from jerky. Marcy described the Plains Indian method:

> *The buffalo meat is cut into thin flakes, and hung up to dry in the sun or before a slow fire; it is then pounded between two stones and reduced to a powder; this powder is placed in a bag of the animal's hide, with the hair on the outside; melted grease is then poured into it, and the bag sewn up. It can be eaten raw, and many prefer it so. Mixed with a little flour and boiled, it is a very wholesome and exceedingly nutritious food, and will keep fresh for a long time.* [52]

Colter likely started out with a pouch of corn to supplement his beef diet and consumed roots, berries, and seeds along the way. Later mountain men often began their journeys with a supply of corn and sometimes procured additional small amounts along the route. Corn was grown in large quantities by the Mandan and Hidatsa villages and was a major trade item for the plains tribes. Frontiersmen cooked it in various forms. One method was to grind it down to cornmeal, add bison fat and water to form thick pancakes, and fry it in the bottom of a kettle.

When the corn supply ran out, frontiersmen subsisted on plants that nature provided. Roots were a primary staple for tribes on both sides of the Continental Divide and served as a supplemental diet or starvation food for western travelers. The root of the prairie turnip (*Psoralea esculenta*) was an essential food source for natives of the Great Plains. It also went by the names bread root and pomme blanche.

Its counterpart in the Rocky Mountains and far west was camas (*Camassia quamash*). The ranges of prairie turnip and camas overlapped in parts of the eastern Rockies and the plants shared similar characteristics. Both could be readily located by their blue or purple flowers. Both were eaten raw, boiled, baked in pit ovens, or dried and pounded into flour for making mush or cakes.

Colter had opportunity to partake of both species. He ate camas while crossing the Rockies with Lewis and Clark, and survived on prairie turnip while returning to Manuel's Fort after one of his escapes from the Blackfoot. He probably consumed these roots on numerous other occasions as well. Lewis brought back specimens of both plants as part of his herbarium, and later frontiersmen made general use of them, sometimes commenting on the sweet and pleasant flavor of both.

Bitterroot (*Lewisia rediviva*) was another useful plant harvested by indigenous people, but with a more limited range. Lewis had gathered specimens at Traveler's Rest in present-day western Montana and also included this in his herbarium. Flathead Indians harvested the plant in June, at the time of what they called the

Bitterroot Moon, and prepared the roots for consumption much like prairie turnip and camas. Bitterroot had a pleasant enough flavor, but was more of an acquired taste.

Other common food plants included wild onions, plums, currants, chokecherries, gooseberries, serviceberries, buffalo berries, and huckleberries. The berries were eaten fresh or pounded and dried. Or they were added to pounded meat to make pemmican.

Rosehips, sunflower seeds, sunflower roots, grass seeds, mosses, and sap from cottonwood trees and evergreens also served as dietary supplements. According to Rufus Sage: "Rosebuds are found in great quantities in many places, throughout the mountains, during the winter . . . and have not unfrequently been the means of preserving life in cases of extreme hunger."[53]

Salt for preservation and seasoning was carried as an essential supply in many backpacks. Among the men of the Corps of Discovery, some insisted on salt in their diets while others did not. The fact that Colter helped boil seawater into salt for the expedition might hint at his personal preference. Other condiments are rarely mentioned in frontier journals.

Colter's pack perhaps included the typical metal cup, fork, and spoon for making food preparation and consumption easier. These, along with his hunting knife, would meet all his needs.

To add to his larder when times were hard, he certainly carried tools for fishing, as he did while traveling with the Corps of Discovery. A few metal hooks and a piece of string would allow him to fish in the manner of Indians along the Missouri River. Or he could spear fish with a gig like the Columbia Basin natives.

An assortment of metal hooks and gigs also made attractive trade items to display to Indians, although the Crow and Blackfoot cared little for fishing.[54] All were impressed by the pins and needles, the awl and thimble, and the roll of thread that Colter carried for clothing repairs or suturing wounds. These and the full assortment of trade items were sure to draw long stares and covetous murmurs.

For people who made fire by friction with a stick spun between the palms of their hands, flint and steel appeared as a miracle. For those who boiled meat in a rawhide container with hot rocks dropped into the broth, brass kettles came as a godsend. For those who combed their hair with a porcupine tail or buffalo tongue, the ivory comb looked like a luxury.

Neat and tidy hair was important to most tribes of the northern plains and mountains. Indian sign language for the word *woman* can be literally translated as *hair comber*. Women of the Crow, Blackfoot, and other nations typically parted their hair on the forehead down the middle, then painted the part with vermilion. Some native people, male and female alike, groomed their spouse or lover in a similar manner as a sign of affection.[55]

In addition to combs, there were other trade items used for personal adornment: colorful flannel cloths, silk handkerchiefs, and ribbons. There were shiny rings that could be poked into clothing, ears, and noses. These rings were highly prized. Rufus Sage noted that an Indian woman "prides herself much upon the number of rings in her ears and upon her fingers." Among wealthier tribes like the Blackfoot, women sometimes wore six to eight rings on each finger.[56]

Trade items also included tiny brass bells and buttons. There were pewter mirrors that offered a first look at oneself or provided a means of signaling to friends by reflecting the sun. The Crow, Shoshone, and other tribes later learned to use mirrors for conveying messages at a distance. Jim Beckwourth said they "telegraphed with the aid of a small looking-glass, which the Crow scouts usually carry, and every motion of which is understood in the village."[57]

Other items included whole strings of wampum and perfectly spherical beads manufactured in several hues, including the favorite color of blue.[58] Vermilion was available in one-ounce portions to be painted on cheeks as a sign of friendship. Two years earlier, when Meriwether Lewis came upon three Shoshone women, they had fallen down and wailed aloud for fear of the white-skinned stranger. But he soon gained their trust with a few trade items, especially when he "painted their tawny cheeks with some vermilion, which," he explained, "with this nation is emblematic of peace."[59]

To clinch trade negotiations, Colter would have carried a supply of tobacco. The dried plant was essential for establishing diplomacy and formalizing commercial transactions. It was also a provision eagerly sought among tribes of the plains, who often had nothing more than a pungent local plant to smoke.

John Townsend spoke for many western traders when he said, "No trade, of consequence, can ever be effected with Indians, unless the pipe be first smoked, and the matter calmly and seriously deliberated upon." For Native Americans, tobacco served many purposes. Physically, it provided a soothing effect. Mentally, it symbolized goodwill during serious deliberations. Spiritually, it served as an important element of prayer.

P. J. De Smet, a Jesuit missionary among the northern tribes, explained: "The smoking of the calumet forms a part of all their religious ceremonies. It is a kind of sacred rite which they perform when they prepare themselves to invoke the Great Spirit, and take the sun and moon, the earth and the water as witnesses of the sincerity of their intentions, and the fidelity with which they promise to comply with their engagements."[60]

The tobacco plants cultivated by Indians on the eastern plains along the Missouri River included the species *Nicotiana quadrival-*

vis, as well as the closely related species *Nicotiana multivalvis* and *Nicotiana attenuate*. Lewis collected *Nicotiana quadrivalvis* in South Dakota on October 12, 1804, and placed a sample in his herbarium.

These plants provided the primary ingredient of native tobacco. But Indians almost always combined this with parts of other plants to form a tobacco mixture some called *kinnikinik*. They produced favorite blends by adding bearberry or the inner bark of red osier dogwood (also known as red willow). Other plants used for this purpose included black willow, sumac, pokeweed, and various herbs.[61]

With an essential supply of tobacco, Colter's bundle of trade goods was complete—representing a sampling of items that would be available at Manuel's Fort in the spring. The inventory of trade items remained basically the same on the frontier through the first half of the nineteenth century. The goods that Lewis and Clark carried westward as gifts for native tribes remained popular among indigenous people for many years.

As a result of this continuity, the Corps of Discovery's list of trade goods in 1804 closely matched those of François Larocque in 1805, William Ashley in 1825, and Jedediah Smith in 1826. In the 1830s, Robert Campbell, John Townsend, Nathaniel Wyeth, William Anderson, and Alfred Jacob Miller noted trade items practically identical to those of their predecessors. The same held true in the records of Rufus Sage in the 1840s and Kit Carson in the 1850s.[62]

In addition to standard trade items, Colter's pack probably held an extra shirt and pair of pants, or patches of cloth and leather that allowed for repairs while on the trail. With snowshoes strapped on top, the pack weighed some thirty pounds and contained all that Colter needed for a trek of several months in the mountains.[63]

Chapter Three

GOING NATIVE

COLTER WANDERED INTO THE UNKNOWN WEST WITH all the supplies and skills he required for survival, supplemented by the knowledge and assistance he received from native people. To endure in this wilderness, one was wise to adopt the ways of an indigenous culture that had refined the art of survival over a thousand generations.

Colter paid heed and learned Indian lore and customs.[1] Later frontiersmen followed his lead and took pride in assuming native ways. Washington Irving wrote in 1837, "You cannot pay a free trapper a greater compliment, than to persuade him you have mistaken him for an Indian brave."[2]

Native Americans understood many vital aspects of living in nature that exceeded the knowledge of civilized society. Their senses remained acute to sights and sounds; to touch, taste, and smell. They remained closely attuned to their surroundings, with survival skills aided by an intimate knowledge of the environment.

According to P. J. De Smet,

Experience and observation render him [the Indian] conversant with things that are unknown to the civilized man.

Thus, he will traverse a plain or forest one or two hundred miles in extent, and will arrive at a particular place with as much precision as the mariner by the aid of the compass. . . . He acquires this knowledge from a constant application of the intellectual faculties.

Others agreed that this knowledge came from a lifetime of close attention to detail for the sake of survival: "Exposed to constant danger, their wits become sharpened, making them keen observers of nature." Many frontiersmen acquired the same traits, "owing to a careful attention" to minute sensory observations.[3]

Newcomers to the West often expressed pleasant surprise at how quickly and willingly their bodies and minds returned to a sharpened primitive existence after a life dulled by pampered society. The process was aided by the immediate presence of an indigenous culture living close to nature. Much was learned from the native example, and it soon became obvious that theirs was the most expedient means of survival.

Narcissa Whitman, early in her travels, became fully enchanted with life in the wilderness and wrote, "Our manner of living is far preferable to any in the States. I never was so contented and happy before." Even those people who had been thoroughly immersed in civilized society soon adjusted to a more natural existence.

De Smet said: "In the midst of so much game, we scarcely felt the want of bread, sugar or coffee. The haunches, tongues and ribs replaced these. And the bed? It is soon arranged. . . . You wrap your buffalo robe around you, the saddle serves as a pillow, and . . . you have scarcely laid your head upon it before you are asleep."

Western travelers also became conditioned to the extremities of weather. Rufus Sage remembered a time when he "was forced to pass the night among the mountains, without even a robe or a blanket to screen me from the severities of a pitiless snow-storm that fell in the mean time. Strange as it may seem, I experienced not the slightest ill effect in consequence."[4]

Colter was well adapted to a native life in the wilderness and seemed to develop a true admiration for it. Among the Indians, times could be hard. Scarcity brought starvation. Dangers lurked nearby. Life was precarious. But when meat was abundant and tribes at peace, happiness often prevailed and sometimes showed forth in heartfelt joy.

The native life was one of sharp contrasts, tottering constantly between peaceful repose and intense excitement. In a split second, a quiet camp could become a scene of hysteria. Nathaniel Wyeth described one such night in an Indian village. A gun discharged somewhere in camp, which was not at all unusual. But the noise frightened several horses, causing them to pull free of their pickets. Their neighing and panic began a general stampede. Then the dogs all began to howl and the men, fearing an enemy attack, grabbed their guns and mayhem broke loose.

Jim Beckwourth noted the dramatic contrast between the dark and dangerous aspects of Indian life on the one hand and exuberant joy on the other. At all times this contrast was expressed by the full spectrum of unrestrained emotion. Beckwourth explained that, "being untutored and natural, and not restricted by any considerations of grace or propriety, they abandon themselves to their emotions, and no gesture is too exaggerated."[5]

During intervening periods of calm, Plains Indians enjoyed their leisure and rarely used their time to craft items for trade. There was no metallurgy or coiling of pottery, and little woodwork, weaving, or basketry. There was no reason to produce goods for profit.[6] Profit came from the more direct and dangerous tasks of hunting and plundering.

Early plains culture was less driven toward the idea of material success. Nomads had little desire to be encumbered by property. The main exception was ownership of the horse—a wonderfully mobile and advantageous possession.

The horse was a newcomer to the northern plains, having arrived en masse only about a century before Colter appeared on the scene. Horses were such a recent innovation in indigenous culture that many still called them by the name of the beast of burden they largely replaced—the dog. As late as the 1830s, they still called horses *big dog* or *medicine dog*.

At first, native people primarily used horses to haul loads, like dogs. But the burdens horses carried and the travois they pulled could be made much larger. One horse could pull the poles and hides of an entire lodge. This was a great convenience for plains tribes that frequently changed campsites in their relentless search for game.[7]

Horses soon proved their worth as mounts, and Indians of every age learned to ride them. Many children of both genders rode before they could walk and quickly became proficient in handling a horse. Robert Stuart recalled how the Crow Indians

> *were all on horseback. Even the children do not go afoot. These Indians are such good horsemen that they climb and descend the mountains and rocks as though they were galloping in a riding school. . . . It was really unbelievable. There was, among others, a child tied to a two-year-old colt. He held the reins in one hand and frequently plied his whip. I inquired his age; they told me that he had seen two winters. He did not talk as yet.*

Fur trader Edwin Denig described a similar scene: "On top of the saddle is either one large child fit to guide the horse, or two or three small children so enveloped and well tied as to be in no danger of falling. Often the heads of children are seen popping up alongside of pup dogs or cub bears on the same horse." William Anderson said of the Rocky Mountain Indian women, "They are perfect riders. They mount and dismount with the ease and more than the grace of the men."

The horse immediately transformed the lifestyle and material culture of the Plains Indians. Pliable rawhide and braided bison hair came into great demand for making long cords for lassoing wild horses. The same cord could be fastened to the under-jaw of a tame horse to serve as a bit and bridle.

While the horse grazed, the cord was tied around the neck and allowed to drag on the ground to make the animal easier to catch. Crow Indians kept spare lariats handily tucked in their breech-cloth belts, which allowed them to catch their own horses or steal those of an enemy band if the opportunity arose.[8]

The Crow soon became wealthy in horses. Near their camps, hundreds of the animals cropped the grass under the watchful eyes of their owners. These nomadic people always kept their horses close and excelled at keeping them healthy while increasing the size of the herd. Some families owned more than one hundred. François Larocque claimed that among the Crow, "He is reckoned a poor man that has not ten horses."

A person could increase the number of horses in his possession by maintaining breeding herds or by catching and taming wild horses. Or he could acquire them by stealing. Among the Crow, a brave warrior was respected for his daring, while a successful hunter was praised as a good provider. But a talented horse-thief was considered the epitome of both qualities. Horse-theft was esteemed as an honorable trade. It was often justified as the right-ing of past wrongs or on the grounds that the neighboring tribes owned more than their fair share. The only dishonor was in getting caught.

Jim Beckwourth observed that "the large majority of Indian troubles arise from their unrestrained appropriation of each other's horses. It is their only branch of wealth. . . . All their other wants are merely attended to from day to day; their need supplied, they look no farther; but their appetite for horses is insatiable." This created tremendous problems between the Crow and Blackfoot, and produced a ripple effect among their neighbors.

Edwin Denig explained:

> *Whatever losses in horses the Crows sustain, they are supplied by yearly peregrinations to the Flat Heads and Nez Perces with whom they exchange . . . for these animals. On their return the same scenes are enacted over again. The Blackfeet, being four times more numerous than the Crows, gain by these expeditions. The latter are gradually becoming weaker in men from this and other causes. The Assiniboines supply themselves with horses by stealing from the Blackfeet, and the Sioux in their turn take them from the Assiniboines. Thus the poor animals are run from one nation to another, frequently in this way returning to their original owners several times.*

The Crow had deftly stolen two dozen horses from William Clark's men as the Corps of Discovery descended the Yellowstone River in 1806. Four years later, despite cordial trade relations, they relieved the Andrew Henry party of its drove. Horse theft was fast becoming a primary reason for conflict among the plains tribes, and between Indians and whites.[9]

Besides their desire for horses, Plains Indians had little need to amass property. The two physical necessities of life—the sustenance provided by water and food, and the shelter provided by cover and clothing—remained ever close at hand. Water sources were known to all. Game abounded. And the horse made procuring them easier than ever.

For a person like Colter who loved the wilderness, the Crow world was paradise. He must have enjoyed the lifestyle and admired the native values that upheld it. Strength, stamina, courage, and fortitude defined the character of the ideal person.[10] Colter had long since learned that native people embraced these qualities. When confrontations had arisen, he had known the importance of a show of strength and steadfast control of the situation.

On one occasion while traveling with the Corps of Discovery, local Indians had stolen his knife and gig. Upon locating the culprits he confronted them—not with violence, but with unflinching resolve—and took the goods back into his possession. After treating the Indians well, they parted in peace.[11]

At another time, Meriwether Lewis recorded in his journal, "We halted and took breakfast. John Colter, one of our party, observed the tomahawk in one of the lodges which had been stolen from us on the fourth of November last as we descended this river." He immediately snatched it up. "The natives attempted to wrest the tomahawk from him but he retained it."[12]

Again, two years later, "an Indian seized the rifle belonging to Potts"—Colter's friend. "But Colter, who is a remarkably strong man, immediately retook it, and handed it to Potts."[13] Such shows of strength and resolve drew admiration from native people.

Thomas Leforge, who later lived among the Crow, explained that when a warrior wrested a weapon from the hands of an enemy he counted coup, that is, he demonstrated superior strength and daring over his opponent. If one of his companions, in turn, was able to seize it from his grip, he too was allowed to count coup.

Thus, Colter's ability to take back his tomahawk and Potts' rifle had a powerful effect on the Indians, for he had counted coup on them.[14] The Crow admired such demonstrations of prowess and the daring nature of these fair-skinned wanderers from the east. Edwin Denig reported that the Crow "ascribe powers to whites ... far beyond those admitted by any other nation."

But other tribes felt similarly. When Warren Ferris calmly approached a rumbling geyser that had overawed his Kalispel companions, he reported that,

> *The Indians who were with me, were quite appalled, and could not by any means be induced to approach them. They seemed astonished at my presumption in advancing up to the large one, and when I safely returned, congratulated me on my 'narrow escape.' They believed them to be supernatural, and supposed them to be the production of the Evil Spirit.*

In battle, frontiersmen seemed equally undaunted. The indigenous method of warfare usually demanded caution except when they were outnumbered and facing annihilation, or when they easily outnumbered their enemy and rushed forward, confident of victory. In comparison, the fighting method of the western explorers appeared bold and reckless.

When Irish frontiersman Robert Campbell and his party of mountain men were surrounded by a superior number of Blackfoot, he described how he and another man volunteered to break through and go for reinforcements: "We dashed right in the face of the enemy! As it is not their mode to stand a charge, they separated." Similarly, Joe Meek reported that when a man appears undeterred by an Indian threat, his "coolness confounds and awes" them.[15]

Colter exhibited these traits. He had the added advantage of being one of the first white men to visit the northern plains and mountain tribes and bring amazing trade items to the Crow, Flathead, and Shoshone. The Corps of Discovery had passed quickly through their lands, and François Larocque had made one brief visit in 1805. Larocque reported that the Crow "have never had any traders with them." They had received a few thirdhand items from the Spanish, French, and English, but this was only enough to whet their appetites.

While Larocque was with the Crow, "a Snake [Shoshone] Indian arrived. He had been absent since the spring and had seen part of his nation who traded with the Spaniards. He brought a Spanish bridle and battle ax, a large thick blanket, striped white and black, and a few other articles." Larocque promised to return to the Crow the following year and bring similar items. But he failed to do so. Instead, Colter appeared unannounced on the scene with the goods that the Crow coveted. He endeared himself to them by introducing amazing new weapons, tools, and other trade items that far exceeded their lithic culture and gave power and prestige to those who owned them.

The Crow probably responded to Colter in the manner described by a Flathead who had visited with Lewis and Clark. He said, "They were unlike any people we had hitherto seen, fairer than ourselves, and clothed with skins unknown to us. . . . They gave us things like solid water [mirrors], which were sometimes brilliant as the sun, and which sometimes showed us our own faces. Nothing could equal our wonder and delight. We thought them the children of the Great Spirit." Years later, white traders continued to be favored among the northern tribes. Leforge recalled, "As I now look back at the situation, I can but believe that many girls chatted and coquetted with me only because I usually had plenty of store-bought little presents to give away."[16]

The admiration between the Crow and Colter was mutual. Perhaps Colter felt the same sentiment as his friend and fellow trapper, Thomas James, who later said, "I began to be reconciled to a savage life and enamored with the simplicity of nature. Here were no debts, no sheriffs or marshals, no hypocrisies or false friendships. With these simple children of the mountains and prairies love and hate are honestly felt and exerted in their full intensity."[17]

In Colter's time, before the natives of the plains became devastated by military defeat, exploitative commerce, and alcohol, many of their leaders had reputations for speaking and acting with profound nobility. James observed:

> I have seen some of the finest specimens of men among our North American Indians. I have seen chiefs with the dignity of real princes and the eloquence of real orators, and braves with the valor of the ancient Spartans. Their manner of speaking is extremely dignified and energetic. They gesticulate with infinite grace, freedom, and animation. Their words flow deliberately, conveying their ideas with great force and vividness of expression deep into the hearts of their hearers.

Other western travelers agreed with his description of tribal leaders. They admired the intellect, nobility, and spirituality of the Flatheads and the "fine, poetic imaginations" and eloquence of the Crow. Rufus Sage praised a Sioux chief's manner of speech:

> He commenced in a low, distinct tone of voice. His robe, drawn loosely around him, was held to its place by the left hand, exposing his right arm and shoulder. As he proceeded he became

more animated, and seemed to enter into the full spirit of his discourse. The modulations of his voice, its deep intonations and expressive cadences, coupled with a corresponding appropriateness of every look and gesture, presented one of the most perfect specimens of delivery I ever witnessed.

Nathaniel Wyeth mentioned another tribal leader who was "very intelligent and the President would do well if he could preserve the respect of his subjects as well or maintain as much dignity." William Anderson said of a Shoshone chief, "In postures and gesticulation he is extremely graceful and expressive. These are things however by no means confined to him. Every savage of these deserts, is as graceful and dignified, as a Roman Senator."

Anderson noted that Indian sign language was equally eloquent: "The language of signs which is understood by all savages, gives grace, flexibility and impressiveness to every possible motion of the head, hands, arms and body. . . . Their pause is peculiarly forcible." And then, "after an animated harangue," they take leave of their spellbound audience with a pronounced "I have done!"[18]

In later years, the loss of dignity caused by defeat and subordination weighed heavily on native people and often manifested itself in alcoholism. Charles Larpenteur, a French frontiersman and fur trader, noted that the Crow did not drink or trade in liquor until the mid-nineteenth century. In the early days they profited from trade. But later they became devastated by the effects of liquor and the unfavorable trade for it that netted no profitable material increase. Sage lamented the encroachment of eastern civilization and its negative effects. The Indian, he declared, "has a heart instinctive of more genuine good feeling than his white neighbor—a soul of more firm integrity—a spirit of more unyielding independence."[19]

Colter experienced Plains Indian culture in its prime. His admiration perhaps moved beyond the physical attributes and mental values to include their spiritual beliefs as well. He must have respected the warrior's valor that resulted from fearlessness in the face of death. Native Americans thought of the end of life as a step toward a greater existence where every person, despite deeds and misdeeds, anticipated the same eternal destination.

Colter might have admired a spirituality that acknowledged the oneness of nature and of all things tangible and intangible. He likely respected the freedom from religious dogma, coercion, and fear of eternal damnation. And he probably approved of the open, unabashed devotion toward friend, family, and divine spirit alike.

Spirituality was central to indigenous beliefs. Jim Beckwourth said, "I have lived among Indians in the Eastern and Western States, on the Rocky Mountains, and in California. . . . All believe in the same Great Spirit." They declare that he "sees and knows all things."

Other observers added that Native Americans universally believed "in one Great Spirit, who has created all things, governs all important events, who is the author of all good, and the only object of religious homage." They say he made "the light and the darkness, the fire and the water," and that it is this "Great Superintendent of all things, whose power sustains the universe, causing day and night with the varying seasons, making the grass grow, the water to run, and the rains to fall, for the good of man and beast." Accordingly, "all their worship . . . is offered to . . . the Great Spirit," and they "never pronounce the name of the Big Medicine, or Great Spirit, other than in a reverential manner, nor upon trivial occasions."

Sage said that some Indians believed the Great Spirit "lives in the sun; others, in the air; others, in the ground; and others in the immensity of His works." Regardless of where he resides, he takes a personal interest in his creation.

One Sioux chief offered homage by saying,

The Great Spirit is good to His children. To us He has given the buffalo, the elk, the deer, and the antelope, that we may be fed and clothed, and furnished with lodges to shelter us from the storms and cold. To us He has given the mountains and prairies, for hunting grounds. For us He has taught the streams to flow, and planted trees upon their banks, to give us food and drink, that we may meet around our lodge-fires with comfort and rejoice in His goodness, even while He spreads his white robe upon the hills, and lays the couch of winter upon the plains.

Native worship was offered personally and directly to the Great Spirit through open and unabashed praise and through simple ritual offerings of first portions of meat or puffs of tobacco smoke. Otherwise, there were no religious sacrifices, no idols, no sacred objects except those found in nature, and no materialistic manifestations of religion.

There also was no dogma. Although indigenous people shared theological sentiments, the manner in which they worshipped the Great Spirit differed among tribes, families, and individuals. Thus, they revealed a remarkable degree of tolerance. According to Presbyterian missionary Samuel Parker: "Their minds are perfectly open to receive any truth in regard to the character and worship of God."

Nor did they tend to be judgmental. Charles Larpenteur observed that, since they made no distinction between the eternal fate of good and bad people, they had nothing to fear in the afterlife. As a result, they had little fear of death. In fact, death could be welcomed as a journey to a greater existence.

Warren Ferris declared that all Indians believed in "a future state of existence . . . and in a great spirit, by whose bounty they will be permitted to inhabit that delightful region." Crow men envisioned the afterlife as a place where they would be equipped with horses, bows, and arrows, which is "all that a man requires to perfect his happiness and peace." Others imagined they would dwell in a paradise where they would ride "fleet horses that never tire, and roam amid the fruits and flowers, the sweet waters and pleasure-groves of that lovely clime." There they would be reunited with loved ones who went before them.

One Sioux story told of a maiden named Chischille who mourned the death of her youthful lover, Wahuspa. Unable to continue in life without him, she chanted her death song before leaping off a precipice to her own demise:

> *Spirit of Death, set me free! Dreary is earth. Joyless is time. . . .*
> *Farewell, oh sun! Vain is your light. Farewell, oh earth! Vain*
> *are your plains, your flowers, your grassy dales, your purling*
> *streams, and shady groves! I loved you once, but now no longer*
> *love! Tasteless are your sweets—cheerless your pleasures! Thee I*
> *woo, kind Death! Wahuspa calls me hence. In life we were one.*
> *We'll bask together in the Spirit Land.*[20]

Colter's friend, Thomas James, was one of many who spoke highly of the spirituality of these supposedly godless pagans:

> *At their meals, the Indians on the Missouri throw the first piece*
> *of meat in the direction of an absent friend. In smoking, they*
> *send the first whiff upwards in honor of the Great Spirit, the*

*second downward as a tribute to their great mother, the third
to the right and the fourth to the left, in thanks to the Great
Spirit for the game he sends them so abundantly on the bosom
of the earth.* [21]

★   ★   ★   ★

COLTER SPENT much time with the Crow. He had ample opportunity to become immersed in the spiritual, mental, and physical
aspects of Plains Indian culture. He learned to think and act in the
native way and survive in a dangerous world just as the indigenous
people had long survived.

Before leaving their camps to resume his trek, he almost certainly called upon their knowledge of watering holes and gatherings of game, and inquired about trails, fords, and passes through
the mountains. He would note the locations of winter encampments where he could find refuge and spread the word about Manuel's trading post. A helpful Crow perhaps marked these sites on a
map made of hide, as others had done for Lewis and Clark.

Colter probably carried a compass for finding cardinal directions. But even without one, he could rely on native navigational
techniques. The western tribes had a well-known ability to find
their way on the trackless plains and in the jumbled confusion
of the Rocky Mountains. They had an uncanny sense of location
based partly on familiar landforms. William Clark told Alfred
Jacob Miller that Indians "will start on a journey for over a 100
miles either through forests or over a plain and reach their destination without any material deviation from a straight line; and it
will make no difference in the result whether the sun shines or is
obscured by clouds."

When the sun did shine, they used it to mark east, south, and west as it moved across the sky. They knew that if they faced the direction of the midday sun, then sunrise had occurred on the horizon to the left, and sunset would occur on the horizon to the right. Their sign language reflected this. With the index finger and thumb of the right hand forming a circle to represent the sun, they pointed it left to indicate sunrise, ahead and above to indicate midday, and right to indicate sunset. After white explorers made them familiar with cardinal compass points, they related these positions of the sun to the directions—east, south, and west, respectively.

Native people also had a concept of the cardinal direction north, and often used the North Star (Polaris) as a nighttime pointer. Rufus Sage suggested that they even determined the passage of time at night by the rotation of the Little Dipper (the constellation Ursa Minor) around the North Star. Trappers adopted this native lore and learned to roam the western wilderness "without chart or compass."[22]

Indians also proved willing to share their knowledge by providing cartographic information in various forms. Sometimes they made charcoal drawings on hides or bark. At other times they fashioned trails, landmarks, and topography in the sand. In addition, they offered verbal descriptions.

When the Corps of Discovery passed through their lands, the captains requested and received all these forms of cartographic data on more than thirty occasions. Clark incorporated this wealth of information into his own maps, as did later explorers.

P. J. De Smet said, "When in their councils they decide on war or on distant excursions, they lay off these journeys with astonishing accuracy on a kind of map, which they trace on bark or skins." Some even oriented their drawings to sunrise and sunset—east and west—and measured distances by days required for travel.[23]

There is little doubt that Colter had native help laying out his route. The paths he took made so much sense and followed the lay of the land so well that he must have received directions from those who knew the way. It seems unlikely that one person could work all this out through the puzzling maze of mountains, ravines, and rivers, and traverse this terrain in such a timely manner.[24]

He was aided by indigenous information refined over generations that specified the best routes to follow and the best places to find water, timber, and game. He also had well-marked trails to guide him. As late as the 1950s, an experienced tracker could still follow the century-old remnants of native trails that traversed the upper Yellowstone country.

Colter could readily pick out the worn pathways marked here and there with the charred rocks of a campfire, the bleached bones of a butchering site, or the chipped flint that a toolmaker left behind. Even in snowy passes, the fresh blazes that Indians notched on tree trunks pointed the way. Their travois trails, in particular, were easy to recognize and follow. Colter would have had no trouble finding the parallel marks made by horses and dogs dragging heavily loaded travois poles.[25] In addition, an occasional Crow guide might have trudged by his side from one village to another.

But could Colter have covered a thousand miles from October 1807 to the following spring? The simple answer is yes. If he traveled eight months, for example, then he needed to average only four miles a day. In Colter's time, an experienced frontiersman typically covered about thirty miles a day in the wilderness, whether on foot or horseback.

Western explorers often found traveling by foot preferable to riding a horse or hauling a boat upstream. On foot, they could move more quickly over greater distances in rugged country. They could wriggle through thickets, scramble across ravines, glide over deep snow, and slip stealthily through hostile territory. Many travelers reported covering distances on foot up to fifty miles or more in one day, although thirty miles was the norm, day after day, in difficult terrain.[26]

Native people often covered more ground than that, traveling up to fifty or sixty miles a day. When they raided for horses, they usually left their own mounts behind. They moved individually or in small groups on foot for substantial distances and slipped quietly into an enemy's herd under cover of darkness. Even large groups could cover impressive ground. Whole Indian villages typically traveled fifteen to twenty-five miles a day or more. Pioneer caravans covered similar distances on the plains.[27]

Colter knew well the advantages of foot travel over riding horseback. Horses were often thwarted by rugged trails and slippery slopes. Colter himself had taken a tumble off a mountainside while riding through the Rockies with the Corps of Discovery. Horses also hampered progress in rugged, brushy, heavily timbered areas; in muddy, snowy, icy conditions; or in arid lands without forage.

The Rocky Mountains featured all these types of terrain. Even on the plains, horses frequently had to be walked far from rivers because of the numerous ravines formed by tributaries. The only option when confronted with an obstacle was to backtrack, often many miles, and find another route. To make matters worse, the plains were covered with prickly pears from which horses had little protection. If wounded, they sometimes bucked and threw their riders into the thorny patches.

In rocky country, mangled hooves caused horses to become lame. Riders often had to make moccasins for them. Horses in bad condition kept men in camp for days. Horses in good condition created tempting targets for thieves. They had to be hobbled and staked at night for fear of theft and to prevent thunderstorms from scattering them. To lose the horses meant having to abandon the supplies they carried.[28]

Horses became a greater problem in deep snow. First, it was difficult to find forage for them. Robert Newell said, "Our time is principally spent in peeling cotton wood bark for our horses as that is their principal food." Second, they were more susceptible to the cold than other animals. Dogs were hardier in that regard and were often used in winter to haul goods in place of horses.

Third, horses often became snowbound in the mountains, unable to travel over passes for months at a time while men on snowshoes could cross with ease. Dogs could carry a backpack or pull a sled on top of the snow without bogging down. But horses often sank in deep snow and could not get out. Even two feet of snow was sometimes enough to prevent further progress. Too often, men had to stamp roads for horses and pull them out of deeper spots where they became mired.

On one occasion, Warren Ferris said,

Our horses plunged in at every step, and speedily became quite exhausted from the excessive fatigue of constantly breaking through, and forcing their way under such disadvantage. There was no alternative but for us to carry them, since they could neither carry us nor themselves even, and we therefore procured poles, and transported them two miles through the snow to a hill side, which was accomplished only at the cost of incredible labour, hardship, and misery. In addition to this, we had our baggage . . . to collect and bring in on our shoulders.

Sometimes horses had to be abandoned. Or, if the men were in luck, a bison herd might pass through and create a road in the snow that horses could follow. At times, bison were stampeded for that very purpose.[29]

Even under seemingly impossible conditions, frontiersmen often made reasonable progress on snowy trails. Despite having to tramp roads for horses over the Sierra Nevada range, Joseph Walker's party still made eight to ten miles a day. Likewise, Nathaniel Wyeth's men, though exhausted and starving, made six miles in rough, snow-packed country, on foot and carrying sixty-pound packs.

Colter endured a similar experience on a later trek. During a blizzard at Bozeman Pass, he led an expedition through deep snow. Even on the most brutal day they made four miles. One man recorded:

> We entered an opening or gap in the mountains, where it commenced snowing most violently and so continued all night. The morning showed us the heads and backs of our horses just visible above the snow, which had crushed down all our tents. We proceeded on with the greatest difficulty. . . . The strongest horses took the front to make a road for us, but soon gave out and the ablest-bodied men took their places as pioneers. A horse occasionally stepped out of the beaten track and sunk entirely out of sight in the snow. By night we had made about four miles for that day's travel.[30]

A man alone, on snowshoes and packing light, could do much better. With snowshoes as standard equipment, and with different designs for varying conditions, the northern Plains Indians traveled freely in winter.[31] It is no surprise that Colter encountered a Blackfoot party in the dead of winter of 1808–9, and met a band of Shoshone in deep snow the following year.

In milder weather on smoother trails, Colter occasionally might have opted to travel by horseback. While horses proved problematic in rugged country and snowy passes, they made good time in broad grasslands and basins. George Drouillard later mentioned to Clark that an expedition could travel by horseback through the open country near Manuel's Fort that he had traversed.[32] He further reported that "the Indians of this country live on horses altogether."[33] The Crow admiration for horses stood in Colter's favor. They had plenty to spare for a friend. Colter could have taken advantage.

In fact, Colter had many advantages. He packed lightly and could travel swiftly on foot, snowshoe, or horseback. He typically traveled alone, inconspicuous in hostile territory, and unhampered by the slower progress of a large group. Rufus Sage explained that a small party "can pass through a dangerous country and avoid coming in contact with enemies . . . much more easily than one of larger numbers." Not only are they less conspicuous, but more cautious than a larger party that relies too much on strength in numbers. An individual or small party must "trust exclusively to their own personal vigilance" and remain "keenly alive to every suspicious appearance."[34]

Colter also had the advantage of access to native information and guides, and could find supplies and shelter at Crow villages along the way. Furthermore, his route passed through a country abounding in game. Living off the land in Crow country was not a difficult proposition. Edwin Denig described it as

> *perhaps the best game country in the world. From the base of the mountains to the mouth of the Yellowstone buffalo are always to be found in immense herds. Along that river elk may be seen in droves of several hundred at a time, also large bands*

of deer both of black-tailed and white-tailed species. Antelope cover the prairies, and in the badlands near the mountains are found in great plenty bighorn sheep and grizzly bear. Every creek and river teems with beaver, and good fish and fowl can be had at any stream in the proper season.

The Crow were justifiably proud of their land of plenty. One chief said of it,

The Great Spirit has put it exactly in the right place; while you are in it you fare well; whenever you go out of it, which-ever way you travel, you fare worse. If you go to the south, you have to wander over great barren plains; the water is warm and bad, and you meet the fever and ague. To the north it is cold; the winters are long and bitter, with no grass; you cannot keep horses there, but must travel with dogs. What is a country without horses?

On the Columbia they are poor and dirty, paddle about in canoes, and eat fish. Their teeth are worn out; they are always taking fish-bones out of their mouths. Fish is poor food. To the east, they dwell in villages; they live well; but they drink the muddy water of the Missouri—that is bad. A Crow's dog would not drink such water. About the forks of the Missouri is a fine country; good water; good grass; plenty of buffalo. In summer, it is almost as good as the Crow country; but in winter it is cold; the grass is gone; and there is no salt weed for the horses.

The Crow country is exactly in the right place. It has snowy mountains and sunny plains; all kinds of climates and good things for every season. When the summer heats scorch the prairies, you can draw up under the mountains, where the air is sweet and cool, the grass fresh, and the bright streams

come tumbling out of the snow-banks. There you can hunt the
elk, the deer, and the antelope, when their skins are fit for
dressing; there you will find plenty of white [grizzly] bears
and mountain sheep.

In the autumn, when your horses are fat and strong from
the mountain pastures, you can go down into the plains and
hunt the buffalo, or trap beaver on the streams. And when win-
ter comes on, you can take shelter in the woody bottoms along
the rivers; there you will find buffalo meat for yourselves, and
cotton-wood bark for your horses: or you may winter in the
Wind River valley, where there is salt weed in abundance. The
Crow country is exactly in the right place. Everything good is
to be found there. There is no country like the Crow country.[35]

Colter combined all these advantages with his own excellent
survival skills. Most of all, he was motivated to the task at hand.
His own love of discovery must have compelled him to take the
journey. No outsider had seen the lands he would enter. He was
not commissioned to make geographic observations, measure distances, or mark watersheds and passes in a formal sense. But his
profound interest in exploring new country resulted in his route
and the landmarks he saw being recorded on important maps.

Beyond the thrill of discovery, Colter recognized the possibil-
ity of profitable trade. Manuel Lisa had stressed this aspect. While
Lisa hoped to locate lucrative beaver sites, he preferred to leave the
grueling task of trapping beaver to Indians and company hirelings.
Then he planned to acquire their catches in return for trinkets or
supplies that enabled them to continue trapping.

Lisa's main ambition, for which he commissioned Colter, was
to open trade. The Crow nation was his first objective. The Flathead and Shoshone came second. Colter would need to travel great

distances to reach their scattered winter encampments. But at least their mobile villages remained stationary during the cold months of the year.

Blackfoot trade also appealed to Lisa. The nation was powerful on the northern plains and would make good commercial allies. But they had strong ties with the British in Canada who encouraged hostilities with Americans. Colter soon could attest to the problems of dealing with the Blackfoot nation.

More alluring were rumors of Spanish settlement southwest of Manuel's Fort. One of Lisa's scouts, George Drouillard, received word from the Crow that "a man on horseback can travel to the Spanish country in 14 days" from the fort.[36] At about thirty miles a day, this represented a distance of several hundred miles. Colter must have heard the same native rumors and searched for the Spanish. He certainly ventured far to the southwest—upward of five hundred miles, according to Henry Brackenridge.[37] With these objectives in mind, and with every reason to hope for success in making new discoveries, Colter departed Manuel's Fort in October 1807.

Chapter Four

A WINTER TREK AND
A RACE FOR LIFE

AS FALL FOLIAGE SIGNALED THE APPROACH OF colder weather in 1807, Colter shouldered his pack and worked his way westward along the Yellowstone's south bank. He left behind comrades chopping logs for the construction of huts and a defensive stockade. As the sound of axes faded in the distance, he made his path alone. This was nothing new or unwelcome to him; he enjoyed the solitude and anticipated the discoveries that waited around every hill and bend.

In unfamiliar lands, Colter knew to remain close to watercourses that formed a green belt of vegetation through the surrounding arid plains. This is where he could find game and winter villages of the Crow. In a day or two he crossed a stream called Shannon's Creek that meandered from the south through tall prairie grasses to join the main river.

The year before, William Clark had hacked canoes from cottonwoods and floated down this stretch of the Yellowstone with a small detachment of the Corps of Discovery. Colter was not with him at the time, but was descending the Missouri River under John Ordway's command. As Clark explored the Yellowstone, he named landmarks and creeks after the men who accompanied him.[1] This stream got its name from young George Shannon.[2]

Upon wading the Shannon, Colter beheld a sandstone bluff rising gracefully alongside the Yellowstone. Clark had also marked this feature on his map the previous year and had labeled it Pompey's Tower after Sacagawea's infant son. Sacagawea— the young Shoshone mother—had carried her baby thousands of miles while helping to guide Lewis and Clark to the Pacific Ocean and back.[3] At Pompey's Tower, the mother, child, and men of the Corps had rested along the shore while the captain climbed to the summit and carved: Wm. Clark, July 25th 1806. The inscription remains to this day—a rare remnant of the Lewis and Clark Expedition.

Pompey's Tower later became an important landmark used by explorers, trappers, traders, cavalrymen, cowboys, and settlers for a hundred years. In 1876, some of George Custer's cavalrymen climbed the rock to gaze upon the inscription of Clark—their frontier hero—before they marched off to die at Little Bighorn.

Colter continued westward from Pompey's Tower and made another day's march to Pryor's Fork, named for one of Clark's trusted sergeants, Nathaniel Pryor. Like Colter, Pryor had been an essential member of the Corps of Discovery. And like Colter, he became enraptured with the West and returned on later expeditions.

Many frontiersmen developed a similar "irresistible fascination" for the western wilderness and refused to return to the East, or only did so reluctantly. Daniel Potts wrote home, explaining to his family, "I have been on the very eve of returning this summer, but owing to this unexplored country, which I have a great curiosity to see, I have concluded to remain one or two years."

Others remained for the adventure or because they found the nomadic Indian lifestyle preferable to civilization. Those who did return often regretted it and found that they were "weary of rest" or lacked the "contentment and inward satisfaction" they had enjoyed. After sixteen years in the wilderness, Kit Carson wandered to St. Louis. But after only a few days, he proclaimed that he was "tired of the settlements" and headed westward again.[4]

Pryor's frontier adventures almost rank with those of Colter. While ascending the Missouri River with the Corps of Discovery in 1804, he dislocated a shoulder. His companions made four attempts before they were able to reset it, and it bothered him for the remainder of his life.

On the return journey in 1806, Pryor and his squad of men lost their horses to a native band. The following night, while Pryor slept, a wolf attacked and bit him through the hand. The wolf then mauled another man before being shot by Shannon.

Bad luck continued to follow Pryor after the expedition's return to St. Louis. In 1807, he led a small military force toward the Mandan villages, but was attacked by the Arikara Indians. Shannon and two others under his command were wounded, and Shannon's leg had to be amputated. In addition, four members of a small accompanying party of trappers and traders were killed and six wounded in the fight. Pryor was forced to retreat downriver.

In 1809, Pryor was assigned to Fort Madison on the Mississippi River. He was present when the entire garrison barely averted a Sauk Indian attack. The following year, he resigned from the army and began trading with native people near present-day Dubuque, Iowa. On January 1, 1812, about a hundred Winnebago Indians attacked his establishment, killing two men and plundering Pryor's stores.

After a harrowing escape across the ice on the Mississippi River, Pryor rejoined the army and served as an officer during the War of 1812. Achieving the rank of captain, he fought under

Andrew Jackson at the Battle of New Orleans. Sam Houston later informed Jackson that "a braver man never fought" under the general's command.[5]

At war's end, Pryor returned to the frontier to trade with Indians along the Arkansas River. By 1820, he was permanently established on the Verdigris River near Three Forks of the Arkansas in present-day Oklahoma. Here he maintained a trading post, married an Osage woman, and became a valued trader and liaison with her tribe.

Pryor persisted in the trade for eleven more years and was named US subagent to the Osage in 1831. As such, he helped maintain peace between their nation and the United States. He died soon afterward and was buried near present-day Pryor, Oklahoma, where his gravesite may still be seen.

Pryor's namesake in Montana is a sparkling creek that waters a gentle valley. Colter resumed his journey by following Pryor's Fork southward, away from the Yellowstone.[6] Here his route departed from what William Clark and company had followed the year before. Colter knew that the Pryor Valley provided the Crow with favorite campsites shaded by cottonwoods and edged by a half-mile swath of grassland.[7] The bluffs along both sides gave shelter from winter storms and seclusion from enemy eyes.

Native people often established encampments near hilltops or bluffs that provided protection and allowed a view of the surrounding countryside. From here they could oversee their herds of horses while watching for marauding bands and wandering bison herds. They could discern anxious behavior among horses or bison that indicated the presence of an intruder.

Thomas Leforge recalled using this technique: "When we got to the top of Pryor Mountain we stayed there all night and until after noon the next day. Our main object was to watch the buffalo, to see if they were in agitation. That is the best way to discover the presence of human beings in any wild country." François Larocque recalled an anxious moment while visiting a Crow camp: "In the evening news came that the buffalos were in motion on the Large Horn River, and harangues were made to guard the camp."

A spooked bison herd not only suggested the presence of men but also their direction, as the men were likely to be windward of the keen-scented beasts. In this case, the hilltop observer would keep a watchful eye to locate the intruders. At first, in the distance, he might not be able to distinguish bison or elk from horseback riders. Elk, in particular, were often mistaken for men on horses. The confusion came from the manner in which elk throw back their antlers above their shoulders while running. But if the distant objects revealed glinting metal or splashes of bright color, the lookout sounded the alarm.

Smoke was another telltale sign to watch for from atop a bluff. Early morning was the best time to look for strange sources of smoke because "a freshly kindled fire makes more smoke and also the morning atmosphere is more clear."[8] While the bluffs along Pryor's Fork provided vantage points for the Crow, thick stands of timber offered plentiful shelter and fuel down below.[9]

Here, Colter perhaps reunited with the people who had befriended him the winter before while he was in the company of Dickson and Hancock. Under the cottonwoods, he showed the Crow his tempting array of trinkets and wares, and encouraged them to trade at Manuel's Fort once the "green grass" season arrived.[10]

Colter's visit was short. The crisp autumn air urged him along to cover ground before cold weather set in. From halfway up the valley he could already see the Red Mountains (Pryor Mountains)—the source of Pryor's Fork—flecked with patches of snow.[11]

George Drouillard followed Colter's trail some weeks later and marked this small range of mountains on his map. The name he assigned must have come from the red sandstone deposits that appear here and there along the foothills. A person may still admire the distinctive formations now known as the Red Cliffs on the southeast end at the Bighorn River.[12]

Colter followed Pryor's Fork to its headwaters in the Red Mountains. Then he left the valley and turned southwest into the elevated expanse of Pryor Gap. After a short march through an arid prairie he came upon Gap Creek. Here he quenched his thirst and filled a canteen while surveying the prospects ahead.

A desert basin lay below, with the lofty, snowcapped, seemingly endless Absaroka Range beyond. From Gap Creek, a single breach appeared in the natural rock fortress. Despite the hazy distance, Colter could see the V-shaped gap that marks the mouth of Clark's Fork Canyon. The waters of the Clark's Fork pour from this spout to exit the Absaroka Mountains. Then the fork swings north to journey toward a juncture with the Yellowstone River.

From Gap Creek, a two-day march across the Bighorn Basin through soil and rock bereft of vegetation brought Colter to the waters of Clark's Fork. After another day of walking along the bank, he stood at the mouth of Blue Bead River, which flows into Clark's Fork from the south. William Clark's Map of 1810 shows the southern headwaters of Clark's Fork in a way that corresponds closely with present-day Pat O'Hara Creek, its tributary Blaine Creek, and Paint Creek. If this correspondence is accurate, Blue Bead River is today's Pat O'Hara Creek, and Blue Bead Mountain is Pat O'Hara Mountain. This interpretation is reinforced by the existence of blue serpentine rock deposits in the vicinity.[13]

Sighting southward along the Blue Bead River, Colter could see another distinctive landmark: Heart Mountain. This unique desert peak rises from the basin in the center of a circuit that Colter followed for the next dozen days or so. As he caught glimpses of its summit through gaps and valleys, he could determine his direction and progress.

Drouillard and Clark later confirmed the importance of this feature by noting Heart Mountain on their maps. Drouillard's later route took him past Heart Mountain, but this was an arid trail. Colter followed Crow advice and took the watered, timbered, and game-rich route along Clark's Fork, Dead Indian Creek, and Valley River.[14]

For now, Colter left Heart Mountain behind and directed his path upriver to Clark's Fork Canyon. He might have passed the previous winter with Dickson and Hancock inside these protective walls. Or perhaps the Crow living on Pryor's Fork directed him to the site, with its plentiful water and winter encampments. The canyon offered access to verdant valleys nestled deep in the mountains.

Within its steep walls, Colter found fast-flowing waters and plenty of game and fish. He was tempted to dally here awhile and resupply his pack. Then, after a tough day's march up and out of the canyon, he came to Sunlight Basin—a lush, secluded valley and a hidden jewel of the Absaroka Range.

Hunting was good and attracted Crow bands to settle for the winter. After a hospitable welcome and talk of trade, the Indians pointed south and encouraged Colter to descend from the mountains before heavy snowfalls set in. Southward was the surest and straightest route from Sunlight Basin to the next gathering of Crow encampments near present-day Cody, Wyoming.

Following this trail, Colter clambered up Dead Indian Creek to a pass on the western slope of Blue Bead Mountain. Drouillard later noted that near here "the Indians obtain a clear and solid substance like glass which they manufacture into pipes." Presumably, they fashioned blue beads from the same or similar material. Out-crops of blue rock are still prominent features along this route.

The *blue* mentioned by George Drouillard might be what we would describe today as aquamarine or blue-green. The Crow used the same word—*shua*—for both *blue* and *green*, and their sign language left much room for interpretation. To express a color in Indian sign language, one simply pointed at an object of similar color. The lack of distinction between blue and green is common in Native American languages and other languages worldwide.

Meriwether Lewis, in his journals, described the highly pol-ished, translucent, green stone pipes of the Shoshone. François Larocque made similar mention. These pipes probably were fash-ioned from serpentine, which occurs in colors ranging from green to blue.

Years later, Thomas Leforge, who lived with the Crow Indi-ans for six decades, described Crow pipes: "The pipe ordinarily was of red soapstone, but sometimes a blue pipe was preferred. The blue material was what the miners call serpentine. I know a mine of it near the present town of Red Lodge." This town, at the time of Leforge's account, was the closest one to Blue Bead Mountain (present-day Pat O'Hara Mountain). Cody, Wyo-ming, did not yet exist.

A natural source of light-blue serpentine rock is found today in the vicinity of Pat O'Hara Mountain and is also visible in the metamorphic strata of neighboring White Mountain. Another well-known quarry was located in Shoshone country, fifteen miles downstream from Beaverhead Rock on the Beaverhead Fork of the Jefferson River. Samuel Parker observed still another vein while trav-eling on the Sweetwater River near Independence Rock. He said, "I saw today . . . a quantity of the most beautiful serpentine I ever beheld. It was semi-transparent and of a deep green hue."

Indigenous people of various tribes carved serpentine into tube-shaped pipe bowls like the one described by Lewis. The tube pipe, according to archaeologist George West, was "the most primitive form of smoking pipe. Its antiquity is indicated by its general distribution over the greater part of the United States and Canada. . . . Most of them were employed as smoking pipes, and others as medicine tubes. Very short elliptical ones were probably worn as beads." In this context, George Drouillard's mention of Blue Bead Mountain, where pipe bowls are made, makes perfect sense.[15]

From the top of the pass above Dead Indian Creek, Colter gazed down upon the headwaters of Blue Bead River. The stream originated in springs and snowmelt on the slopes of Blue Bead Mountain. Farther to the east, Heart Mountain reflected a reddish glow in the setting sun.

Colter continued southward. The trail steadily descended along the cold and gloomy Valley River, with Rattlesnake Mountain looming to the west and blocking sunlight through late afternoon. Colter hurried on and soon approached the valley's lower end.[16]

Near the mouth of Valley River, the stench of sulfur shocked his senses after days in the fresh mountain air. Noxious pits pockmarked the north bank of the Stinking Water River, releasing geothermal gas and steam. Here Colter gazed with amazement on sulfur domes and fumaroles—a landscape unlike any he had seen or smelled. Nor had his countrymen witnessed such a sight. Some would find it hard to believe his tale.

As for the Crow, they preferred to camp somewhere else. They avoided the area not only because of the forbidding fumes but for fear of any spirit that would dare to dwell in such a place. Drouillard reported to Clark the next year: "The natives give an account that there is frequently heard a loud noise, like thunder, which makes the earth tremble. They state that they seldom go there because their children cannot sleep—and conceive it possessed of spirits, who were averse that men should be near them."[17]

The unpleasant smells even tainted the name of the graceful river that flows swiftly by. Washington Irving, writing thirty years later, said the "Stinking River . . . takes its unhappy name from the odor derived from sulphurous springs and streams." He reported that Colter came upon the area "in the course of his lonely wanderings, and gave such an account of its gloomy terrors, its hidden fires, smoking pits, noxious streams, and the all-pervading 'smell of brimstone,' that it received, and has ever since retained among trappers, the name of 'Colter's Hell!'"[18]

The Crow encampment could be found a comfortable distance upstream, where two forks converged to form the river. To reach it, Colter had to cross the rapid current to the south bank of the Stinking Water River. From there he could skirt the southern slope of Spirits' Mountain to arrive at the native camp. Fording a rushing watercourse was always a dangerous proposition, but Colter had ample experience doing just that on the Missouri, the Columbia, and the Snake Rivers.

He probably forded in the manner of the Crow. Thomas James described how they

> stripped themselves entirely naked and every ten piled their accouterments together, blankets, saddles, weapons, etc. on a tent skin made of buffalo robes, and tying it up in a large round bundle threw it into the river and plunged after it, some swimming with these huge heaps, floating like corks, and others riding the horses or holding by the tails till they had all crossed the river. Arrived on the opposite bank, which they reached in little less time than I have taken to describe their passage, they dressed, mounted their horses, and marched off.[19]

Frontiersmen used a similar method by bundling clothing and goods inside hides, oil cloths, buckskin shirts, or cloaks, and pushing them ahead for a float as they swam the river.[20] Fording was also accomplished with rafts made of logs or river canes. The Corps of Discovery used these methods, and later explorers followed their example. Another alternative was to build boats for making a crossing or for a longer trip by river. Frontiersmen became expert at fashioning dugouts, skin boats, or rafts, depending on available materials.

The Corps of Discovery constructed a total of ten dugouts from cottonwood and six from ponderosa pine. They also built four bull boats. Dugouts of ponderosa pine were burned and gouged. Cottonwood, being less combustible, was shaped solely by gouging and chiseling. Cottonwood was the preferred material because it was light, buoyant, and easily carved. A thickness of one to several inches was left in dugouts, depending on the projected needs of sturdiness, stability, and portability. Colter was present at the manufacture of at least eight cottonwood dugouts and the six pine dugouts. He had ample experience making them, although he probably had no need while in the presence of Indian villages.[21]

Another option was the bull boat, or skin boat, made in the shape of a round or elongated tub from one or more hides. A bull boat was fashioned from green bison hides stretched over a frame of willow or other flexible wood. It was then allowed to dry in the sun or over a low fire until snug. Bull boat seams were waterproofed with bison or elk tallow and ashes. The skins could be carried on horseback until needed. Then a frame was made from the ever-present willow and the skin was stretched over. The makeshift boat carried a surprisingly large cargo.[22]

Still, the use of boats could be difficult and dangerous. Heavy currents and headwinds were common on the western rivers. Boats often had to be portaged over sandbars or other obstacles. Banks collapsed without warning, dropping huge trees into the water. Floating trees and driftwood rammed boats, while sawyers and snags ripped the bottoms out of them.

Bull boats were especially vulnerable because of their soft hulls and round bottoms, which created a deeper draft. Seams sometimes leaked and cargo suffered damage. Worst of all, gunpowder often got wet, leaving the men without effective weapons. The powder had to be poured out and spread in the sun to dry.[23]

Whether by boating or floating, Colter crossed the Stinking Water River and moved upstream to arrive on the west side of Spirits' Mountain. This otherworldly geologic formation has rocks that reach toward heaven like the spires of a Gothic cathedral. To the Crow, Spirits' Mountain marked a holy site.

Strange and lofty peaks have long been revered as divine habitations. Many tribes of the northern plains and mountains believed such places possessed special powers granted to them by the Great Spirit.[24] Beyond that, Spirits' Mountain had the advantage of another supernatural feature. At its base rose smoke and steam from a gurgling tar pit called Boiling Spring.

The construction of Buffalo Bill Reservoir in 1906 inundated this site. But those who lived in earlier times recalled the boiling, oozing tar surrounded by a number of hot springs and geysers. The tar spring, in particular, stood out for its unique character and medicinal value.

Early frontiersmen learned from the Indians how to make use of the warm and sticky pitch. They rubbed it on their horses' backs to heal saddle sores. And they applied it with equal vigor to their own aches and pains.

The Arapaho venerated one "medicine fountain" as a "manifestation of the immediate presence of the Great Spirit." As such, they made offerings to it of "robes, blankets, arrows, bows, knives, beads, moccasins," and other goods, which they dropped into the divine spring or hung in nearby trees. Another famous medicinal site was found in Crow country on the Popo Agie River. Mountain man Zenas Leonard claimed that the oil from the spring at Popo Agie effectively cured rheumatism.[25]

At Boiling Spring, under the watchful gaze of Spirits' Mountain, the Crow dwelt in a favorite encampment. Here the Mick-ka-ap-ha (*Grass House*) River descended from the Absaroka Mountains and flowed past their lodges to form the northern branch of the Stinking Water River. Springs were plentiful and grasslands lush, and villagers could graze large herds of horses.

Deer and elk wandered close to nibble the abundant forage, and furbearing animals built dams and lodges in the marshes and waterways. Drouillard described the stream as having "much beaver and otter."

The Crow camp on the Mick-ka-ap-ha might have been Colter's primary objective. A large encampment surrounded by an abundance of pelts for trade would bring easy profits for Manuel Lisa's enterprise.

Just to the south ran another branch—the Salt Fork of the Stinking Water River. This stream also provided a home for the Crow. And if rumors proved true, it promised a route to more riches.

The natives reported a natural cache of "fossil salt" tucked away in a cave upstream. Apparently they knew of a deposit of fossilized bones they thought had broken down to salt. The mistake could be easily made. Salt licks attract mammals in large numbers. They graze nearby and eventually die, leaving scattered skeletal remains among the salt.

Drouillard later reported the rumor. The Salt Fork, he said, provided a path through the Absarokas to a "salt cave on the north side of a mountain where the salt is found pure or perfect." A supply like this would be priceless for preserving and seasoning meat. Better yet, he added, the "Spaniards obtain it from this place by passing over from the river Colorado."[26]

Colter almost certainly heard the same rumors. Perhaps he attempted to ascend the Salt Fork. He possibly even reached Castle Rock—a distinctive landmark fifteen miles upriver.[27] But the trail becomes rugged after that and snow makes the route impractical in winter. Besides, Colter had unfinished business in Crow camps that dotted the Absaroka foothills.

Still, the tantalizing tales of a cave of pure salt must have lingered in his mind. Like Drouillard, Colter probably reported the site to William Clark, who marked it on his map as FOSSILS and underneath wrote SALT.[28] To this day, the site remains undiscovered.

*   *   *   *

FROM THE Salt Fork, Colter skirted the east slope of present-day Carter Mountain. Then he followed the Absaroka foothills, wading several creeks that water a grassy highland. This was a favorite Crow hunting ground, and deer and pronghorn can still be seen in large numbers here.

A few days' trek through this country brought him to the Owl Creek Mountains—a low range extending east from the Absarokas. At a distance an obvious gap came to view, providing easy access to Blondy Pass and the Wind River valley beyond. Colter crossed the low mountains and descended to the watercourse. As he approached, he gazed upon a scenic backdrop—the snowcapped Wind River Range that rises majestically to the southwest.

The Wind River Valley provided another natural paradise and winter campsite for the Crow. Zenas Leonard called it "one of the most beautiful formations of nature . . . with the margin of the river evenly ornamented with thriving cotton wood," and an "abundance of buffalo and other game."

Higher up, toward Togwotee Pass, the valley continued to present a narrow, grassy plain populated by large bison herds. To ascend the valley, Colter turned northwestward. Water and food remained in good supply. Pronghorn roamed the broad, open spaces while deer took shelter in the timber.

Following a well-marked Indian trail, Colter came to Togwotee Pass in a few days. Perhaps to his surprise, he discovered a mild mountain crossing along a well-watered, grassy plain a quarter-mile wide. A thick fringe of forest stood on each side, inhabited by plentiful game.[29]

At the top of the pass, Colter discerned a gently descending slope that beckoned the curious explorer onward. In contrast, the southward route to Union Pass looked too steep and heavily wooded. He would have needed a guide and a good excuse to take that path. Wilson Price Hunt was compelled to take the Overland Astorians that direction four years later only out of desperation to reach the Green River and resupply his expedition.

Hunt recorded in his journal of late September, "We should have continued at that time to follow Wind River and to cross one of the mountains [at Togwotee Pass] because we would have reached the headwaters of this river [Snake River]; but lack of provisions forced us to make for the banks of Spanish River [Green River]." There, Hunt had the best chance of finding bison, beaver, otter, waterfowl, and several varieties of berries in enough quantity to feed his large expedition. The Green River later became a favorite rendezvous site for mountain men for that very reason.[30] But Colter had no need to go that direction now.

A northward trail looked even less inviting. The climb toward

Brooks Lake is steep, thickly timbered, and ringed with forbidding peaks. A better option lay plainly ahead. Togwotee Pass allowed easy access to a watered plain where Indian encampments and Spanish traders might be found.

Colter's route to Jackson Hole is rather well established. Historians have carefully studied William Clark's 1810 map, including, in recent years, Yale University's digitally enhanced image of the map. In addition, they have made careful reconnaissance of Colter's route, largely on foot. Most historians, including the major biographers—Hiram Chittenden, Stallo Vinto, and Burton Harris—have concluded, based on independent research, that Lake Eustis on Clark's map is present-day Lake Yellowstone, and Lake Biddle represents present-day Lake Jackson in Grand Teton National Park.

When comparing the western portion of Clark's 1810 map to a modern map, the four key features—Teton Pass, Lake Biddle (Lake Jackson), Lake Eustis (Lake Yellowstone), and Hot Spring Brimstone (Tower Falls)—are properly spaced, properly oriented, and in the case of the two lakes, properly proportional in size, as well as can be expected from ground-level perspectives. Lake Jackson was substantially smaller in 1807–8, before being dammed in the early twentieth century. The diminished size of Lake Jackson is reflected on Clark's 1810 map.

A look at the four key features on Clark's map reveals one error in orientation that occurs north of Lake Eustis, where Clark depicts the Yellowstone River flowing northeast instead of north. Otherwise, Clark's map is surprisingly accurate considering he drew it, sight unseen, from second- and thirdhand sources.

Despite this evidence, a recent study claims that Lake Biddle is what we now call Brooks Lake, near Togwotee Pass. This would make Brooks Lake Colter's point of return. There are significant problems with this theory. First, Brooks Lake did not provide a natural and obvious route to potential trading villages as Togwotee Pass did. Second, whereas the relative sizes and positions of Lake Biddle and Lake Eustis correspond closely to those of present-day Lake Jackson and Lake Yellowstone, Brooks Lake does not correspond well at all.

Not only does Brooks Lake lie in the wrong direction, far to the southeast of Lake Yellowstone, but its surface area is only about one percent of Lake Jackson's. Brooks Lake is so small that it rarely appears on a modern map of Wyoming. Why, then, would Clark exaggerate its size one hundred times and include it on his map as a major landmark? If Clark had drawn Lake Biddle to represent modern Brooks Lake, this would have constituted perhaps his greatest blunder on the 1810 manuscript map.[31]

Togwotee Pass provided a better route. Archaeologists have defined Togwotee Pass as a major east-west thoroughfare for native travelers. From a topographic viewpoint, it is also the most logical means of passage from the Wind River Valley to Jackson Hole. For this very reason, US Highways 26 and 287 now traverse the pass.

West of the pass, Jackson Hole offered sufficient provisions to sustain small groups. It was known to have, in addition to game, an autumn supply of serviceberries and various types of currants. The Shoshone frequently visited the area of Jackson Hole and Pierre's Hole, and "showed a perfect knowledge" of the route from one hole to the other.

Four years after Colter passed this way, Wilson Price Hunt's expedition came upon a Shoshone camp that "had dealt with white men, and knew them to be friendly, and to abound with articles of singular value." It is quite likely the Shoshone were referring to Colter. Later explorers followed the same trail. In 1829, a trapper named David Jackson searched for beaver in the hole that now bears his name. Incidentally, Jackson had a young nephew named Thomas (b. 1824) back home in Virginia, who later gained fame in the Civil War as "Stonewall" Jackson.[32]

As Colter began to descend Mule River toward Jackson Hole, the Teton Range suddenly loomed. Despite the number of geographic wonders that Colter had beheld in his travels, he must have been taken aback by the majestic peaks that are forever breathtaking, from the moment they reflect the first light of morning to the end of the day, when they are silhouetted by the setting sun. The lofty mountains provided him with a prominent and picturesque landmark that he worked his way around over the next few months.

Once he reached the open expanse of Jackson Hole, Colter kept to the fringe of timber as he slipped stealthily southward. A good hunter stays near cover, as does a wary trespasser. He had now left the land of the Crow and was entering a country that might be inhabited by unknown and unpredictable native bands. The Spanish might also be nearby. As much as he wanted to contact these people, common sense demanded caution.

Earlier that year, while exploring what would become Colorado, Zebulon Pike had clandestinely crossed from the United States into Spanish territory. Spanish officials promptly arrested him and the men of his expedition. After marching them to Santa Fe, then far south to Chihuahua, the Spaniards finally escorted the men to the American outpost of Natchitoches with a stern warning not to return.

When Colter traversed Togwotee Pass he too entered Spanish territory. He might or might not have realized the transgression. But either way, he would have thought it wise to quietly scout the area and measure the strength of strangers before making his presence known.

To remain concealed, he headed south from the Mule River. He would not set eyes on Lake Biddle yet, but instead encountered the swift-flowing stream of the Snake River. Near present-day Jackson, Wyoming, he crossed at an established Indian ford.

Western travelers, Indian and white, preferred to make river crossings at sites such as this where the waters divided into manageable channels. Robert Stuart described the Snake River ford as having "five channels of from 30 to 60 yards wide each, and from 1½ to 3 feet water." Later frontiersmen likewise followed this "well known ford."[33]

Colter continued to push westward. The lower Teton Range loomed ahead. But a well-marked trail through Teton Pass offered a way through the mountains. Teton Pass is steeper and narrower than Togwotee Pass. Still, the route is short and often free of snow until late fall. Once on top, the descent is moderate, with gentle slopes and a creek that trickles through grassy meadows.

The pass was a favorite native crossing. It offered wandering bands a sure supply of water and game, as well as access to an obsidian quarry that was widely known and often used for making weapons and tools.[34] Colter had no trouble picking his way along the route from the Snake River over Teton Pass.

Wilson Price Hunt's expedition crossed snow-covered Teton Pass in October four years later with no difficulty. The following October, Robert Stuart and company traversed the pass in the opposite direction and found negligible amounts of snow. On the same day, they crossed the Snake River ford. Thus, in one day, they traveled twenty-four miles from the Teton River, over Teton Pass, and across the Snake River while carrying a sick man on a litter. Later explorers confirmed that the route was "an easy crossing" following "an easy and well-beaten trail" often used by the Shoshone.[35]

Colter's use of the pass appears verified on the maps later drawn by William Clark. These show the pass properly placed in relative distance and direction from present-day Jackson and Yellowstone Lakes. With dotted lines, Clark marked Colter's route in association with those of the later expeditions of Wilson Price Hunt and Andrew Henry. Just before crossing the Tetons westward, the paths of Colter and Hunt converge at the only nearby place to cross the range—clearly at Teton Pass.

On the range's western slope, Colter followed the South Fork of Crook's River downhill to the broad and fertile valley of Pierre's Hole. What he observed was aptly described later by Osborne Russell—a member of the 1834 Nathaniel Wyeth expedition:

> *This valley lies north and south in an oblong form about thirty miles long and ten wide, surrounded except on the north by wild and rugged mountains. The east range resembles mountains piled on mountains and capped with three spiral peaks which pierce the cloud. These peaks bear the French name of Tetons, or Teats. The Snake Indians call them the Hoary-headed Fathers. This is a beautiful valley consisting of a smooth plain intersected by small streams, and thickly clothed with grass and herbage; and abounds with buffalo, elk, deer, antelope, etc.*

Pierre's Hole later became a favorite campsite for fur traders because of its abundance of water, grassland, timber, and game, encompassed by majestic scenery. Beaver were plentiful in the marshy waters that drained from the surrounding mountains. And the extensive grasslands attracted bison, elk, deer, pronghorn, bear, and waterfowl. Wild cherries were common along with berries and other edible plants. To add to the allure, a neighboring hot spring provided a favorite year-round bathing ground for native people and frontiersmen alike.

But the popularity of Pierre's Hole contributed to occasional bloody clashes. It was the scene of a battle between Robert Campbell's company and a band of Blackfoot Indians in 1827. During the fight, Pierre, an Iroquois member of Campbell's party, was killed. Pierre's Hole was named in his memory. Five years later, during the mountain man Rendezvous of 1832, the more famous Battle of Pierre's Hole was fought between a Blackfoot band and an alliance of Indians, trappers, and traders.[36]

Clark's 1810 map shows Colter's route making a loop south and west around Pierre's Hole through the fringe of encircling mountains. As at Jackson Hole, he kept cautiously close to the tree line and remained concealed while watching for game and seeking an Indian or Spanish presence.

Bands of Shoshone frequently visited the region. Their Lemhi band, living farther northwest, had befriended the Corps of Discovery two years earlier. Colter probably hoped their southern bands or other local tribes would prove equally amiable. If so, they might be persuaded to trap these valleys and become partners in trade.

At the same time, if native rumors held true, Spanish settlement could not be far away. Trade with Spain's colonies in the Southwest would ensure continuing profits and fulfill one of Manuel Lisa's pervading hopes and objectives. As early as August 1806, Lisa had determined "to open some commercial intercourse with Santa Fe."[37]

In that same month, while William Clark led the Corps of Discovery's return voyage down the Yellowstone, Clark had a similar thought in mind. He noted, "This delightful river, from Indian information, has its extreme sources with the North River [Rio Grande] in the Rocky Mountains on the confines of New Mexico."[38] Clark, Lisa, and others believed that a feasible route might be established from a post on the Yellowstone, such as Manuel's Fort. The anticipated route would extend up tributaries like the Bighorn and Wind Rivers, then to the upper Rio Grande Valley and downstream to Santa Fe.

George Drouillard, while employed by Manuel Lisa, seemed to confirm what everyone wanted to believe. After he traversed the country and gathered local lore, he brought back native stories of a feasible route to Spanish settlements. Drouillard reported the same to William Clark, who enthusiastically imagined a link between Manuel's Fort and the Rio Grande. He wrote, "From the Fort or entrance of Bighorn River the Indians say a man on horseback can travel to the Spanish settlements in fourteen days on the head of Del Norte [Rio Grande]."[39]

Drouillard's report seemed verified by Spanish trade items that occasionally appeared among the possessions of the Crow, Shoshone, Blackfoot, and neighboring tribes. They had actually received these items thirdhand, but the presence of Spanish merchandise nevertheless tempted white traders on the Yellowstone to believe that the Spanish settlements were close.

Zebulon Pike raised such hopes to fever pitch after returning from his expedition of 1806–7. He erroneously declared in his official report that the headwaters of the Yellowstone and Rio Grande were no more than two days' march apart: "The same chain of mountains . . . gives birth on its northeastern side to the . . . yellow stone river . . . and on its south the Rio del Norte of North Mexico," as well as to the Platte, Arkansas, and Colorado Rivers. "I have no hesitation in asserting that I can take a position in the mountains, whence I can visit the source of any of those rivers in one day."[40]

Interest in a trade route to the Spanish settlements lingered for years. Doctor Thomas served as surgeon on Manuel Lisa's 1809 expedition. While the party halted at the mouth of the Platte, he

Roaming herds of bison and wide-open spaces would have been a common site for the Corps of Discovery. *Photograph by author.*

Bison were the most prized animal among natives and mountain men alike. George Catlin (1796–1872). *Buffalo Hunt. A Surround.* Toned lithograph with applied watercolor, 1844. *Courtesy of the Amon Carter Museum of American Art, Fort Worth, Texas. 1972.46.9.*

Far easier to hunt, elk and deer provided much of the sustenance needed to survive in the harsh Western wilderness. *Photograph by author.*

Colter would have used various types of shelter depending on the conditions. The simplest, the half-face tent, is seen here. *Photograph by author.*

Barrel-vault tent, another common portable shelter. *Photograph by author.*

A one-person wigwam, which can be used as a sweat lodge for recuperation. *Photograph by author.*

The tipi provides the most protection from the elements. *Photograph by author.*

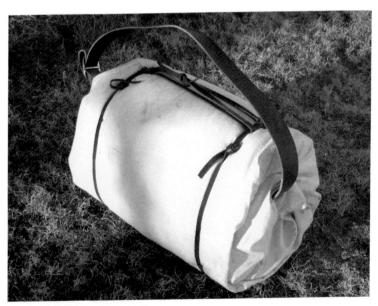

Pack roll. *Photograph by author.*

Canteens from the American Revolution and Frontier: one with wooden hoops, the other with iron hoops. Marchall Collection, Loma Paloma, Texas. *Photograph by author.*

Shoshone family in Willow Thicket Shelter. Photograph by William Henry Jackson. *Courtesy of Yellowstone National Park.*

The ancient Bannock Trail Crossing in Yellowstone National Park. *Photograph by author.*

Beaver gnawings in the Lamar Valley along Colter's winter route. *Photograph by author.*

The site of Colter's capture by eight hundred Blackfoot warriors.
Photograph by author.

Pryor's Fork,
a favorite of
the Crow who
befriended and
traded with Colter.
*Photograph by
author.*

The famous stone on which John Colter allegedly carved his name near South Leigh Creek in 1808 inter route. *Photograph by author.*

Grand Teton National Park, whose inclusion in Clark's original 1810 map of the West is largely due to Colter's later remembrance. *Photograph by author.*

wrote in his journal, "The Pawnees reside a considerable distance above [upstream on the River Platte] ... in the neighborhood of the Spanish villages, near Santa Fe. . . . Through them we may obtain an extensive trade with that portion of Mexico, most adjacent to the mines."[41]

Manuel Lisa finally took direct action to establish a route in 1812 when he dispatched an emissary with a letter addressed "To the Spaniards of New Mexico." He wrote, "My Dear Sirs: Ever since my first journey among the forks [or bends] of the Missouri [in 1807] ... I have desired to find an opportunity to communicate with my compatriots, the Spaniards."

He explained that he was sending the letter to be put "into the hands of some Spaniard who may be worthy ... to engage in business and open up a new commerce, which might easily be done." He concluded with an eager tone, "I propose to you gentlemen that if you wish to trade and deal with me, for whatever quantity of goods it may be, I will oblige myself to fill each year any bill of goods which shall be given me, and all shall be delivered ... at the place nearest and most convenient for both parties."[42]

Despite Lisa's efforts, profitable trade with Santa Fe did not begin until 1821. Late that year, William Becknell reached the town with a load of goods via the newly blazed Santa Fe Trail. Beneath the adobe portico, alongside the Spanish plaza that was already more than two centuries old, he traded wares with the Mexican residents and Pueblo Indians.

Following close on Becknell's heels was Thomas James, an old acquaintance of Colter. By this time, Spain, with its mercantile trade restrictions, was out of the picture. Mexico had won its independence and Santa Fe was free to indulge in commerce with the United States.

But all this happened fourteen years after Colter's expedition.

In 1807, the lonely wanderer had no idea of the long road that lay ahead before commerce could be established. For now, he pushed beyond the land of the Crow to search on Lisa's behalf for Spanish frontier traders. Colter found none, and no sign of Spanish settlement has been discovered in the vicinity of Pierre's Hole.

Clark's maps suggest that Colter circled south in search of the elusive settlements, following the low-lying Big Hole Mountains that fringe Pierre's Hole. There he came to an inviting gap called Pine Creek Pass, sprinkled with rustling Aspen groves. Peering beyond for Spanish and native villages, or perhaps for elk and deer, he discovered present-day Pine Creek—a mountain stream that flows south into the Snake River. William Clark later labeled the stream on his map as Colter's River.

This route marked a well-used Indian trail. It provided the most logical path from the Snake River headwaters in Jackson Hole to the lower Snake River—just below present-day Palisades Reservoir. Rugged canyons that now enclose Palisades Reservoir presented an impassable barrier to a water route, forcing one to detour from the Snake River ford through Teton Pass to Pierre's Hole, then south through Pine Creek Pass and down Colter's River to the lower Snake River. At the juncture of Colter's River and Snake River, Robert Stuart's expedition later camped "on a beautiful low point" in an area abounding with deer, elk, beaver, and trout.[43]

Clark's maps indicate that Colter did not descend as far as the lower Snake River. Instead, he wandered a few miles down this gentle valley before turning northwest, probably up the Pine Creek North Fork. From here, he looped northeast, possibly descending Horseshoe Creek South Fork to its juncture with the Teton River.

The present-day Teton River was called Crooks River on Clark's 1810 map. It received its original name from Ramsay Crooks, who traveled through Pierre's Hole with Wilson Price Hunt in 1811 and returned along the same route with Robert Stuart the following year. Crooks' return passage through this valley was worth noting because he almost perished from fever and was revived by an Indian sweat bath. His name was probably assigned to the river because of this memorable occurrence.

Near Horseshoe Creek's juncture, Clark's maps show Colter following Crooks River North Fork, which is probably today's South Leigh Creek.[44] Here in Pierre's Hole, Colter had reached the western extreme of his journey. It is easy to imagine him having been drawn southward and westward a little farther, and farther, to see what might lie beyond the next pass or bend. Perhaps a lush valley waited just over the rise. Or maybe the Spanish inhabited the next river bend. But at some point Colter had to turn back to complete his mission. And by now, winter was bearing down hard.

☆   ☆   ☆   ☆

COLTER TOOK refuge from the brutal storms either in a native lodge or in his own lonely hovel as he had done many times before. Rufus Sage described the typical setting:

> *The winter-camp of a hunter of the Rocky Mountains . . . is usually located in some spot sheltered by hills or rocks, for the double purpose of securing the full warmth of the sun's rays, and screening it from the notice of strolling Indians that may happen in its vicinity. Within a convenient proximity to it stands some grove, from which an abundance of dry fuel is procurable when needed; and equally close the ripplings of a watercourse. . . .*
>
> *His shantee faces a huge fire, and is formed of skins carefully extended over an arched frame-work of slender poles, which are bent in the form of a semicircle and kept to their places by insert-*

*ing their extremities in the ground. Near this is his 'graining
block,' planted aslope, for the ease of . . . preparing his skins for
the finishing process in the art of dressing. . . . Facing his shantee
upon the opposite side of the fire, a pole is reared upon crotches
five or six feet high, across which reposes a choice selection of . . .
'side ribs,' shoulders, heads, and 'rump-cuts' of deer and sheep,
or the 'depouille' and 'fleeces' of buffalo. . . . Close at hand, his
rifle awaits his use, and by it his powder-horn, bullet-pouch,
and tomahawk.*

Winter encampment allowed time for rest and relaxation with minimal exertion. Sage continued, "Game was plenty, and wood abundant; nothing, therefore, remained for us to do but to . . . eat of the best the prairie afforded, drink of the crystal waters that rolled by our side, and enjoy life in true mountain style. . . . The effort of a few hours was sufficient to procure a month's supply." Often, herds became snowbound in the vicinity of camps, sometimes for the entire winter. This made meat even easier to procure and left plenty of time for making moccasins and repairing clothing and weapons.[45]

In his winter camp, Colter watched the year 1807 come to an end and 1808 begin. The first frozen months brought bitter cold. But warmer weather was ahead with snowmelt in spring that offered a chance to return over the Teton Range.

Meanwhile, he had plenty of time to rest and reflect. Perhaps he recalled similar situations—the frozen plains that first winter with the Corps of Discovery at the Mandan villages, or the chilling, relentless rains at Fort Clatsop by the sea. Or maybe he longed for places he loved—the Three Forks of the Missouri with its limitless game, or that fertile bottomland so far away downriver where a shady bluff watched over the surrounding woodlands near La Charette.

If he was in the company of natives, he would hear ancient tales and learn their lore and legends. With their help he could map out routes and landmarks. He could reconnoiter the countryside to discover thawing pools of water and gatherings of game that would help him in his return trek come spring. And still he had time to spare.

Perhaps he took up carving. A tantalizing object surfaced in 1931 on a site near South Leigh Creek. A man and his son were plowing a field when they pulled up a stone from beneath the soil. They immediately noticed that the piece of rhyolite had been fashioned into the profile of a human head. It was carefully carved in three dimensions with a heavy brow, prominent nose, and protruding lower lip, suggesting the artist's sense of humor. Across the eight-inch width of the profile, a man had engraved a name—JOHN COLTER. On the other side he carved the year—1808.

On May 8, 1934, F. M. Fryxell, a ranger-naturalist at Grand Teton National Park, sent a letter to Arno Cammerer, director of the National Park Service, describing the Colter Stone and its discovery. Fryxell explained that "the stone was found in the summer of 1931 when Mr. [William] Beard and his son . . . were plowing the land . . . three or four miles east of Tetonia [Idaho], just east of the state line [on the Wyoming side]." When they unearthed it, they were "mildly interested" in this strange rock that resembled a human head.

They took it home as a curiosity piece, where it sat neglected for two years. Eventually, their neighbor, Aubrey Lyon, who ran the horseback-riding concession for the national park, became aware of the stone. In 1933, Lyon "chanced to mention [to Fryxell] that one of his neighbors over in Teton Basin had a few years prior found a stone on which was carved the name of John Colter." Fryxell asked Lyon to acquire the stone, if possible, so he could take a look. A week later, Lyon showed up with the Colter Stone. He had swapped an old pair of boots for the slab of rock that has since become an intriguing artifact of frontier history.

The stone aroused Fryxell's interest. He and an associate soon made a trip to the far side of the Tetons to interview Mr. Beard, Mrs. Beard, and their son, all separately without each other's knowledge. Fryxell found that their stories of the stone's discovery corroborated. He also became aware that "the finders did not know who John Colter was and had no interest whatever in the inscription. Their curiosity grew solely out of the fact that they had found a 'stone head' as they put it."

When the Beards pointed out the discovery site to Fryxell, he found the outcrop from which the stone had originated. He also noted active springs nearby, two of which flowed within one hundred yards of the location. He concluded that the springs, the sheltering terrain, and the abundance of game in the area made an ideal campsite.

Later, Fryxell and his associate examined the artifact in greater detail, and "excellent photographs of the stone were obtained." He reported that JOHN COLTER was engraved on one side "in letters which are still very easy to decipher," and 1808 appeared more faintly on the back. He added that the whole piece was "rudely carved, probably with a hunting knife or some such instrument." Fryxell had been skeptical when he first heard of the stone, but after closely examining its weathered carvings and the circumstances of its discovery, he "became convinced it could not be a fake."[46]

More recently, the artifact has drawn skepticism. Today, some dismiss it as a hoax perpetrated in the 1870s by a member of the Hayden expedition. But no evidence exists to support the charge.

On the contrary, Colter's name was rarely known at that time and not worth the trouble of a prank. One recent study has disavowed the Colter Stone, not based primarily on the evidence at hand, but because the stone thwarts its theory that Colter never entered Jackson Hole, the Tetons, or Pierre's Hole.

Others have made the baffling claim that the carving must be a fake because Colter could not write or even sign his name. This opinion is unfortunate and uninformed—the product of an enduring stereotype that declares frontiersmen uncouth and unlearned. To counter this, some have posited that Colter came from an educated family in Virginia. What is known for certain is that Colter owned a small collection of books, which suggests his literacy. In addition, his signature appears on several public documents signed at Three Forks and St. Louis.[47]

Many frontiersmen were literate and even well-educated. This is evident in the polished narratives they wrote describing their travels. Indeed, the numerous quotes that appear in this book attest to the fact. William Anderson said, of his travels across the Great Plains and Rockies, I saw "gentlemen and men of genteel deportment wherever I have been."

Joe Meek told how the mountain men gathered about the evening campfire and "told tales of marvelous adventures, or sang some old-remembered song, or were absorbed in games of chance. Some of the better educated men, who had once known and loved books, but whom some mishap in life had banished to the wilderness, recalled their favorite authors, and recited passages once treasured, now growing unfamiliar." Others related stories they had read in their youth, including *Robinson Crusoe*, *The Arabian Nights*, and *The Pilgrim's Progress*.

The rugged frontiersmen who traveled with William Sublette, Jedediah Smith, and David Jackson carried a copy of the Bible and the works of Shakespeare. From these, Joe Meek learned to read by the light of the campfire while in the mountains. Osborne Russell said of one winter encampment on the Snake River, "We had nothing to do but to eat, attend to the horses, and procure firewood. We had some few books to read, such as Byron's, Shakespeare's, and Scott's works, the Bible, and Clark's Commentary on it, and other small works on geology, chemistry, and philosophy." At another camp at Fort Laramie, leisure time was spent in typical pursuits: "story-telling, ball-playing, foot-racing, target-shooting." But several men formed a debate club and "the merits of the arguments presented were decided upon by a committee of three."[48]

Others who had received less education still left abundant signed records of various transactions. Even those who were illiterate often learned the letters that made up their names. Explorers of Colter's time frequently proved this ability by carving their names on trees, rocks, and anything else that stood still long enough to allow it.

While probing along the mouth of the Columbia River, men of the Corps of Discovery had taken the time to do just that. William Clark wrote, "We passed at each point a soft cliff of yellow, brown and dark soft stones. Here Captain Lewis and myself, and several of the men marked our names, day of the month, and by land, etc., etc."

This was a common occurrence, perhaps more so than today. Lewis carried a brand for the specific purpose of blazing trees with his name. And Clark often mentioned carving his name on this or that. There is no reason to doubt that Colter did the same.

In addition to carvings and brandings, travelers often scribbled their names on rocks or on peeled tree trunks using a makeshift ink of bison grease mixed with charcoal or gunpowder. Frontier graffiti may still be seen at Pompey's Pillar, Independence Rock, Register Cliffs, and other sites along historic trails.[49]

Another baffling claim states that Colter would not have had the ability to carve the face on the stone. Detractors say the work required a degree of skill. That may be true. Still, it is no masterpiece. One could easily contend that a person like Colter, who had crafted canoes out of cottonwoods, could certainly have carved this rock.

The fact that a barrage of skepticism and dubious disgruntlement has failed to doom the Colter Stone might even hint at its authenticity. Meanwhile, the rock rests unperturbed in the Teton Valley Museum in Driggs, Idaho, on loan from the national park. On one side, the name JOHN COLTER is still quite visible.

Whether Colter occupied his time by carving or keeping camp, a few frigid months of sitting around made him restless and ready to begin his return journey. At last, in April, as endless formations of wild geese passed northward overhead, he slung a pack over his shoulder and headed out.[50] With native advice or well-marked indigenous trails, he had little trouble finding a route through the Tetons.

The Shoshone knew these mountains well. For ages they had traversed the range along several routes and had pursued vision quests on the lofty heights under the approving gaze of the Hoary-headed Fathers. They believed that these jagged spires of the Tetons led them to the spirit world. Today, the remains of scattered rings of stone mark the sites of their solitary vigils, where they passed the days and nights in a trance induced by lack of food and shelter.[51]

Colter was ready to follow their trails and was well-equipped with snowshoes for the crossing. A logical route was to continue the ascent of South Leigh Creek to its headwaters in Granite Basin. From there, Colter could cross the divide to Moran Creek South Fork and descend through Moran Canyon—marked on Clark's 1810 map as GAP and DRAW.

Or Colter might have followed a different route, such as Teton Creek or North Leigh Creek. These lead over the Teton Range to Cascade, Leigh, and Moran Canyons. Archaeologist Charles Love noted multiple routes through the Tetons to Jackson Hole and said "nearly every mountain pass reported or visited had some form of artifact material associated with it." The Shoshone commonly ventured into all parts of the Teton Range. Their stone circles are found at high altitudes, even above 13,000 feet. In addition, hunters followed the high elevation routes in their autumn pursuit of bighorn sheep as they left Lake Jackson (Lake Biddle) to traverse the Tetons westward.

Colter possibly even traveled north to a point where the height of the range visibly diminishes. In this case he would have intercepted North Bitch Creek and followed it over Conant Pass to Berry Creek, then to Owl Creek and on to Lake Biddle. The Conant Pass route was an important crossing point with relatively easy climbs and quarries of chert, steatite, obsidian, and ignimbrite in the general area. The Lawrence archaeological site in the Snake River delta, now underwater, was likely a natural stopping point for people crossing east and west along this route. According to Charles Love, Togwotee and Conant Passes marked the easiest east-west route through northern Jackson Hole.

But there is a problem with the theory of Colter following the Conant Pass route. Before the twentieth century damming of Lake Biddle, Berry Creek flowed into the Snake River north of the lake. Clark's 1810 map, however, distinctly shows that Colter's route approached Lake Biddle from the southwest.

It seems most logical, then, that Colter descended Horseshoe Creek South Fork to its juncture with Teton (Crooks) River near the mouth of Leigh Creek. Then he ascended South Leigh Creek (Crooks River North Fork), roughly following the present-day

Andy Stone Creek trail to Granite Basin. From there he crossed to Moran Creek South Fork and descended to Lake Biddle.

According to archaeologist Deward Walker, the abundance of archaeological sites at Moran Bay and the direct access provided by Moran Creek to the Bighorn Range suggest the use of this watercourse as a route over the Tetons.[52] This would account for the general shape of the westward loop on Clark's maps and the approach to Lake Biddle from the southwest. Incidentally, the Colter Stone discovery site lies on this very route.

At last, Colter arrived on the shore of Lake Biddle for a few days of much-needed rest. The rugged traverse over snowy passes must have tested his strength and endurance. But Colter had surmounted as big a challenge in the Bitterroots—while starving, no less. Later, he would scale a similar range with "rugged and perpendicular sides" that a companion reported as seemingly "impassable, even by the mountain goat."[53]

After refitting and repacking at Lake Biddle, Colter made his way northward along the western shore. From there he could not see the lake's eastern drainage into the Snake River. Nor could he see how the Snake turns south to run through Jackson Hole. In fact, he had no evidence that the two bodies of water even drained the same watershed.

This led to a discrepancy on William Clark's maps. Clark relied on Colter for information on this region. But Colter lacked knowledge of the eastern shore. Clark was left to assume that Lake Biddle drained eastward, maybe through a canyon, to join the Bighorn River system.

In hindsight, much has been made of Clark's mistake. But in reality the error is easily understood. After all, Lake Biddle and the Bighorn watershed are only thirty miles apart. Without a clear picture of the geography, Clark speculated that the two were linked.

This would seem to support his theory—and that of George Drouillard and Zebulon Pike—that the headwaters of the Bighorn branch of the Yellowstone River was not far from the headwaters of the Rio Grande. Only later, after further exploration of the region, was the map corrected to place Lake Biddle and the Yellowstone River system in separate watersheds, and to place the Rio Grande headwaters far to the south.

The fact is, Clark's Map of 1810, despite errors and distorted distances, is remarkably accurate. He drew large portions of the map sight unseen, based on verbal information from various sources over several years. Yet he placed most mountain passes, rivers, lakes, and other features in proper orientation and relation to each other.[54]

Perhaps this should not be surprising. After all, William Clark had used nothing more than dead reckoning to estimate the distance traveled by the Corps of Discovery from St. Louis to the Pacific Ocean. Over an eighteen-month period of wandering in every direction, he had calculated a distance of 4,162 miles. He was only off by forty miles—an error of less than one percent.

Clark's navigational and cartographic talents are obvious on the 1810 map in spite of the lack of geographical information at his disposal. For a person to judge him in hindsight, while holding a modern atlas in hand, is simply unfair. As Burton Harris correctly stated, "condemnation of Clark's map because it cannot be superimposed upon a modern map is carping criticism at its irrational worst."[55]

Colter was not in the position to provide Clark with information on Lake Biddle's drainage because he never laid eyes on the lake's lower reaches. Instead, he moved northward along an Indian trail that followed the natural corridor of the upper Snake and Lewis Rivers. This took him straight to Lake Eustis—known today as Yellowstone Lake. Having observed portions of Lakes Biddle and Eustis, he could later report to Clark their relative size and direction from one another. Clark duly marked them on his map.[56]

Already, Colter had traipsed back and forth across country later designated as Grand Teton National Park. Now he wandered from south to northeast through what would be Yellowstone National Park. He was the first non-native explorer of this extensive region, which has since become world famous for its natural beauty.

As he followed the western shore of Lake Eustis, the geysers and mud pots he encountered must have reminded him of Boiling Spring and Colter's Hell. On the north side of the lake he came to a point where it narrowed to form a river channel. Whether he knew it or not, he now stood at the headwaters of the Yellowstone River. From here it wound hundreds of miles through mountains and basins, past Pompey's Tower and Manuel's Fort, and on to join the Missouri.

As Colter followed the banks of the upper river the land became more pleasant—a paradise for bison, elk, and deer. Then an amazing site came into view. The rushing river began to drop in a succession of cascades into a deep gorge—the Grand Canyon of the Yellowstone.

Colter followed the rim, unable to access the riverbank. He depended instead on upland springs to fill his canteen. After a day or two of struggling through rugged country, he noticed the canyon depth diminish. At last he came to a place where the rim sloped gently down to the water's edge at the mouth of Tower Creek. Steaming geysers and sulfurous formations left strange specters on the landscape. Colter called the area Hot Spring Brimstone, and so it appears on Clark's maps.

When the Washburn Expedition wandered through the same country sixty-two years later, Gustavus Doane, who commanded the military escort, penned a description of the surreal surroundings. On August 26, 1870, the party encountered their first geo-thermal site. It was a small spring with "a temperature milk warm," and "highly impregnated with sulphur."

Close by flowed a creek through a gorge that the men called Warm Spring Creek. They camped there for the night near "the 'wickey ups' of fifteen lodges of Crows." The Indians likely favored the spot for the warm water in winter and for medicinal and spiritual purposes. Nearby ran a native trail that traversed the Yellowstone River.

The following day, Doane reported more discoveries: "At the mouth of Hot Spring Creek we found a system of sulphurous and mineral springs, distributed for a distance of two miles" northward toward the Lamar River juncture. Some of these had a "temperature at the boiling point." The scalding water explains why Doane changed the name of the main stream from Warm Spring Creek one day to Hot Spring Creek the next.

The creek and the neighboring springs carried such an abundance of sulfur that they emitted fumes for a half mile and deposited the mineral "in yellowish beds along their courses," giving "a brilliant yellow color to rocks in many places." But the most amazing spectacles were the "masses of a more solid nature" that formed along the riverbank and "projected from the wall in curious shapes of towers, minarets, etc."[57] From these formations, the nearby stream received a third appellation—its present name—Tower Creek.

This area, first explored by Colter in 1808 and described by Doane in 1870, remained geologically active through the twentieth century, as it does today. In 2012, a Yellowstone National Park geologist confirmed that "an active acid-sulfate hydrothermal area exists along the Yellowstone River from approximately one-half-mile south of Tower Falls to two-and-a-quarter-miles north."[58] This matches Doane's description and suggests that Colter aptly described the area when he named it Hot Spring Brimstone.

Near the mouth of Tower Creek the banks of the Yellowstone slope gently toward the river. At midstream, a series of sandbars served as stepping stones for travelers on the ancient Bannock Trail. The Bannock, Shoshone, and Nez Perce tribes all used this major route to reach the bison ranges in the Lamar Valley and east of the Absaroka Mountains.[59] It provided a passage comfortably south of the dangerous Blackfoot territory. After fording the Yellowstone River from west to east, the native bands would regroup and begin the easy climb to Specimen Ridge.[60]

Colter followed the same well-marked route. Upon gaining the ridge, he continued along the Bannock Trail by dropping into the undulating grasslands of the Lamar River valley. In his mind, this landscape must have stood out as another treasure hidden within the forbidding folds of the mountains.

Osborne Russell followed the path a generation after Colter. He described it just as it appears today, as "a beautiful valley about eight miles long and three or four wide, surrounded by dark and lofty mountains . . . and skirted in many places with beautiful cottonwood groves." Grassland game roamed leisurely in large numbers. Bison, elk, deer, and pronghorn abounded. Bighorn sheep inhabited the valley rim.

Russell continued:

Here we found a few Snake Indians comprising six men, seven women, and eight or ten children who were the only inhabitants of this lonely and secluded spot. They were all neatly clothed in dressed deer and sheep skins of the best quality and seemed to be perfectly contented and happy. . . .

> *Their personal property consisted of one old butcher knife*
> *nearly worn to the back. . . . They were well armed with bows*
> *and arrows pointed with obsidian. . . . They said there had been*
> *a great many beaver on the branches of this stream but they*
> *had killed nearly all of them.* [61]

One has to wonder how these lithic people living in a remote valley obtained the butcher knife. Colter wandered the valley twenty-six years before Russell. Could he have traded it to a local Shoshone for food or hides? Could the knife have survived so many years of use? The thought is intriguing but unanswerable.

Colter probably took his time hunting his way up the Lamar River. Where it forked, he headed northeast along the Soda Butte branch.[62] Passing Trout Lake and Pebble Creek, he made the moderate climb out of the narrowing northeast neck of the valley.[63] At a highpoint on the Soda Butte headwaters he crossed a rise that still bears his name—Colter Pass. A few more paces brought him to the upper reaches of Clark's Fork of the Yellowstone. An easy descent now followed.

After meandering several miles, the valley broadened into a mile-wide grassy plain. Wildlife grazed in large numbers and timber skirted the fringe. From here, Colter needed no more than a day to reach Sunlight Basin. He had hunted this valley at least once before. Now he was practically home.

After renewing acquaintances at Crow lodges, he encouraged them to pack up camp and prepare for a journey—a trading venture down the Clark's Fork and Yellowstone River to Manuel's Fort. Then, slinging his pack, he retraced his route up Dead Indian Creek. A pause at the pass west of Blue Bead Mountain allowed another view of Heart Mountain in the distance. From here, he descended the Valley River.

The familiar route brought him once more to Colter's Hell on the Stinking Water. Again he visited the large encampment near Boiling Spring under the gaze of Spirits' Mountain. Again he prompted the Indians to trade—encouraging them to gather their pelts and robes and float down the Stinking Water and Bighorn Rivers to Manuel's Fort.

Colter headed this direction himself as he left the juncture of the Mick-ka-ap-ha and Salt Fork and followed the flow of the main river channel. He must have heard about the large Crow villages only two days' downriver. He had missed visiting them the previous fall when he cut across country from upper Gap Creek toward Clark's Fork Canyon. But now the Stinking Water River offered a direct and easy route on the way to Manuel's Fort.

Two encampments with a total of "two hundred and eighty lodges of dressed leather" occupied the riverbank from the mouth of Gap Creek to the Stinking Water's juncture with the Bighorn River. It was a major gathering of Ap-sha-roo-kee Crow, and might have included other tribes as well. The hides that covered so many lodges suggested that these people dwelled near the bison range and excelled as hunters.

Considering their proximity to Manuel's Fort, they would make ideal trading partners and allies. Colter encouraged them to descend the Bighorn without delay to visit the trading post. Then he returned upstream and ascended Gap Creek into the arid upland of the Bighorn Basin.[64] At Pryor Gap he again reached familiar ground.

After filling a canteen, he took a last look at the majestic Absarokas and the V-shaped mouth of Clark's Fork Canyon in the distance. Then he turned northeast for the final leg of the journey. The Pryor's Fork valley was in springtime bloom as he walked once more through familiar villages and enjoyed native hospitality. At his encouragement, some Crow warriors might have packed up at once and accompanied him along the remaining route to Manuel's Fort.

Soon Colter came to the Yellowstone, swollen by snowmelt and making its rapid descent. The last time he had seen the river was far west of the Absaroka Range when he forded at Bannock Trail crossing. Now he followed along the south bank, passing Pompey's Tower and splashing across Shannon's Creek.

A day or two later he reached the mouth of the Bighorn River and strode into the stockade at Manuel's Fort. No doubt the men watched his return with wide eyes after an absence of about eight months in the frozen mountains. He would have had little time to rest before Manuel Lisa plied him for news. Had he encouraged the Crow to come to trade? Had he encountered other Indian nations or Spanish settlements along the way?

The tales that followed must have kept the men on the edge of their seats—tales of lush valleys and jagged peaks, of comfortable lodges and howling blizzards, of fossilized bones and caves of pure salt, of herds of bison and elk without end, of valiant warriors and comely women.

Some stories brought a few skeptical sighs. He certainly told of smoking tar pits and boiling mud pots, of steaming geysers and yellow towers of sulfur. What did he care if they believed him or not? He had seen it for himself.

Most of his companions must have sat in silent amazement at the accomplishment. A century later, Hiram Chittenden called it a "remarkable achievement—remarkable in the courage and hardihood of this lone adventurer and remarkable in its unexpected results in geographical discovery"—an achievement that "deserves to be classed among the most celebrated performances in the history of American exploration."[65]

★   ★   ★   ★

AFTER A FEW weeks at Manuel's Fort, Colter must have grown bored and restless. Early summer arrived, and the grasses and trees turned a deep green. Fish jumped in the streams, birds sang in the trees, and the mountains called him back.

Obedient to nature's irresistible charms, he rolled up his pack, grabbed his gun, and turned his gaze westward again. As before, he followed the Yellowstone River past Shannon's Creek and Pompey's Tower to the mouth of Pryor's Fork.

But this time he continued to ascend the Yellowstone. Soon he crossed its juncture with the Clark's Fork—the river whose headwaters he knew so well. Several days later he came to a point where the Yellowstone bends south toward the Lamar River valley, Hot Spring Brimstone, and the headwaters at Lake Eustis.

Colter left the river at the bend and continued his westward trek. Crossing the mountains at Bozeman Pass, he followed the flow of the Gallatin River's east fork to arrive at the bountiful, game-rich basin of Three Forks of the Missouri. Somewhere nearby he came across a large band of Flathead Indians.

Three years earlier, in the autumn of 1805, Colter had encountered three Flatheads while hunting near Traveler's Rest. By making a peaceful approach he had assured their friendship. He must have done the same this time.

Soon he and hundreds of the Flathead tribe were on the move eastward together. The trail up the Gallatin east fork and back through Bozeman Pass would lead them to the Yellowstone River. From here, they could follow an easy route to the bison hunting grounds and to trade at Manuel's Fort.

But the party did not make it that far. This was Blackfoot country. The Blackfoot had become a powerful nation through trade with the British—a trade that brought them guns and dominion over the weaker tribes around them.

The Blackfoot, like the Sioux nation of the middle Missouri River, made frequent forays against neighboring bands and attacked any newcomers who befriended them. Edwin Denig explained that, among the Crow,

> *Traffic is carried on with the Flat Heads in St. Mary's Valley, or with the Snake and Nez Perce Indians on the headwaters of the Yellowstone. With the natives named, the Crows have been at peace for a long time. . . . But their natural and eternal enemies are the Blackfeet on the west and the Sioux on the east, with both of whom war has continued from time immemorial without being varied by even a transient peace.*

In the early nineteenth century, much of Blackfoot hostility toward traders and trappers from the United States was incited by British fur companies attempting to frighten off competition. In 1818, John C. Calhoun addressed the problem:

> *It is expected the English traders will take unusual pains to make a contrary impression. They have great advantages in controlling the savages through their commanding station on Red River [of the North], and as our contemplated establishment at Yellowstone, will greatly curtail their trade towards the head of the Missouri, we must expect every opposition from them. No pains must be spared to counteract such efforts.*

Calhoun's solution was to send an expedition to establish military posts reaching to the mouth of the Yellowstone River. Andrew

Jackson, in typical fashion, spoke out more forcefully against the threat:

> *The British traders will no doubt excite the Indians to hostility. They ought in my opinion to be hung wherever they are found among the Indian tribes within our territory. A few examples would be sufficient and the commanding officer of the troops is the proper authority to judge of their guilt and order their execution. But the over cautious policy of the Executive [President James Monroe], has directed that they only be arrested and reported to him.*

In the end, the US military expedition only made it as far as Council Bluffs near present-day Omaha, Nebraska. Hampered by scurvy and thefts by Indians, it only served to prove the ineffectiveness of the US military in that region.[66]

Western travelers were left to their own defenses. They, like their native allies, knew that the Blackfoot threat was real and imminent. "They are the sworn enemies of all—Indians and white men alike," declared Alfred Jacob Miller. George Catlin agreed, calling them "warlike and ferocious." Prince Maximilian of Wied added that they "are always dangerous."

Even John Townsend, who was not prone to exaggeration or overexcitement, said, "The Blackfoot is a sworn and determined foe to all white men, and he has often been heard to declare that he would rather hang the scalp of a "pale face" to his girdle, than kill a buffalo to prevent his starving."

To defend against this threat, trappers sometimes worked in groups rather than pairs. After one tragic Blackfoot attack in which several men were killed, Pierre Menard commanded his company to trap in groups of fifteen, with another fifteen guarding the camp.

Expeditions often attempted to avoid surprise attacks by encamping on islands in a river. Some established decoy camps in the open, but scattered to sleep in the brush around the perimeter where they could watch for intruders during the night. Others routinely traveled until after dark and camped without fires in order to obscure their location from watchful eyes.

When fires were needed for preparing food, "cooking was all done at midday when the fire makes no glare, and a moderate smoke cannot be perceived at any great distance. In the morning and the evening, when the wind is lulled, the smoke rises perpendicularly in a blue column, or floats in light clouds above the treetops, and can be discovered from afar."

Another common precaution when danger lurked nearby was to make a roaring fire in the evening, eat dinner, and slip away from camp with the fire still burning. After traveling for some time in the dark, a camp was made without benefit of fire. In this way, any marauders would be duped when trying to steal horses after the camp was asleep, or when launching an attack at dawn.[67]

Such precaution was warranted. The Blackfoot resented trespassers, whether native or white, and defended their territory furiously. Most tribes gave them a wide berth. Others, like the Flathead and Crow, frightened less easily, especially when traveling in large numbers.

Only one day's march from Three Forks, on the Gallatin east fork, a Blackfoot army suddenly fell upon the Flathead band with whom Colter was traveling. Colter fought alongside his new friends and barely survived the onslaught. He returned to the site less than two years later in the company of a trapping expedition and pointed out the particulars of the battle to his friend, Thomas James, who described the scene in detail:

We passed a battlefield of the Indians, where the skulls and bones were lying around on the ground in vast numbers. The battle which had caused this terrible slaughter took place in 1808, the year but one before, between the Blackfeet to the number of fifteen hundred on the one side, and the Flatheads and Crows, numbering together about eight hundred, on the other.

Colter was in the battle on the side of the latter, and was wounded in the leg, and thus disabled from standing. He crawled to a small thicket and there loaded and fired while sitting on the ground. The battle was desperately fought on both sides, but victory remained with the weaker party.

The Blackfeet engaged at first with about five hundred Flatheads, whom they attacked in great fury. The noise, shouts, and firing brought a reinforcement of Crows to the Flatheads, who were fighting with great spirit and defending the ground manfully. The Blackfeet, who are the Arabs of this region, were at length repulsed, but retired in perfect order and could hardly be said to have been defeated.

The Flatheads are a noble race of men, brave, generous and hospitable. They might be called the Spartans of Oregon. Lewis and Clark had received much kindness from them in their expedition to the Columbia, which waters their country, and at the time of this well-fought battle Colter was leading them to Manuel's fort to trade with the Americans, when the Blackfeet fell upon them in such numbers as seemingly to make their destruction certain. Their desperate courage saved them from a general massacre. [68]

After this horrific battle in the summer of 1808, Colter wrapped his wounded leg and limped the long trail back to Manuel's Fort. But as soon as his leg healed he was ready again to escape the dull routine of camp life and the doldrums of being bedridden. Undaunted by recent events, he packed his gear that autumn and prepared to return to the beaver-rich streams of Three Forks.[69]

This time he hoped to trap for pelts and trade them directly at Manuel's Fort. The best trapping took place in the colder months, when beaver pelts reached their prime, so Colter had time to gather supplies and make the trip in good season.

But first he needed to find a partner. At the time, most trappers worked in pairs. In typical fashion, the two would select a site and pitch a small shelter at the mouth of a creek. From there they worked opposite banks, struggling upstream with a set of five or more traps apiece plus weapons and gear.

Each man trapped the tributaries that flowed in on his side of the stream. The work required long hours of wading icy waters and setting traps beneath the surface. To make trapping effective, they used castoreum—a secretion from the animal's scent glands—which they smeared on a willow stick and floated or hung above the trap to attract beavers.[70] At the top of the stream, the men would meet and return to camp to rest and prepare the pelts. Then they would move to the next stream to begin the process again.

Finding a worthy partner was essential. He must know how to trap, and to do so stealthily to avoid the dangers that lurked all about. A trapper might need to depend on his partner's cool judgment, courage, and marksmanship.

Colter chose John Potts, an acquaintance since their days with Lewis and Clark.[71] The two had served under Sgt. Ordway's command in the Corps of Discovery. As close companions for two and a half years, they knew each other well. Often they had shared assigned duties, including scouting ahead of the expedition in canoes.[72]

On one of these ventures, Ordway had commanded his men to float six canoes down the Missouri River from Three Forks to the waters below the Great Falls. The task became more dangerous as the men approached treacherous rapids and cataracts near the end of their journey. Most of them chose to portage the canoes and use ropes to lower the boats over difficult stretches. But Ordway noted in his journal that the more adventurous Colter and Potts "went at running the canoes down the rapids."[73]

Now, two years later, with high hopes of success, the two returned to Three Forks on their own accord. There they launched canoes upstream to work the tributaries of the Jefferson River. Colter later stood with Thomas James and others at the site and told of the tragedy that ensued. According to James, Colter spoke with emotion as he described the events in detail, and "his veracity was never questioned among us." The following is James' record of Colter's account "precisely as he related it":[74]

> [Colter] had gone with a companion named Potts to the Jefferson River, which is the most western of the Three Forks, and runs near the base of the mountains.[75] They were both proceeding up the river in search of beaver, each in his own canoe, when a war party of about eight hundred Blackfoot Indians suddenly appeared on the east bank of the river. The chiefs ordered them to come ashore, and apprehending robbery only and knowing the utter hopelessness of flight, and having dropped his traps over the side of the canoe from the Indians into the water, which was here quite shallow, he hastened to obey their mandate.[76]

On reaching the shore he was seized, disarmed, and stripped entirely naked. Potts was still in his canoe in the middle of the stream, where he remained stationary, watching the result. Colter requested him to come ashore, which he refused to do, saying he might as well lose his life at once as be stripped and robbed in the manner Colter had been.

An Indian immediately fired and shot him about the hip; he dropped down in the canoe, but instantly rose with his rifle in his hands. 'Are you hurt,' said Colter. 'Yes,' said he, 'too much hurt to escape; if you can get away, do so. I will kill at least one of them.'

He leveled his rifle and shot an Indian dead. In an instant at least a hundred bullets pierced his body, and as many savages rushed into the stream and pulled the canoe, containing his riddled corpse, ashore.[77] They dragged the body up onto the bank and with their hatchets and knives cut and hacked it all to pieces, and limb from limb. The entrails, heart, lungs, etc., they threw into Colter's face.[78]

The relations of the killed Indian were furious with rage and struggled, with tomahawk in hand, to reach Colter, while others held them back. He was every moment expecting the death blow or the fatal shot that should lay him beside his companion. A council was hastily held over him and his fate quickly determined upon.

He expected to die by torture, slow, lingering, and horrible. But they had magnanimously determined to give him a chance, though a slight one, for his life. After the council a chief pointed to the prairie and motioned him away with his hand, saying in the Crow language, 'go—go away.'

He supposed they intended to shoot him as soon as he was out of the crowd and presented a fair mark to their guns. He started in a walk and an old Indian, with impatient signs and exclamations, told him to go faster, and as he still kept a walk the same Indian manifested his wishes by still more violent gestures and adjurations.

When he had gone a distance of eighty or a hundred yards from the army of his enemies he saw the younger Indians throwing off their blankets, leggings, and other encumbrances, as if for a race. Now he knew their object. He was to run a race, of which the prize was to be his own life and scalp.[79]

Off he started with the speed of the wind.[80] The war-whoop and yell immediately arose behind him, and looking back he saw a large company of young warriors, with spears, in rapid pursuit. He ran with all the strength that nature, excited to the utmost, could give; fear and hope lent a supernatural vigor to his limbs, and the rapidity of his flight astonished himself.

The Madison Fork lay directly before him, five miles from his starting place. He had run half the distance when his strength began to fail and the blood to gush from his nostrils. At every leap the red stream spurted before him, and his limbs were growing rapidly weaker and weaker.[81]

He stopped and looked back; he had far outstripped all his pursuers and could get off if his strength would only hold out. One solitary Indian, far ahead of the others, was rapidly approaching, with a spear in his right hand and a blanket streaming behind from his left hand and shoulder.

Despairing of escape, Colter awaited his pursuer and called to him in the Crow language to save his life. The savage did not seem to hear him, but letting go his blanket and seizing his spear with both hands he rushed at Colter, naked and defenseless as he stood before him, and made a desperate *lunge to transfix him. Colter seized the spear near the head with his right hand, and exerting his whole strength, aided by the weight of the falling Indian, who had lost his balance in the fury of the onset, he broke off the iron head or blade which remained in his hand, while the savage fell to the ground and lay prostrate and disarmed before him.*

Now was his turn to beg for his life, which he did in the Crow language, and held up his hands imploringly, but Colter was not in a mood to remember the golden rule, and pinned his adversary through the body to the earth by one stab with the spear head. He quickly drew the weapon from the body of the now dying Indian, and seizing his blanket as lawful spoil, he again set out with renewed strength, feeling, he said to me, as if he had not run a mile. A shout and yell arose from the pursuing army in his rear as from a legion of devils, and he saw the prairie behind him covered with Indians in full and rapid chase.

Before him, if anywhere, was life and safety; behind him, certain death; and running as never man before sped the foot, except, perhaps, at the Olympic Games, he reached his goal, the Madison River, and the end of his five-mile heat. Dashing through the willows on the bank, he plunged into the stream and saw close beside him a beaver house, standing like a coalpit about ten feet above the surface of the water, which was here of about the same depth.[82] This presented to him a refuge from his ferocious enemies, of which he immediately availed himself. . . .

The Indians soon came up, and in their search for him they stood upon the roof of his house of refuge, which he expected every moment to hear them breaking open. He also feared that they would set it on fire. After a diligent search on that side of the river, they crossed over, and in about two hours returned again to his temporary habitation, in which he was enjoying bodily rest, though with much anxious foreboding. . . .

In this asylum Colter kept fast till night. The cries of his terrible enemies had gradually died away and all was still around him when he ventured out of his hiding place by the same opening under the water by which he had entered and which admits the beavers to their building.

He swam the river and hastened towards the mountain gap or ravine, about thirty miles above on the river, through which our company passed in the snow with so much difficulty. Fearing that the Indians might have guarded this pass, which was the only outlet from the valley, and to avoid the danger of a surprise, Colter ascended the almost perpendicular mountain before him, the tops and sides of which a great way down were covered with perpetual snow. He clambered up this fearful ascent about four miles below the gap, holding on by the rocks, shrubs, and branches of trees, and by morning had reached the top.

He lay there concealed all that day, and at night proceeded on in the descent of the mountain, which he accomplished by dawn. He now hastened on in the open plain towards Manuel's fort on the Big Horn, about three hundred miles ahead in the northeast.[83] He travelled day and night, stopping only for necessary repose and eating roots and the bark of trees, for eleven days.[84]

He reached the fort, nearly exhausted by hunger, fatigue, and excitement. His only clothing was the Indian's blanket, whom he had killed in the race, and his only weapon the same Indian's spear, which he brought to the fort as a trophy. His beard was long, his face and whole body were thin and emaciated by hunger, and his limbs and feet swollen and sore.[85] The *company at the fort did not recognize him in this dismal plight until he had made himself known.*

Colter, now with me, passed over the scene of his capture and wonderful escape, and described his emotions during the whole adventure with great minuteness. Not the least of his exploits was the scaling of the mountain, which seemed to me impassable, even by the mountain goat. As I looked at its rugged and perpendicular sides I wondered how he ever reached the top, a feat probably never performed before by mortal man.

The whole affair is a fine example of the quick and ready thoughtfulness and presence of mind in a desperate situation, and the power of endurance, which characterize the western pioneer. As we passed over the ground where Colter ran his race and listened to his story an indefinable fear crept over all. We felt awestruck by the nameless and numerous dangers that evidently beset us on every side.[86]

Perhaps Colter's story should have ended right then, with a safe float downriver to the settlements. There he could have lived to a ripe old age, held in high esteem, recounting his adventures and writing his memoirs. But that was not Colter.

Instead, he gathered his supplies and returned—alone—to the very country inhabited by the same people who had twice almost cost him his life. Thomas James continued his record of Colter's account:

In the winter, when he had recovered from the fatigues of his long race and journey, he wished to recover the traps which he had dropped into the Jefferson Fork on the first appearance of the Indians who captured him. He supposed the Indians were all quiet in winter quarters, and retraced his steps to the Gallatin Fork.

> *He had just passed the mountain gap and encamped on the bank of the river for the night and kindled a fire to cook his supper of buffalo meat when he heard the crackling of leaves and branches behind him in the direction of the river. He could see nothing, it being quite dark, but he quickly heard the cocking of guns and instantly leaped over the fire. Several shots followed and bullets whistled around him, knocking the coals off his fire over the ground.*
>
> *Again he fled for life, and the second time ascended the perpendicular mountain which he had gone up in his former flight, fearing now, as then, that the pass might be guarded by Indians. He reached the top before morning and resting for the day descended the next night, and then made his way with all possible speed to the fort.*[87]

After three close calls in the span of eight months, Colter finally took leave of the country and departed Manuel's Fort. This time he headed east—not west—riding the spring floodwaters toward home. Whether he intended to reach St. Louis is not known.

He took shelter in a Hidatsa village near the earth lodge towns of the Mandans.[88] Here, on the Knife River, he had survived his first winter on the northern plains in 1804 with the Corps of Discovery. That must have seemed a lifetime ago. Much had happened in the past four years—amazing discoveries and brushes with death. It was a long time to survive in the wild, rugged mountains. But now it seemed all behind him.

Most of his comrades had long returned to a semblance of civilized life. Lewis and Clark held administrative posts in St. Louis. Ordway had gone home to New Hampshire, then retraced his steps to Missouri. Pryor was still in the army, moving from one frontier post to another. Shannon was in St. Louis, having lost a leg in a fight with Arikara Indians while serving under Pryor's command.

Even Manuel Lisa and George Drouillard had returned to St. Louis, but only briefly. Lisa was busy organizing another venture for the purpose of trapping and trading on the upper Missouri and its tributaries. His flotilla departed in May 1809 and arrived at the Platte River that August.[89]

In addition to Lisa and Drouillard, this Missouri Fur Company expedition included Pierre Chouteau, Pierre Menard, Andrew Henry, Thomas James, and the party's surgeon, Doctor Thomas. In late September, they navigated past the Mandans and moored along the south bank at the Hidatsa village.

At the time, several British employees of the Hudson's Bay Company resided there in order to trade with the native people. But when they saw an American force ascending the river they quickly stole away. Tensions ran high among Americans and British at the time. The Revolutionary War had ended twenty-six years before, but lingering hostilities would soon flame into the War of 1812.

Most frontiersmen continued to complain that the trespassing British not only sought to dominate the indigenous trade, but to encourage Indian attacks on Americans. Some British sources admitted as much.[90] But Colter appeared oblivious to these matters. After all, he was staying in the same village with the British traders before the American expedition arrived.

Colter's solitary lifestyle came with a strong sense of independence, a willingness to live outside social norms, and a seeming aloofness from political concerns. His work with the fur companies suggested the same. Although he might contract to scout or hunt, he always remained his own person. When he went in search of beaver pelts, he did so of his own accord.

Colter operated as a free trapper from beginning to end. He owned his own equipment and sold pelts to whomever he pleased. Others, who remained bound as employees to the fur companies, often remained in perpetual debt. By contract, they could only sell pelts to their companies, and always received low prices in return. Yet the same companies sold traps and supplies to them and made them pay exorbitant rates.

As a free trapper, Colter must have been doing quite well. Despite the setbacks of 1808 and the loss of his traps in the Jefferson River, he possessed a surplus of supplies and equipment by the following September. Thomas James first met Colter at that time.

James recalled, "On arriving at the Gros Ventres [Hidatsa] village we had found a hunter and trapper named Colter, who had been one of Lewis and Clark's men, and had returned thus far with them in 1806. Of him I purchased a set of beaver traps for $120, a pound and a half of powder for $6, and a gun for $40."[91]

The bustle and excitement of this new expedition no doubt captured Colter's interest. Manuel Lisa surely plied him for information and once more requested his participation as a hunter and scout. Or Colter might have decided to join the flotilla when he first saw it coming upriver. Either way, he could not resist the allure, and soon he prepared to head upstream again.

Chapter Five

A BEAUTIFUL, HOSTILE LAND

COLTER LIVED AT EASE IN THE WILD. HE LIKELY took comfort in his skills of survival and his abilities as a scout and hunter. He likely took pride in his knowledge of the landscape, the environment, and Indian ways. Leaving the wilderness and losing the independence it offered would not sound to him like a good option. He had little use for human comforts. They seemed small and superficial compared to his freedom and the enjoyment of the natural wonders that surrounded him.

And what natural wonders he encountered! The snowcapped Tetons and the Yellowstone landscapes; the geysers and sparkling rivers and waterfalls; the bison, elk, and pronghorn—today these draw throngs of admirers from around the world. Colter and the native inhabitants had this unspoiled beauty all to themselves. What a shame it would be to leave it.

But did rugged frontiersmen appreciate lovely landscapes and rosy sunsets? Oh yes! And they often recorded these sentiments in their journals.

The life of the true frontiersman was not a mere show of

machismo or bravado. They proved themselves through action. They were not afraid of blizzards and bears, and they were not afraid to express their emotions. Those who scoffed be damned!

Meriwether Lewis waxed eloquent during his first weeks on the western prairie: "The scenery, already rich, pleasing and beautiful, was still further heightened by immense herds of buffalo, deer, elk and antelopes, which we saw in every direction feeding on the hills and plains."[1] Later, Lewis marveled at the White Cliffs upstream from the Mandans: "The hills and river cliffs which we passed today exhibit a most romantic appearance. . . . As we passed on it seemed as if those scenes of visionary enchantment would never have an end."[2]

Farther upriver, he described the Great Falls of the Missouri as a "sublimely grand spectacle . . . which at this moment fills me with such pleasure and astonishment." He wrote about the cascading, glittering waters at great length: "From the reflection of the sun on the spray or mist which arises from these falls there is a beautiful rainbow produced which adds not a little to the beauty of this majestically grand scenery."[3]

William Clark was rarely as verbose as Lewis. But he certainly portrayed the same sentiments. He too was struck by the awesome grandeur of the Great Plains:

> *I had an extensive view of the surrounding plains, which afforded one of the most pleasing prospects I ever beheld; under me a beautiful river of clear water . . . meandering through a level and extensive meadow . . . much enlivened by the fine trees and shrubs . . . bordering the bank of the river. . . . The bottom land is covered with grass of about four-and-a-half feet high . . . interspersed with . . . groves of trees . . . grapes . . . wild cherry.*[4]

The emotions of these men show forth in long, babbling sentences and passages. For them, writing was painstaking—an activity squeezed into a rigorous schedule of marching, canoeing, hunting, and camping. Their days often began before light and ended after dark. They wrote while on a halt or resting in camp, in fair or foul weather, and often by the light of a candle or campfire. The landscape must have been exciting indeed to warrant lengthy descriptions.

Clark's vocabulary was more limited than that of Lewis, but he compensated by using the word *beautiful* hundreds of times in his journals. With this one word he described beautiful mornings, days, evenings, and nights. He wrote of a beautiful moon.

He also noted beautiful landscapes, plains, prairies, glades, valleys, and bottomlands, all adorned with beautiful rivers, streams, creeks, and islands. The ocean, he declared, had beautiful shores and beaches. And dozens of plants and animals of every kind were described by him as beautiful. Even two tough years in the wilderness did not diminish his admiration of the western frontier. On the return trip he wrote of the "beautiful, fertile, picturesque country."[5]

Later explorers reacted to the land in a similar way. Thomas James held a soft spot in his heart for the Missouri Valley downriver from Three Forks. He wrote,

> *On the third day we issued from very high and desolate mountains on both sides of us, whose tops are covered with snow throughout the year, and came upon a scene of beauty and magnificence combined, unequalled by any other view of nature that I ever beheld. It really realized all my conceptions of the Garden of Eden.*
>
> *In the west the peaks and pinnacles of the Rocky Mountains*

shone resplendent in the sun. The snow on their tops sent back
a beautiful reflection of the rays of the morning sun. From the
sides of the dividing ridge between the waters of the Missouri
and Columbia there sloped gradually down to the bank of the
river we were on, a plain, then covered with every variety of
wild animals peculiar to this region . . . buffaloes, elk, deer,
moose, wild goats, and wild sheep; some grazing, some lying
down under the trees, and all enjoying a perfect millennium of
peace and quiet. . . .

The stillness, beauty, and loveliness of this scene struck us all
with indescribable emotions. We rested on the oars and enjoyed
the whole view in silent astonishment and admiration. Nature
seemed to have rested here, after creating the wild mountains
and chasms. [6]

Osborne Russell felt likewise toward the Lamar Valley: "For
my own part I almost wished I could spend the remainder of my
days in a place like this where happiness and contentment seemed
to reign in wild romantic splendor surrounded by majestic bat-
tlements which seemed to support the heavens and shut out all
hostile intruders."

The journals and letters of western travelers often provided
descriptions of the enchanting plains and mountains. The "endless,
everlasting prairies" mesmerized them. And the "beautiful flowers
of various colors" that blanketed the wide-open spaces presented
"an appearance, which for beauty and charms, is beyond the art
of man to depict." Jim Beckwourth said, "Nature presented so
many charms that my previous sufferings were obliterated from
my mind. The trees were clothing themselves with freshest verdure,
flowers were unveiling their beauties on every side, and birds were
caroling their sweetest songs from every bough."

Even Alfred Jacob Miller, the artist, freely admitted the superiority of nature to art: "The sketch, although conveying some idea, must of necessity fall short of enchanting reality." In particular, the snowcapped mountains amazed him with their play of light, from "frosted silver" in the morning to a "rosy tint" in the evening. Frontiersmen sometimes ascended these precipitous peaks just to enjoy the views. Osborne Russell, after climbing to an elevation of six thousand feet to a point overlooking the Great Salt Lake, spent a bitter cold night there for the sole purpose of observing the lake in the light of the morning sun.

Nighttime in the Rockies was equally enchanting. William Anderson exclaimed, "How lovely are the nights! The moon and stars shine with a purer and brighter light than I ever saw them before." To which Joe Meek added, "The northern lights blazed up the sky! It was the most beautiful sight I ever saw."[7]

Night sounds added to the mystical aura. The "woebegone howlings" of wolves seemed to capture the essence of the remote vastness of the wilderness, and the hoot of the owl deepened the melancholy chorus. To this was added the voice of the ever-present prairie wind, "whose whistling moan . . . makes loneliness more lone!" F. A. Wislizenus became accustomed to the "nocturnal music" of the howling wolves, "and found a sort of enjoyment in the long-drawn wails . . . which run through all the minor chords." In later life, he longed for the sound.

Other men described lying awake at night listening to the bellowing of bison, the snuffing of grizzly bears as they nosed about camp, and the slap of beaver tails on nearby ponds. Coyotes were the favorite night visitors to native and white encampments. Rufus Sage reported that "the Indians cherish many superstitious notions in regard to this animal, and hold it in great veneration. They consider it as the messenger employed by the Great Spirit, on special occasions, to herald the approach of events interesting to the welfare of his red children, and for that reason they are never known to harm or molest it."

According to the Flathead Indians, the Great Spirit appointed Coyote to bring order to the earth. In obedience, Coyote gave the native people fire and showed them how to make tools and weapons. Coyote also protected them by yipping at the approach of strangers and howling at impeding dangers. Many tribes of the plains and mountains believed that a coyote yipping near camp was a sign of strangers in the vicinity, and some claimed to know from the tone of the yip whether the stranger was friend or foe. Because of their many services, the natives called coyotes *medicine wolves*.

The men of the Corps of Discovery encountered their first coyote on August 12, 1804, as they traveled up the Missouri River. None had seen one before. At the time, coyotes lived only west of the Mississippi. Meriwether Lewis was the first to describe the species for science. William Clark called the coyote a *prairie wolf* and said it barked like a feist. Wislizenus, a German adventurer, called the coyote a *barking wolf* and said it barked like a *dachs*, or dachshund.

Instances of an Indian or mountain man eating a coyote are practically unheard of, although they ate dogs and sometimes wolves. The exception occurred with the men of the Corps of Discovery, who simply had to sample one or two of these strange new creatures. Otherwise, coyotes were universally revered, and the enchantment of their nightly serenades brought smiles to many faces huddled around campfires.[8]

★   ★   ★   ★

THE WESTERN frontier was a place of serenity and beauty, but could quickly turn hostile and brutal. No one knew better

than Colter about the deadly climate and dangerous enemies—
both man and beast—that lay in the wild. He wrote no account
of the hardships he endured. But others of that era faced similar
trials, and their recollections provide a glimpse into the perilous
world Colter inhabited. Winter storms in the northern plains and
mountains proved to be among the deadliest threats of all, as this
account recalls:

> *The snow blew directly in our faces and ice was formed on our
> lips and eyebrows. In this high latitude and in the open prairies
> in the vicinity of the mountains, where we then were, the win-
> ters are very cold. On the first night we were covered where we
> lay to the depth of three feet by the snow. No game was to be seen
> and we were destitute of provisions. For five days we tasted not
> a morsel of food, and had not even the means of making a fire.*
>
> *We saw not a mound or hill, tree or shrub, not a beast nor
> a bird. . . . We were destitute, alone in that vast, desolate, and
> to us limitless, expanse of drifting snow, which the winds drove
> into our faces and heaped around our steps. Snow was our only
> food and drink, and snow made our covering at night. We
> suffered dreadfully from hunger. . . . A languor and faintness
> succeeded, which made travelling most laborious and painful.*[9]

Equally dangerous and more dreadful was the threat of being
devoured by a bear. Many considered the grizzly more deadly than
hostile Indians. At the time, they were numerous and often insen-
sitive to danger. Most had never heard a gunshot. For ages on end,
they had ruled unchallenged and hunted at leisure at the top of the
food chain—a food chain that included humans.

Encounters with grizzlies had always been frequent among
native people, but they first entered the historical record in the

journals of Lewis and Clark. The journals noted numerous clashes between grizzlies and the men of the Corps of Discovery. Later frontiersmen continued to warn of this horrific threat to anyone daring to enter their habitat.

Grizzlies were huge, stealthy, and fast as a horse. They were often ill-tempered and easily angered. When wounded, some went berserk with fury—snapping their jaws and running full speed at their tormentors.

They were also hard to kill. The first shot rarely proved fatal. This was something to think about in an age of single-shot, muzzling-loading, flintlock rifles. Thomas James left a vivid account of the grizzly bear's nature:

> *Marie and St. John, my two Canadian companions on the route from my winter quarters on the Missouri to the Big Horn, came to the fort at the Forks. Marie's right eye was out and he carried the yet fresh marks of a horrible wound on his head and under his jaw. . . . One morning, after setting his traps, Marie strolled out into the prairie for game and soon perceived a large white [grizzly] bear rolling on the ground in the shade of a tree. Marie fired at and missed him. The bear snuffed around him without rising, and did not see the hunter until he had re-loaded, fired again, and wounded him.*
>
> *His Majesty instantly, with ears set back, flew towards his enemy like an arrow, who ran for his life, reached a beaver dam across the river, and seeing no escape by land, plunged into the water above the dam. The bear followed and soon proved himself as much superior to his adversary in swimming as in running.*
>
> *Marie dove and swam under the water as long as he could, when he rose to the surface near the bear. He saved himself by*

diving and swimming in this manner several times, but his enemy followed close upon him and watched his motions with the sagacity which distinguishes these animals. At last he came up from under the water directly beneath the jaws of the monster, which seized him by the head, the tusks piercing the scalp and neck under the right jaw and crushing the ball of his right eye.

In this situation, with his head in the bear's mouth and he swimming with him ashore, St. John, having heard his two shots in quick succession, came running to his rescue. St. John leveled his rifle and shot the bear in the head, and then dragged out Marie from the water, more dead than alive. I saw him six days afterwards, with a swelling on his head an inch thick, and his food and drink gushed through the opening under his jaw made by the teeth of his terrible enemy.[10]

Encounters such as this continued for many years. In the fall of 1823, Jedediah Smith and a company of men stumbled upon a large grizzly bear west of the Black Hills. According to one of the men, James Clyman, Captain Smith was leading his men single file through a brushy river bottom when the bear attacked: "As he emerged from the thicket, he and the bear met face to face. Grizzly did not hesitate a moment but sprang on the captain, taking him by the head first." The bear took "nearly all of his head in his capacious mouth, close to the left eye on one side and close to his right ear on the other, and laid the skull bare to near the crown of the head, leaving a white streak where his teeth passed. One of his ears was torn from his head out to the outer rim," and several ribs were shattered.

Despite the excruciating pain, Smith demanded that someone take needle and thread and sew his bloody head back together. After some hesitation among the men, Clyman stepped up to the task and proceeded in his first ever attempt at surgery. Smith remained conscious throughout and provided instructions. At last, Clyman came to the dangling ear and announced there was nothing he could do for it. Smith insisted that he proceed, so the reluctant surgeon took the needle in one hand and the ear in the other, "stitching it through and through, and over and over, laying the lacerated parts together" as best he could.

Afterward, Smith climbed on his horse and rode with his men to the nearest water source, a mile away.[11] He recuperated fully, and for eight more years carried his scars as he explored the West from the Mississippi to the Pacific. No man of his generation gained a broader knowledge of the mountains, rivers, valleys, and basins of that vast extent of land. He died in 1831 at the hands of a band of Comanche on the Santa Fe Trail.

The same autumn that Jedediah Smith ran afoul of the grizzly, Hugh Glass, a trapper with the Andrew Henry expedition, was attacked by a she-bear with cubs. According to the accounts of fur trapper George Yount and others, Glass was "reckless and eccentric to a high degree." On this particular day, "Glass, as was usual, could not be kept, in obedience to orders, with the band, but persevered to thread his way alone through the bushes. . . . A white bear, that had imbedded herself in the sand, arose within three yards of him, and before he could 'set his triggers,' or turn to retreat, he was seized by the throat."

By the time the men reached him, "the monster had . . . torn the flesh from the lower part of the body, and from the lower limbs. He also had his neck shockingly torn, even to the degree that an aperture appeared to have been made into the windpipe, and his breath to exude at the side of his neck. . . . Blood flowed freely, but fortunately no bone was broken, and his hands and arms were not disabled."

As he lay there gasping for breath, the party debated what to do. "To remove the lacerated and scarcely breathing Glass, seemed certain death to him." And to slowly transport him through hostile territory would endanger the entire party. Glass was "too feeble to walk or help himself at all." Some of the men bandaged his wounds as best they could. Then they courteously waited for him to expire before continuing on their way.

But Glass refused to accommodate them. For several days he clung to life as his companions obligingly toted him on a litter. At last, the slowness of their progress and the signs of hostile Arikara Indians nearby forced Andrew Henry to make a difficult decision.

He chose to push on, leaving John Fitzgerald and young Jim Bridger to watch over Glass until he died. Then the two were to bury him and hurry to rejoin the outfit. As Glass remained unconscious and all but dead, the two laid low in concealment for fear of the warlike bands.

They waited and waited for Glass to die while their nerves grew increasingly frayed. Finally, they decided he was close enough to joining his Maker. So they helped themselves to his weapons and left him for dead beside the spring where they had taken refuge.

After catching up with Henry, they reported that Glass had expired. By then they were sure he had. But Glass was a stubborn cuss. Soon he regained consciousness and found himself alone and defenseless in a country that teemed with keen-scented bears and wolves, and with a hostile band close by.

"As he lay by the spring, buffalo berries hung in clusters and in great profusion over him and around his bed." Glass helped himself to the cool water and ripe berries, and slowly began to recoup his strength.

Finally, with festering wounds, Glass began to stagger toward

Fort Kiowa two hundred miles away. "With sharp stones he would dig . . . nourishing roots" and supplemented this with berries he found along the way. On the third day he watched a pack of wolves bring down a bison calf. He waited until they had satiated their appetite by eating half the carcass. Then he shuffled forward to claim the rest and drive the snarling wolves away. In six weeks he reached the fort.

After a slow recuperation, he hunted the two men who had abandoned him. But at the moment of confrontation, he refrained from taking revenge on Bridger because of his youth, and on Fitzgerald because he had protected himself by joining the army. Glass returned to trapping and remained on the frontier for ten years. During that time, "the same passion for travelling alone never forsook him, and he would never encamp with his fellows, but always miles distant roaming solitary and sleeping in silent loneliness." Finally, one day he was crossing the ice of the frozen Yellowstone River when spotted by a band of Arikara, who pursued and killed him.[12]

Like most mountain men, Rufus Sage showed cautious respect for the grizzly bear. He declared that it "reigns prince of the mountains, and . . . stalks forth at pleasure, in his majesty and strength, lord of the wild solitudes in which he dwells, and none dares oppose him." Sage reported that grizzly bears

frequently kill buffalo, horses, and cattle to gratify their taste for animal food, and, in such cases, always drag their prey to some convenient spot, and perform the task of burial by heaping upon it piles of rock or earth, to a depth of several feet, for protection against the voracity of other beasts of prey. It is not uncommon, even, that they drag the entire carcase [sic] of a full-grown bull a distance of several hundred yards.

Frontiersmen agreed that they were most dangerous when guarding their kill or when wounded—or when surprised, when hungry, when emerging from hibernation, or when their cubs seemed threatened. In short, they posed a danger most always. Famished grizzlies, attracted by the smell of roasting meat, were known to spring on a man while he sat by a fire eating his meal.

Running from a grizzly was not considered cowardly in the least. William Anderson recalled coming upon a bear dining on a carcass. The startled animal immediately ran away. And it's good that he did, said Anderson, for had he not, "I should have taken to my heels with a will—I should have run away 'to live to run another day.'" Kit Carson told a story about two bears that chased him, treed him, and furiously tore at the trunks and roots, hoping to dislodge him. Finally, they wandered off a distance. Carson clung to the tree for a while, fearing their return, then slid down the trunk and ran away.

Joe Meek gave a lighthearted account of his encounter with a grizzly *bar* in 1830:

The first fall hunt on the Yellowstone, Hawkins and myself were coming up the river in search of camp, when we discovered a very large bar on the opposite bank. We shot across, and thought we had killed him, fur he laid quite still. As we wanted to take some trophy of our victory to camp, we tied our mules and left our guns, clothes, and everything except our knives and belts, and swum over to whar the bar war. But instead of being dead, as we expected, he sprung up as we come near him, and took after us. Then you ought to have seen two naked men run!

It war a race for life, and a close one, too. But we made the river first. The bank war about fifteen feet high above the water, and the river ten or twelve feet deep; but we didn't halt.

*Overboard we went, the bar after us, and in the stream about
as quick as we war. The current war very strong, and the bar
war about half way between Hawkins and me. Hawkins was
trying to swim down stream faster than the current war carrying the bar, and I war a trying to hold back. You can reckon
that I swam! Every moment I felt myself being washed into
the yawning jaws of the mighty beast, whose head war up the
stream, and his eyes on me. But the current war too strong for
him, and swept him along as fast as it did me.*

*All this time, not a long one, we war looking for some place
to land where the bar could not overtake us. Hawkins war the
first to make the shore, unknown to the bar, whose head war
still up stream; and he set up such a whooping and yelling that
the bar landed too, but on the opposite side. I made haste to
follow Hawkins, who had landed on the side of the river we
started from, either by design or good luck: and then we traveled back a mile and more to whar our mules war left—a bar
on one side of the river, and "two bares" on the other!* [13]

As Joe Meek and so many others discovered, grizzly bears were
extremely intelligent. Even when bears could not see the man who
had taken a shot at them, they knew to race toward the puff of rifle
smoke and seek him out.

The bears also proved surprisingly resilient. Once, when Jedediah Smith's men killed a large grizzly, they cut it open and found
a stone arrowhead with three inches of shaft still attached. The
formidable weapon was completely embedded in the bear's body,
yet it had lived and the wound had healed. It is no wonder, then,
that Alfred Jacob Miller reported, "It is a rule with the Indians and
white hunters not to attack him without a strong party, and even
then not to press him too closely."

Harrison Rogers and John Hanna, two of Jedediah Smith's men, violated that rule when they wounded a grizzly and unwisely pursued him into a dense thicket. The bear "suddenly rose from his bed and rushed on them. Mr. Rogers fired a moment before the bear caught him. After biting him in several places he went off, but Hanna shot him again," at which point "he returned, caught Mr. Rogers and gave him several additional wounds." Smith "found him very badly wounded, being severely cut in ten or twelve different places." He dressed the wounds with a "salve of sugar and soap." This likely brought back vivid memories to Smith, who still carried his own ghastly scars from a grizzly attack.[14]

Despite its many attractions, the frontier was a dangerous place. In addition to hostile Indians and grizzly bears, there were blizzards, lightning storms, rock slides, flooded rivers, mountain lions, rattlesnakes, and a host of other potentially lethal elements. Even the seemingly benign bison could kill a person in an instant.

Bison, like grizzlies, are surprisingly fast runners despite their bulk, and often charge at intruders. When wounded, they can attack in fury. George Catlin described one encounter:

> *I defy the world to produce another animal that can look so frightful as a huge buffalo bull, when wounded as he was, turned around for battle, and swelling with rage—his eyes bloodshot, and his long shaggy mane hanging to the ground— his mouth open, and his horrid rage hissing in streams of smoke and blood from his mouth and through his nostrils, as he is bending forward to spring upon his assailant.*

An even greater threat came from whole herds of bison, especially when panicked. At times, they ran right over parties of men or flattened encampments.

A more elusive foe was the rattlesnake. Mountain men often encountered them in rugged country and tried to maintain a distance. At night, some men scattered tobacco around their bedroll, trusting that it repelled snakes. The indigenous approach differed. According to Rufus Sage, "the various Indian tribes in the vicinity of the mountains are accustomed to regard the snake with a kind of superstitious veneration, and consider the act of killing it a sure harbinger of calamity." In fact, some Indians looked upon snakes as wise counselors to healers and medicine men, or as intermediaries between them and the Great Spirit. In this regard, the Native American opinion toward snakes was similar to that of other ancient cultures.[15]

Contrary to popular opinion, wolves were not considered much of a threat unless rabid, though it is true that western travelers sometimes suffered bites. Nathaniel Pryor, while with the Corps of Discovery, was attacked and bitten by a wolf while he slept. But accounts of people killed by wolves remained rare. Instead, wolves were rather shy and aloof, keeping distant during the day and prowling and howling nearby at night.

Normally, they fit the behavioral description left by John Townsend, who wrote,

> *I have often been surprised at the perseverance and tenacity with which these animals will sometimes follow the hunter for a whole day, to feed upon the carcass he may leave behind him. When an animal is killed, they . . . stand still at a most respectful distance. . . . Thus will they stand until the game is butchered, the meat placed upon the saddle, and the hunter is mounted and on his way.*

Wolves proved more of a nuisance than a threat. Packs often hovered close to camp, searching for scraps. As a result of the wolves' proximity, native children often found wolf pups and domesticated them, so that there was no shortage of Indian dogs. Of course, the dogs resembled wolves of the prairie in behavior as well as appearance. Wolves would "hold familiar intercourse with the village dogs, and associate with them on friendly terms."

Whether wild or domestic, *Canis lupus* enjoyed chewing up animal furs, including valuable beaver pelts. They sometimes stripped a camp of its rawhide cord and skins and treated moccasins as if they were chew-toys. Rufus Sage protected his moccasins by using them as a pillow while sleeping, but sometimes awoke to find them stolen from beneath his head. Wolves and dogs even ate bison-skin boats. Nathaniel Wyeth complained, "We are much annoyed by the dogs of the Indian village, which are numerous. They eat all our cords and fur flesh they can get at in the night. This is always a great trouble while traveling with Indians until you get to buffalo, where they find better food."[16]

On the other hand, dogs were useful in many ways. Sometimes they toted as much as fifty pounds on their backs. When Joe Meek was captured by the Crow, the women attempted to humiliate him by making him carry a pack of spare moccasins on his back, like a dog.

For hauling heavier loads, a dog pulled a travois. Catlin provided a description: "Two poles, about fifteen feet long, are placed upon the dog's shoulders, in the same manner as the lodge poles are attached to the horses, leaving the larger ends to drag upon the ground." Indian sign language indicated the importance of this function. The sign for the word *dog* consisted of two parts. The first part was the sign used for the word *wolf*—two fingers held up and curved forward to represent ears. The second part was the same two fingers slanted downward and pulled across to represent a travois. So the literal translation for the word *dog* can be stated: a wolf subjected to pulling a travois.

The travois worked so well in the rugged western country that native people scoffed when wheeled wagons arrived. Travois jostled easily over broken terrain, while wagon wheels often broke or got stuck. Indians continued to depend on the travois for many years. Dogs, on the other hand, did not think so highly of the travois. They did not accept their role as beasts of burden without complaint. Several witnesses reported that when dogs were caught and harnessed they would "howl most bitterly."

In addition to serving as porters, some dogs proved reliable as sentinels and alerted the village when strangers approached. Others tended to bark at anything and everything. Unfamiliar dogs that wandered into camp with small loads tied to their backs provided an immediate indication of strangers in the vicinity.

Dogs offered companionship, ate butcher scraps and refuse, and served as an emergency food source. Dog flesh was a favored food among some plains tribes and provided survival rations for others. A few of the men of the Corps of Discovery became rather fond of dog meat. Some later frontiersmen agreed, saying, "The flesh of a fat Indian dog, suitably cooked, is not inferior to fresh pork."

Because of their many uses, native people prized their dogs and became angry if someone abused them. When William Anderson wounded a dog that was attacking the company's sheep, he said, "I don't know which howled the loudest, the dog or master."[17]

Wolves and dogs could be a nuisance, but a greater annoyance was mosquitoes. The Corps of Discovery often cursed the biting insects that converged on them in clouds. Later travelers bitterly chimed in. Anderson once wrote: "I fear the musquitoes [sic] to night more a great deal, than I do the savages." While traveling, a handkerchief or cloth was used to conceal exposed skin. In camp, smoke from rotten wood proved the best deterrent. For this purpose, a fire was kindled at the entrance or even inside a tent or shelter. Lice was another hated parasite. Joe Meek offered a solution: "We just took off our clothes and laid them on an ant-hill, and you ought to see how the ants would carry off the lice!"[18]

Colter understood better than most about the multitude of discomforts and dangers in the western wilderness. Yet he, and men like him, could not stay away, even on pain of death. Washington Irving called Colter and those who followed in his footsteps a "fearless class of men."[19]

Others agreed that fear did not seem to enter into their equation. Henry Brackenridge traveled on the frontier and saw for himself that, for Colter and his kind, dangerous endeavors "would not be regarded . . . as any way extraordinary."[20] Likewise, Thomas James declared that "hair-breadth escapes from death are so frequent in the life of a hunter in this wild region as to lose all novelty and may seem unworthy of mention."

James watched as Colter made narrow escapes and came right back for more. This life of danger, he said, "seemed to have for him a kind of fascination. Such men . . . can only live in a state of excitement and constant action. Perils and danger are their natural element and their familiarity with them, and indifference to their fate, are well illustrated in these adventures of Colter."

Familiarity diminishes fear. This certainly was the case on the frontier. Deep curiosity and constant exposure to hazards made otherwise-normal people indifferent to danger. Before long, the western traveler could make his fire at the end of the day, cook his hump ribs, and throw himself wearily on the ground, "oblivious to all trouble present and prospective."

F. A. Wislizenus said one becomes so accustomed to danger that, even without the protection of shelter, he sleeps soundly: "As disquieting as such conditions would be in civilized life, here one becomes so habituated to them that I do not remember to have ever slept more peacefully in my life. We no longer used tents, but slept quite unprotected in the open air."[21]

Dangers sometimes became intoxicating. Kit Carson claimed, "There is always a brotherly affection existing among trappers and the side of danger is always their choice." Others agreed that mountain men were "rather stimulated than appalled by danger." For this breed of men, said Wislizenus, "daily danger seems to exercise a magic attraction over most of them. Only with reluctance does a trapper abandon his dangerous craft; and a sort of serious home-sickness seizes him when he retires from his mountain life to civilization."[22]

These men preferred an intense, exhilarating life in the wilderness, with its extremes of unbounded freedom and euphoric love of nature on the one hand and imminent danger on the other. They often lived their lives like a shooting spark—flaming brightly, then quickly snuffed out. They cared not at all for a dull, drab, lingering existence. They preferred to venture out rather than cower inside. They refused to let fear of death keep them from living.

A person in present times might make the mistake of viewing a life like Colter's as a series of hardships reluctantly endured in anticipation of eventual retirement to a soft, civilized existence. But Colter's adventures were not so much a hardship as a lifestyle. He chose to live in the wilderness and preferred it to civilization.

Here, he was in his element. A lifetime on the frontier had molded him physically, mentally, and emotionally to a wilderness existence. His sensory perceptions were well-attuned to hearing, seeing, smelling, and feeling the presence of game, or a change in the weather, or a danger that lurked nearby. His mind knew how to interpret the data and convert it into quick action. His emotions remained steady—without the dangerous extremes of languor or panic.

These were not superhuman traits. They were simply needed at that time and place, and were called upon accordingly. In the twenty-first century, most people no longer depend on their senses for survival. The senses are dulled by lack of use. That makes it difficult to understand how vital they are in the wilderness and how satisfying it is to employ them fully.

*　　*　　*　　*

EQUALLY SATISFYING are the pristine wonders and rugged beauty of the Rocky Mountains. They have a way of grabbing hold of the soul and not letting go. They draw a person back to them time and again. Surely none were surprised when Colter gathered his supplies, rolled them in a pack, and prepared to turn back to the mountains once more. In the autumn of 1809, he joined Manuel Lisa's expedition as it left the Hidatsa village and paddled upriver to Manuel's Fort to wait out the winter.

By March of the following year, a small detachment prepared to continue the upstream journey. Colter guided the party of thirty-two Frenchmen and Americans under the command of Pierre Menard. Andrew Henry was second in charge of the company that also included George Drouillard and Thomas James.

Colter knew the route well—perhaps too well. He led them west up the Yellowstone, through Bozeman Pass, and down the Gallatin's east fork to Three Forks—over the very route by which he had made narrow escapes three times. After pushing through a blinding blizzard in Bozeman Pass, they arrived safely at Three Forks on April 3, 1810.[23]

The company chose a campsite between the Jefferson and Madison Rivers where the waters run a half-mile apart, two miles up from their juncture. This was near the location of Colter's desperate run from the Blackfoot eighteen months before. Because of the native threat, the men immediately began to construct a post with a stockade and called it Henry's Fort.[24]

Their concerns were justified. About nine days after their arrival, several of the men who had been out trapping rushed to the fort as if the whole Blackfoot nation was hot on their heels. Catching their breath, they reported that they were the sole survivors of the large party of men that had gone up the Jefferson River that day.

Colter was among the missing. He had ascended the same river and passed the same spot where John Potts had been killed and where he had been captured before. Odds are good that he stopped to look for the traps he had dropped in the shallow channel a year and a half earlier.

The little garrison of survivors now huddled in the fort, nervously preparing for a general Blackfoot assault. Throughout the day and all that sleepless night they waited. But no attack came.

The next morning they saw movement and detected a few of their own men, including Colter, making their way toward the stockade. As it turned out, most had survived the attack. Two were killed. Three more were never found.

Those that survived, said Thomas James, "had a very narrow escape themselves, as all but Colter probably considered it; he, with his large experience, naturally looked upon the whole as an ordinary occurrence."[25] Caution now prevailed at the fort. The men made shorter forays and stayed close, not just for fear of the Blackfoot, but because the grizzlies were thick and threatening in the woods all around.

At last they got cabin fever. James recalled what happened next:

We all became more venturous. One of our company, a Shawnee half-breed named Druyer [Drouillard], the principal hunter of Lewis and Clark's party, went up the river one day and set his traps about a mile from the camp. In the morning he returned alone and brought back six beavers.

I warned him of his danger. 'I am too much of an Indian to be caught by Indians,' said he. On the next day he repeated the adventure and returned with the product of his traps, saying: 'This is the way to catch beaver.'

On the third morning he started again up the river to examine his traps, when we advised him to wait for the whole party, which was about moving farther up the stream, and at the same time two other Shawnees left us, against our advice, to kill deer. We started forward in company and soon found the dead bodies of the last mentioned hunters, pierced with lances, arrows, and bullets and lying near each other.

Farther on, about one hundred and fifty yards, Druyer and his horse lay dead, the former mangled in a horrible manner; his head was cut off, his entrails torn out, and his body hacked to pieces. We saw from the marks on the ground that he must have fought in a circle on horseback and probably killed some of his enemies. [26]

Within a few miles of John Potts, George Drouillard suffered the same fate. The Blackfoot were taking a toll on the veterans of the Corps of Discovery. But even before Drouillard's death, Colter had left the mountains.

HOME TO THE SHADY BLUFF

COLTER FINALLY GOT HIS FILL OF BLACKFOOT ATTACKS that kept him from setting and checking his traps. So he came to the fort, threw down his hat, and swore he would leave in the morning. According to Stallo Vinton, "Colter was wise enough in his estimate of prevailing conditions to realize that the Lisa expedition was a failure, and that it was only a question of time before the incessant attacks of the Indians would completely wreck the enterprise."

Like Colter, Kit Carson and company later gave up on trapping in Blackfoot country, not out of fear, but because they were unable to make a profit. Jedediah Smith and his men faced the same problem in 1830. They found game and beaver in abundance, but the Blackfoot continuously fired on the men and their camp. On top of that, the incessant thefts of traps and horses made their business impracticable.[1]

Sure enough, a couple months after Colter's departure, Pierre Menard, the commander of the venture, also gave up and returned to St. Louis. Only Andrew Henry and a small detachment remained at Henry's Fort. They too abandoned the site after yet another battle with the Blackfoot.

In the meantime, Colter and two other men had made their way toward Manuel's Fort. While traversing the mountains, a band of Blackfoot attacked them. The three only escaped by slipping into a dense thicket to throw off their pursuers. After that, they traveled more carefully by night and hid out by day.

At last they reached the fort on the Bighorn River. Standing on the bank where the Bighorn flows into the Yellowstone, Colter said goodbye to the land that had figured so large in his life. Perhaps he paused to reflect on the many close scrapes and brutal blizzards, on the lofty ranges and sparkling rivers, on the endless herds of bison and game, and on his Crow friends in their lodges upstream. Then he launched his canoe and began the long descent down the Yellowstone and Missouri toward St. Louis.

As he passed the Mandan villages, he must have thought back to his lone departure from the Corps of Discovery four years before. Now some of his comrades, including Captain Lewis, were dead. Most of the others had scattered along the frontier.[2]

At the mouth of the Platte, Colter may have recalled the day three years earlier when he turned his canoe around to ascend the river with Manuel Lisa and his old friends, Potts and Drouillard. But this time he did not waver. He kept the bow pointed downstream.

On this final canoe trip down the Yellowstone and Missouri Rivers, Colter must have been transfixed by the same nostalgic landscapes and the same emotions described by others:

> *There was something pleasingly solemn and mysterious in thus floating down these wild rivers at night. The purity of the atmosphere in these elevated regions gave additional splendor to the stars, and heightened the magnificence of the firmament. The occasional rush and laving of the waters; the vague sounds*

from the surrounding wilderness; the dreary howl, or rather
whine of wolves from the plains; the low grunting and bellow-
ing of the buffalo, and the shrill neighing of the elk, struck the
ear with an effect unknown in the daytime.

As Colter approached the lower river he encountered hills "all covered with a meadow-like green." Soon he entered familiar woodlands "clothed with timber and verdure of the most luxuriant appearance," with abundance "of oaks and sycamores; of mulberry and basswood trees; of paroquets [sic] and wild turkeys." At last, he came upon small clearings of cornfields on the extreme edge of civilization.[3]

Soon afterward, a shady bluff came into view not far from the town of La Charette. When last he had seen it, the Corps of Discovery was just ten days into a journey to the Pacific Ocean. Now six long years and countless adventures had passed.

At last the lonely wanderer had found a home. Near the shady bluff, close to the juncture of the Missouri River and Boeuf Creek, Colter built a cabin. Here he settled on the fertile bottomlands among thick stands of timber, amid an abundance of game and beaver.

The area had already attracted a small gathering of frontier families, including Daniel and Rebecca Boone and their son Nathan. Daniel, aged seventy-five, had found this to be a hunter's paradise. The next spring he would trap sixty beavers for their pelts.[4]

For two years, Boone and Colter lived as neighbors and wandered the same woodlands and creeks. They undoubtedly crossed paths and swapped tales on occasion. Boone would have described the virgin wilderness of Kentucky; Colter the virgin plains and Rockies. Boone could tell of friendships and fights with Shawnee; Colter of Crow and Blackfoot. How priceless a conversation!

After his return, Colter went to see his old captain, William Clark, in St. Louis. He provided information that Clark incorporated into his manuscript map of 1810. The map already contained data from the sketches and notes that Clark had made while commanding the Corps of Discovery. It also included information that George Drouillard had provided in 1808.[5]

On top of all this, Clark drew additional landmarks that only Colter could describe: the Absaroka Mountain gap at Clark's Fork Canyon, the Owl Creek Mountain crossing, the Wind River, Togwotee Pass, Jackson Hole, the Tetons and Teton Pass, Colter's River, Pierre's Hole, Lake Biddle, Lake Eustis, the upper Yellowstone River, Hot Spring Brimstone, the Bannock Trail Crossing, and the Lamar Valley region. Clark also drew a dotted line that marked Colter's circuitous route. Based on Clark's manuscript map of 1810, a more famous but less accurate map was published in 1814.[6]

Colter also met Henry Brackenridge and John Bradbury.[7] Brackenridge was a young writer from Pittsburgh who had come west to experience the frontier. Bradbury, a botanist, had traveled from Scotland to identify new plants for science. Both gathered information directly from Colter and from those who knew him well. And both were sufficiently intrigued by his adventures to describe them in their publications.

Bradbury was offered the rare opportunity to venture upriver with Wilson Price Hunt's Overland Astorians.[8] The expedition determined to reach the Pacific Ocean by land and establish a fur trading post—Fort Astoria. They departed St. Louis in early 1811 and arrived at La Charette on March 17.

Bradbury recalled that,

> *On leaving Charette, Mr. Hunt pointed out to me an old man standing on the bank, who, he informed me, was Daniel*

Boone, the discoverer of Kentucky. . . . I went ashore to speak to him, and requested that the boat might go on, as I intended to walk until evening. I remained for some time in conversation with him.

He informed me, that he . . . had spent a considerable portion of his time alone in the back woods, and had lately returned from his spring hunt, with nearly sixty beaver skins. On proceeding through the woods I came to the river Charette, which falls into the Missouri about a mile above the village, and was now much swelled by the late rains. . . . I got across by swimming, having tied my clothes together, and enclosed them in my deer skin hunting coat, which I pushed before me.

I overtook the boat in about three hours, and we encamped at the mouth of a creek called Boeuf, near the house of one Sullens. I enquired of Sullens for John Colter, one of Lewis and Clark's party. . . . Sullens informed me that Colter lived about a mile from us, and sent his son to inform him of our arrival; but we did not see him that evening. . . .

At day-break Sullens came to our camp, and informed us that Colter would be with us in a few minutes. Shortly after he arrived, and accompanied us for some miles. . . . He seemed to have a great inclination to accompany the expedition; but having been lately married, he reluctantly took leave of us.[9]

One can well imagine Colter with head hung low as, for the first time, he turned his back on a chance at adventure and sauntered slowly home. It proved to be his last chance. A year later he was dead.

Colter lost his life, not to a howling blizzard, a raging river, or a grizzly on the prowl. Nor could the Blackfoot claim him, though they often had tried. Instead, a malady, probably jaundice, took his life on May 7, 1812. At the time, he was serving in Captain Nathan Boone's company of Mounted Rangers, guarding the frontier during the War of 1812.[10]

No one knows for sure the place of death or where he was buried, any more than they know when or where he was born. No one knows much about his wife or so many other aspects of his life. A reserved man by nature, as well as a man of action, he never cared for keeping records or writing about his adventures.

Colter was anything but a self-promoter. Yet he became a hero in his time and a legend in the years that followed. Almost a century ago, Stallo Vinton paid proper tribute: "Not in any diary or narrative by his hand, but in the history and geography of his country, is his record embedded."[11]

Colter became a legend even to those explorers and mountain men who themselves became legendary. On cold nights for years to come, they would huddle close to a flickering fire and boast of their own adventures. But no one dared to suggest, even in hushed tones, that they could outshine Colter.

Along with Lewis and Clark, Colter was one of the first heroes of the great American West. And in some ways he went far beyond them—in breadth of discovery and narrow escapes. He was the prototype of the western hero—of explorers, mountain men, cavalrymen, and cowboys.

He was the first among them—a lonely wanderer in the western wilderness that others followed but never surpassed in survival skills or adventures. His story was destined to live on, even as they laid him to rest near a shady bluff that stands above the meandering Missouri.

WORKS CITED

Historic Maps (in chronological order)

Lewis, Meriwether, William Clark, and Reuben Thwaites. *Original Journals of the Lewis and Clark Expedition, 1804–1806.* Vol. 8. William Clark Maps of 1806, numbers 50, 51. New York: Dodd, Mead and Company, 1904–5.

Drouillard, George. *Map of August 5, 1808, with William Clark Inscriptions.* Map. From the Library of Congress, *Geography and Map Division.* G4262 B53 1808 D7.

Drouillard, George. *Map of September 6, 1808, with William Clark Inscriptions.* Map. From the Missouri Historical Society. A0289 Clark Family Collection 1766–1991, Box 11; William Clark Papers, Folder 18: 1808.

Clark, William. *Map of 1810.* Map. From Yale University, *Beinecke Rare Book and Manuscript Library, Yale Collection of Western Americana.* WA MSS 303, Image ID 1053073. [Yale University's digital copy is accessible online, currently at http://brbl-zoom.library.yale.edu /viewer/1053073.]

Lewis, Meriwether, William Clark, Nicholas Biddle, and Paul Allen. *History of the Expedition under the Command of Captains Lewis and Clark.* Philadelphia: Bradford and Inskeep, 1814. [A high-resolution copy of the William Clark Map of 1814 may be viewed online at the Library of Congress website, currently at: www.loc.gov/resource/g4126s .ct000028.]

Wyoming Historical Topographic Maps, Grand Teton Quadrangle, 1899. From University of Texas Libraries, *Perry-Castaneda Library*.

Frontier Journals, Correspondence, and Records

Anderson, William Marshall, and Dale Morgan, ed. *The Rocky Mountain Journals of William Marshall Anderson*. Lincoln: University of Nebraska Press, 1987.

Ashley, William, and Dale Morgan, ed. "William H. Ashley Diary, March 25–June 27, 1825." In *The West of William Ashley*. Denver: Old West Publishing Company, 1964.

Ashley, William, Jedediah Smith, and Harrison Dale, ed. *The Ashley-Smith Explorations and the Discovery of a Central Route to the Pacific, 1822–1829*. Cleveland: Arthur H. Clark Company, 1918.

Ball, John. *Autobiography of John Ball*. Grand Rapids: Dean-Hicks Company, 1925.

Baron von Steuben, Friedrich. *Regulations for the Order and Discipline of the Troops of the United States*. 1794. Reprint, Portsmouth, NH: Press of J. Melcher, 1804.

Beall, Thomas. "Recollections of William Craig." *Lewiston Morning Tribune*, March 3, 1918.

Beckwourth, James, and T. D. Bonner. *The Life and Adventures of James P. Beckwourth, Mountaineer, Scout, Pioneer, and Chief of the Crow Nation of Indians*. 1856. Reprint, Williamstown, MA: Corner House Publishers, 1977.

Brackenridge, Henry. "Sketches of the Territory of Louisiana." *Louisiana Gazette*, April 18, 1811.

Brackenridge, Henry. "To Mr. Joseph Charless." *Louisiana Gazette*, August 8, 1811.

Brackenridge, Henry. *Views of Louisiana; together with a Journal of a Voyage up the Missouri River in 1811*. Pittsburgh: Cramer, Spear and Eichbaum, 1814.

Bradbury, John. *Travels in the Interior of America*. 1817. Reprint, London: Sherwood, Neely, and Jones, 1819.

Bradbury, John, and Henry Brackenridge. "From Mr. Bradbury and Mr.

Brackenridge, lately arrived from the Mandan villages." *Louisiana Gazette*, August 8, 1811.

Calhoun, John C. "John Calhoun to Henry Atkinson, 27 March 1819." In *The Missouri Expedition: 1818–1820,* edited by Roger Nichols. Norman: University of Oklahoma Press, 1969.

Calhoun, John C. "John Calhoun to Thomas Smith, 16 March 1818." In *The Missouri Expedition: 1818–1820,* edited by Roger Nichols. Norman: University of Oklahoma Press, 1969.

Camp, Charles. "The Chronicles of George C. Yount." *California Historical Society Quarterly* 2, no. 1 (April 1923): 24–33.

Campbell, Robert, and Drew Holloway, ed. *A Narrative of Colonel Robert Campbell's Experiences in the Rocky Mountain Fur Trade from 1825 to 1835*. Fairfield, WA: Ye Galleon Press, 1991.

Campbell, Robert, and George Brooks, ed. "The Private Journal of Robert Campbell." *Bulletin of the Missouri Historical Society* 20 (October 1963 to July 1964): 3–118.

Carson, Kit, and Milo Quaife, ed. *Kit Carson's Autobiography*. 1935. Reprint, Lincoln: University of Nebraska Press, 1966.

Carter, Clarence, ed. *The Territorial Papers of the United States*. Vol. 14. Washington: United States Government Printing Office, 1949.

Catlin, George. *North American Indians*. 2 vols. 1841. Reprint, Edinburgh: John Grant, 1926.

Clark, William. "Notes on the Chart Obtained from George Drewyard (Drouillard), September 6, 1808." St. Louis, MO: Missouri Historical Society, A0289 Clark Family Collection 1766–1991, Box 11; William Clark Papers, Folder 18: 1808.

Clark, William. "William Clark Journals." In *Journals of the Lewis and Clark Expedition*. Edited by Gary Moulton. 13 vols. Lincoln: University of Nebraska Press, 1983.

Clyman, James, and Charles Camp, ed. *James Clyman, Frontiersman: The Adventures of a Trapper and Covered-Wagon Emigrant as Told in His Own Reminiscences and Diaries*. 1928. Reprint, Portland: Champoeg Press, 1960.

Cooke, Philip. *Scenes and Adventures in the Army*. Philadelphia: Lindsay and Blakiston, 1857.

Cox, Ross. *Adventures on the Columbia River, including the Narrative of a*

Residence of Six Years on the Western Side of the Rocky Mountains. 1831. Reprint, New York: J. & J. Harper, 1832.

De Smet, P. J. *Letters and Sketches, with a Narrative of a Year's Residence among the Indian Tribes of the Rocky Mountains.* 1843. Reprint, New York: AMS Press, 1966.

Denig, Edwin, and John Ewers, ed. *Five Indian Tribes of the Upper Missouri: Sioux, Arickaras, Assiniboines, Crees, Crows.* Norman: University of Oklahoma Press, 1961.

Doane, Gustavus, Orrin Bonney, and Lorraine Bonney. *Battle Drums and Geysers: The Life and Journals of Lt. Gustavus Cheyney Doane.* Chicago: Swallow Press, 1970.

Duane, William. *A Military Dictionary.* Philadelphia: printed and published by William Duane, 1810.

Ferris, Warren. *Life in the Rocky Mountains: A Diary of Wanderings on the Sources of the Rivers Missouri, Columbia, and Colorado, 1830–1835.* 1843–44. Reprint, Denver: Old West Publishing Company, 1940.

Gale, John, and Roger Nichols, ed. *The Missouri Expedition: 1818–1820.* Norman: University of Oklahoma Press, 1969.

Gass, Patrick. "Patrick Gass Journals." In *Journals of the Lewis and Clark Expedition.* Edited by Gary Moulton. 13 vols. Lincoln: University of Nebraska Press, 1983.

Houston, Sam, and Walter Douglas, ed. "Documents: Captain Nathaniel Pryor" in *American Historical Review* 24, no. 2 (January 1919): 253–65.

Irving, Washington. *Astoria, or Enterprise beyond the Rocky Mountains.* 1836. Reprint, London: Richard Bentley, 1839.

Irving, Washington. *The Adventures of Captain Bonneville, U.S.A. in the Rocky Mountains and the Far West.* 1837. Reprint, New York: G. P. Putnam's Sons, 1868.

Jackson, Andrew. "Andrew Jackson to Henry Atkinson, 15 May 1819." In *The Missouri Expedition: 1818–1820,* edited by Roger Nichols. Norman: University of Oklahoma Press, 1969.

Jackson, William Henry. *Jackson Photo of Shoshone Indians.* 1871. Yellowstone National Park Photo Collection, National Park Service Photo 14826.

James, Thomas. *Three Years among the Indians and Mexicans.* 1846. Reprint, New York: Citadel Press, 1966.

Kennerly, James, and Stella Drumm, ed. "Diary of James Kennerly." *Missouri Historical Society Collections* 6 (1928–31): 41–97.

Larocque, François, and L. J. Burpee, ed. *Journal of Larocque from the Assiniboine to the Yellowstone, 1805*. Ottawa: Government Printing Bureau, 1910.

Larpenteur, Charles, and Elliott Coues, ed. *Forty Years a Fur Trader on the Upper Missouri*. 1898. Reprint, Minneapolis: Ross and Haines, 1962.

Leforge, Thomas, and Thomas Marquis. *Memoirs of a White Crow Indian*. 1928. Reprint, Lincoln: University of Nebraska Press, 1974.

Leonard, Zenas, and Milo Quaife, ed. *Narrative of the Adventures of Zenas Leonard*. 1839. Reprint, Chicago: The Lakeside Press, 1934.

Lewis, Meriwether. "Meriwether Lewis Journals." In *Journals of the Lewis and Clark Expedition*. Edited by Gary Moulton. 13 vols. Lincoln: University of Nebraska Press, 1983.

Lewis, Meriwether, William Clark, and Donald Jackson, ed. *Letters of the Lewis and Clark Expedition*. Urbana: University of Illinois Press, 1962.

Lewis, Meriwether, William Clark, and Gary Moulton, ed. *Herbarium of the Lewis and Clark Expedition*. Lincoln: University of Nebraska Press, 1999.

Lewis, Meriwether, William Clark, and Reuben Thwaites, ed. *Original Journals of the Lewis and Clark Expedition, 1804–1806*. Vols. 6, 7. New York: Dodd, Mead and Company, 1904–5.

Lisa, Manuel. "To the Spaniards of New Mexico, September 8, 1812," translated by Herbert Bolton. *Southwestern Historical Quarterly* 17 (July 1913–April 1914): 63–64.

Luttig, John, and Stella Drumm, ed. *Journal of a Fur-Trading Expedition on the Upper Missouri, 1812–13*. 1920. Reprint, New York: Argosy-Antiquarian, 1964.

Marcy, Randolph. *Prairie Traveler*. New York: Harper and Brothers, 1859.

Maximilian von Wied, Alexander. *Travels in the Interior of North America*. 1843. Reprint, New York: AMS Press, 1966.

Menard, Pierre. "Letter to Pierre Chouteau from Three Forks of the Missouri, April 21, 1810." Reprinted in Chittenden, Hiram. *The American Fur Trade of the Far West*. 1902. Reprint, Stanford, CA: Academic Reprints, 1954.

Miles, Nelson. *Personal Recollections*. Chicago: Werner Company, 1896.

Miller, Alfred Jacob, and Marvin Ross, ed. *The West of Alfred Jacob Miller*. Norman: University of Oklahoma Press, 1968.

Munger, Asahel, and Eliza Munger. "Diary of Asahel Munger and Wife." *Quarterly of the Oregon Historical Society* 8, no. 4 (December 1907): 387–405.

Newell, Robert, and Dorothy Johansen, ed. *Memoranda: Travles in the Teritory of Missourie*. Portland, OR: Champoeg Press, 1959.

Ordway, John. "John Ordway Journals." In *Journals of the Lewis and Clark Expedition*. Edited by Gary Moulton. 13 vols. Lincoln: University of Nebraska Press, 1983.

Parker, Samuel. *Journal of an Exploring Tour beyond the Rocky Mountains*. 1838. Reprint, Ithaca: Mack, Andrus, & Woodruff, 1842.

Pike, Zebulon, and Elliott Coues. *The Expeditions of Zebulon Montgomery Pike*. Vol. 2. New York: Francis P. Harper, 1895.

Potts, Daniel. "To Dr. Lukens, July 8, 1827." *Philadelphia Gazette and Daily Advertiser*, October 19, 1827.

Potts, Daniel. "To Robert Potts, July 16, 1826." *Philadelphia Gazette and Daily Advertiser*, November 14, 1826.

Reid, Russell, and Clell Gannon, eds. "Journal of the Atkinson-O'Fallon Expedition." *North Dakota Historical Quarterly* 4, no. 1 (October 1929): 5–56.

Richardson, Daniel. "Notice." *Missouri Gazette*, December 11, 1813.

Ross, Alexander, and T. C. Elliott, ed. "Journal of Alexander Ross: Snake Country Expedition, 1824." *Quarterly of the Oregon Historical Society* 14, no. 4 (December 1913): 366–85.

Russell, Osborne, and Aubrey Haines, ed. *Journal of a Trapper*. Portland: Oregon Historical Society, 1955.

Ruxton, George. *Life in the Far West*. New York: Harper and Brothers, 1849.

Sage, Rufus. *Rocky Mountain Life, or, Startling Scenes and Perilous Adventures in the Far West, during an Expedition of Three Years*. 1857. Reprint, Lincoln: University of Nebraska Press, 1982.

Smith, Jedediah, and Maurice Sullivan, ed. *The Travels of Jedediah Smith*. 1934. Reprint, Lincoln: University of Nebraska Press, 1992.

Spalding, Henry. "A Letter by Henry H. Spalding from the Rocky Mountains, 1836." *Evangelist*, October 22, 1836.

Stuart, Robert, Wilson Price Hunt, and Philip Rollins, ed. *The Discovery of the Oregon Trail: Robert Stuart's Narratives of His Overland Trip Eastward from Astoria in 1812–13*. 1935. Reprint, Lincoln: University of Nebraska Press, 1995.

Thomas, Doctor. "Journal of a Voyage from St. Louis, Louisianna, to the Mandan Village," Part 1. *Louisiana Gazette*, November 30, 1809.

Thomas, Doctor. "Journal of a Voyage from St. Louis, Louisianna, to the Mandan Village," Part 2. *Pittsburgh Gazette*, July 13, 1810.

Thomas, Doctor, and Donald Jackson, ed. "Journey to the Mandans, 1809; The Lost Narrative of Dr. Thomas." *Bulletin of the Missouri Historical Society* 20 (April 1964): 179–92.

Thompson, David, W. Raymond Wood, and Thomas Thiessen, eds. "David Thompson Journal." *Early Fur Trade on the Northern Plains*. Norman: University of Oklahoma Press, 1999.

Townsend, John. *Narrative of a Journey across the Rocky Mountains*. Philadelphia: Henry Perkins, 1839.

Victor, Frances Fuller. *The River of the West: Life and Adventure in the Rocky Mountains and Oregon*. Hartford: Columbian Book Company, 1871.

Wetmore, Alphonso. "The Missouri Trapper." *The Port-folio*, March 1826. Reprinted in Hall, James. *Letters from the West*. London: Henry Colburn, 1828.

Whitehouse, Joseph. "Joseph Whitehouse Journals." In *Journals of the Lewis and Clark Expedition*. Edited by Gary Moulton. 13 vols. Lincoln: University of Nebraska Press, 1983.

Whitman, Narcissa. "A Journey across the Plains in 1836." In *Transactions of the Nineteenth Annual Reunion of the Oregon Pioneer Association for 1891*. Portland: A. Anderson, 1893.

Whitman, Narcissa. "Additional Letters." In *Transactions of the Twenty-first Annual Reunion of the Oregon Pioneer Association for 1893*. Portland: George Himes and Company, 1894.

Wislizenus, F. A. *A Journey to the Rocky Mountains in the Year 1839*. St. Louis: Missouri Historical Society, 1912.

Wyeth, John, *Oregon; or, A Short History of a Long Journey*. Cambridge: printed for John B. Wyeth, 1833.

Wyeth, Nathaniel, and F. G. Young, ed. "The Correspondence and Journals of Captain Nathaniel J. Wyeth, 1831–6." In *Sources of the History of Oregon*. Eugene: University of Oregon Press, 1899.

Additional Cited Sources

Ambrose, Stephen. *Undaunted Courage*. New York: Touchstone, 1996.

Carlson, Paul. *The Plains Indians*. College Station: Texas A&M University Press, 1998.

Chittenden, Hiram. *The American Fur Trade of the Far West*. 2 vols. 1902. Reprint, Stanford, CA: Academic Reprints, 1954.

Colter-Frick, L. R. *Courageous Colter and Companions*. Washington, MO: printed by author, 1997.

Cutright, Paul. "Lewis and Clark and Cottonwood." *Bulletin of the Missouri Historical Society* 22, no. 1 (October 1965): 35–44.

Daugherty, John. *A Place Called Jackson Hole*. Moose, WY: Grand Teton National Park, 1999.

Fahey, John. *The Flathead Indians*. Norman: University of Oklahoma Press, 1974.

Fryxell, F. M. F. M. Fryxell to Arno Cammerer, 8 May 1934. Collections Accession File 63, "The Colter Stone," Grand Teton National Park.

Haines, Aubrey. "John Colter." *The Mountain Men and the Fur Trade of the Far West*. Glendale, California: Arthur H. Clark Company, 1971.

Haines, Aubrey. *Yellowstone National Park: Its Exploration and Establishment*. Washington, DC: US Department of the Interior, National Park Service, 1974.

Hanson, Jeffrey. "The George Drouillard Maps of 1808." *Archaeology in Montana* 21, no. 1 (January–April 1980): 45–53.

Harris, Burton. *John Colter: His Years in the Rockies*. New York: Scribner, 1952.

Heasler, Henry. Henry Heasler to David Marshall, 30 August 2012.

Huser, Verne. *On the River with Lewis and Clark*. College Station: Texas A&M University Press, 2004.

Love, Charles. "Archaeological Survey of the Jackson Hole Region, Wyoming." M.A. thesis, University of Wyoming, 1972.

Lowie, Robert. *The Crow Indians*. New York: Farrar and Rinehart, 1935.

Medicine Crow, Joseph. *From the Heart of the Crow Country: The Crow Indians' Own Stories.* New York: Orion Books, 1992.

Moore, Robert, and Michael Haynes. *Tailor Made, Trail Worn: Army Life, Clothing, and Weapons of the Corps of Discovery.* Helena, MT: Farcountry Press, 2003.

Morgan, Dale, ed. *The West of William Ashley.* Denver: Old West Publishing Company, 1964.

Morris, Larry. *The Fate of the Corps: What Became of the Lewis and Clark Explorers.* New Haven: Yale University Press, 2004.

Nelson, Willis. "White Mountain, Northwestern Wyoming: A Pseudo-Volcanic Neck" in *Geology of the Beartooth Uplift and Adjacent Basins: Montana Geological Society and Yellowstone Bighorn Research Association Joint Field Conference and Symposium.* Billings, MT: Montana Geological Society, 1986.

Neumann, George. *Collector's Illustrated Encyclopedia of the American Revolution.* Harrisburg, PA: Stackpole Books, 1975.

Oglesby, Richard. *Manuel Lisa and the Opening of the Missouri Fur Trade.* Norman: University of Oklahoma Press, 1963.

Reed, George. "Dictionary of the Crow Language." M.A. thesis, Massachusetts Institute of Technology, 1975.

Replogle, Wayne. *Yellowstone's Bannock Indian Trails.* Yellowstone Park, WY: Yellowstone National Park, 1956. Reprinted in Nabokov, Peter, and Lawrence Loendorf. *American Indians and Yellowstone National Park.* Yellowstone National Park, WY: National Park Service, 2002.

Ronda, James. "A Chart in His Way: Indian Cartography and the Lewis and Clark Expedition." *Great Plains Quarterly* 4 no. 1 (Winter 1984): 43–53.

Russell, Carl. *Firearms, Traps, and Tools of the Mountain Men.* 1967. Reprint, New York: Skyhorse Publishing, 2011.

Skarsten, M. O. *George Drouillard: Hunter and Interpreter for Lewis and Clark, and Fur Trader.* 1964. Reprint, Lincoln: University of Nebraska Press, 2005.

Swagerty, William. *Indianization of Lewis and Clark.* 2 vols. Norman, OK: Arthur H. Clark Company, 2012.

Tichenor, Harold. *The Blanket: An Illustrated History of the Hudson's Bay Blanket.* Toronto: Madison Press, 2002.

Tomkins, William. *Indian Sign Language.* 1931. Reprint, New York: Dover Publications, 1969.

Vinton, Stallo. *John Colter: Discoverer of Yellowstone Park.* New York: Edward Eberstadt, 1926.

Walker, Deward. *An Assessment of American Indian Occupation and Uses of the Cultural and Natural Resources of Grand Teton National Park.* Boulder, CO: Walker Research Group, 2007.

West, George. *Tobacco, Pipes, and Smoking Customs of the American Indians.* Milwaukee: Board of the Public Museum of the City of Milwaukee, 1934.

Wright, Gary. *A Preliminary Report on the Archaeology of the Jackson Hole Country, Wyoming.* Moose, WY: Grand Teton National Park, 1975.

APPENDIX

Map Locations, including Modern Names and Coordinates

1) The original names of the sites are used in the text and in this list. The modern site names appear in parentheses in this list when different from the original.
2) Site coordinates allow the reader to pinpoint locations using Google Earth, Google Satellite, or other Internet map searches.

Colter's Winter Trek of 1807–1808

Manuel's Fort
46.146377, -107.476137

Shannon's Creek
45.996712, -107.998332

Pompey's Tower (Pompey's Pillar)
45.995461, -108.005153

Pryor's Fork (Pryor Creek)
45.887634, -108.315747

Pryor Gap in Red Mountains
(Pryor Mountains)
45.287029, -108.610733

Gap Creek Upriver (Sage Creek)
45.239814, -108.671641

Clark's Fork of the Yellowstone
45.226897, -108.947203

Blue Bead River (Pat O'Hara Creek)
44.851442, -109.172297

Clark's Fork Canyon
44.845973, -109.301419

Sunlight Basin
44.770566, -109.425194

Dead Indian Creek
44.754739, -109.417706

Blue Bead Pass
44.653428, -109.382853

Blue Bead Mountain (Pat O'Hara
Mountain)
44.657518, -109.332681

Heart Mountain
44.665866, -109.121376

Valley River (Trail Creek)
44.616243, -109.302850

Stinking Water River (Shoshone
River)
44.521949, -109.103838

Colter's Hell
44.520199, -109.115976

Spirits' Mountain (Cedar
Mountain)
44.493284, -109.169632

Boiling Spring
44.497166, -109.196361

Mick-ka-ap-ha River (Shoshone
River North Fork)
44.482797, -109.331414

Salt Fork (Shoshone River
South Fork)
44.432443, -109.253463

Carter Mountain
44.305119, -109.212072

Absaroka Mountains
43.973305, -109.317381

Blondy Pass in Owl Creek
Mountains
43.599567, -108.841504

Wind River
43.248184, -109.021127

Togwotee Pass
43.752853, -110.068319

Mule River (Blackrock Creek)
43.765828, -110.081329

Jackson Hole
43.825682, -110.495455

Snake River
43.544511, -110.799592

Teton Pass
43.497571, -110.955569

Crooks River South Fork
(Trail Creek)
43.498082, -110.965352

Pierre's Hole
43.580525, -111.085251

Pine Creek Pass
43.571525, -111.215911

Colter's River (Pine Creek)
43.571351, -111.229281

Pine Creek North Fork
43.558817, -111.276780

Horseshoe Creek South Fork
43.684224, -111.315138

Crooks River (Teton River)
43.783986, -111.214435

Crooks River North Fork (South
Leigh Creek)
43.788507, -111.201278

Colter Stone Site
43.812389, -111.046476

Moran Creek South Fork
43.834773, -110.868687

Lake Biddle (Lake Jackson)
43.861602, -110.753812

Snake River Upstream
44.036449, -110.718851

Lewis River
44.141789, -110.663527

Lake Eustis (Lake Yellowstone)
44.397713, -110.563692

Yellowstone River Upstream
44.567040, -110.382799

Grand Canyon of the Yellowstone
44.718016, -110.496249

Hot Spring Brimstone
44.893027, -110.376395

Bannock Trail Crossing
44.893027, -110.376395

Lamar River
44.917180, -110.359150

Soda Butte River
44.870161, -110.192239

Colter Pass
45.026699, -109.890739

Clark's Fork of the Yellowstone
Upriver
45.017241, -109.867708

Sunlight Basin
44.770566, -109.425194

Dead Indian Creek
44.754739, -109.417706

Blue Bead Pass
44.653428, -109.382853

Blue Bead Mountain (Pat O'Hara
Mountain)
44.657518, -109.332681

Heart Mountain
44.665866, -109.121376

Valley River (Trail Creek)
44.616243, -109.302850

Stinking Water River
(Shoshone River)
44.521949, -109.103838

Colter's Hell
44.520199, -109.115976

Spirits' Mountain (Cedar
Mountain)
44.493284, -109.169632

Boiling Spring
44.497166, -109.196361

Gap Creek Downriver
(Sage Creek)
44.846243, -108.409036

Bighorn River
44.868675, -108.197089

Gap Creek Upriver (Sage Creek)
45.239814, -108.671641

Pryor Gap in Red Mountains (Pryor
Mountains)
45.287029, -108.610733

Pryor's Fork (Pryor Creek)
45.887634, -108.315747

Pompey's Tower (Pompey's Pillar)
45.995461, -108.005153

Shannon's Creek
45.996712, -107.998332

Manuel's Fort
46.146377, -107.476137

Other Sites Mentioned in the Text

Ap-so-roo-kah Crow Encampment
45.527009, -108.822510

Red Cliffs
44.959047, -108.266661

Bozeman Pass
45.667712, -110.810036

Bozeman Gap
45.651459, -110.942939

Battle of Flatheads and Crows
against Blackfoot
45.824738, -111.240598

Colter's Capture by Blackfoot
in 1808
45.868791, -111.622765

Colter's Hideout from Blackfoot
45.888575, -111.517687

Colter's Traverse over the Mountains
45.745142, -110.954164

Colter's Campsite and Escape
in 1809
45.710554, -111.035239

Henry's Fort at Three Forks in 1810
45.908432, -111.534127

NOTES

Chapter One: DISCOVERY

1. Henry Brackenridge described some "very handsome bluffs" in the vicinity of Boeuf Creek near La Charette, each "about one hundred feet high" and "covered with oak and other timber." [Henry Brackenridge, *Views of Louisiana together with a Journal of a Voyage up the Missouri River in 1811* (Pittsburgh: Cramer, Spear, and Eichbaum, 1814), pp. 205–6.]

2. Frontiersmen had to be attuned to nature to survive. John Bradbury said: "I often associated with the hunters, to collect information from their united testimony, concerning the nature and habits of animals, with which no men are so well acquainted. This knowledge is absolutely necessary to them, that they may be able to circumvent or surprise those which are the objects of chase, and to avoid such as are dangerous." [John Bradbury, *Travels in the Interior of America* (London: Sherwood, Neely, and Jones, 1819), pp. 114–15.]

3. Thomas James met Colter in 1809 and said he was about thirty-five years old, which suggests he was born about 1774. [Thomas James, *Three Years among the Indians and Mexicans* (New York: Citadel Press, 1966), p. 56; Stallo Vinton, *John Colter: Discoverer of Yellowstone Park* (New York: Edward Eberstadt, 1926), p. 28; Burton Harris, *John Colter: His Years in the Rockies* (New York: Scribner, 1952), p. 12.]

4. The thirty-two included Toussaint Charbonneau, his Shoshone wife, Sacagawea, and their newborn son, Jean Baptiste (nicknamed Pompey),

who joined the expedition at the Mandan villages. With Charles Floyd, the expedition members numbered thirty-three, but Floyd died before the Corps of Discovery reached the Mandans. [Meriwether Lewis, William Clark, and Reuben Thwaites, ed., *Original Journals of the Lewis and Clark Expedition, 1804–1806*, vol. 7 (New York: Dodd, Mead and Company, 1904–5), p. 360]; Stephen Ambrose provides a worthy overview of the Corps of Discovery. [Stephen Ambrose, *Undaunted Courage* (New York: Touchstone, 1996).]

5. Meriwether Lewis to William Clark, 19 June 1803; Lewis, Clark, and Thwaites, *Original Journals*, vol. 7, p. 227.

6. James, *Three Years among the Indians*, p. 56.

7. In a canoe, depending on the season, a person could float down the Missouri River at a rate of a hundred miles a day. William Anderson estimated five miles per hour. [William Marshall Anderson and Dale Morgan, ed., *The Rocky Mountain Journals of William Marshall Anderson* (Lincoln: University of Nebraska Press, 1987), p. 216.]

8. Washington Irving, *The Adventures of Captain Bonneville, U.S.A. in the Rocky Mountains and the Far West* (New York: G. P. Putnam's Sons, 1868), p. 237.

9. Brackenridge, *Views of Louisiana*, p. 92.

10. [Meriwether Lewis, Journals, 3 March 1804, Meriwether Lewis, William Clark, and Gary Moulton, ed., *Journals of the Lewis and Clark Expedition* (Lincoln: University of Nebraska Press, 1983); William Clark, Journals, 31 December 1803, 30 March 1804, Meriwether Lewis, William Clark, and Gary Moulton, ed., *Journals of the Lewis and Clark Expedition* (Lincoln: University of Nebraska Press, 1983)]; Unless otherwise specified, subsequent Lewis and Clark journal citations are from this source. See this source for literal transcripts.

11. William Clark, Journals, 29 June 1804.

12. [William Clark, Journals, 15 August 1806]; In later years, William Clark continued to be impressed by Colter's accomplishments and trusted the accuracy of the information he provided. This became obvious when he added Colter's 1807–8 route as a key feature on his 1810 manuscript map of the West. The journals of Colter's other commanders, Lewis and Ordway, offer the same opinion.

13. James, *Three Years among the Indians*, p. 56.

14. Meriwether Lewis to Unknown Correspondent, 14 October 1806, Meriwether Lewis, William Clark, and Donald Jackson, ed., *Letters of the Lewis and Clark Expedition* (Urbana: University of Illinois Press, 1962), p. 339.

15. William Clark, Journals, 17 September 1804.

16. William Clark, Journals, 1 to 2 August 1804.

17. Meriwether Lewis, Journals, 29 June 1806.

18. William Clark, Journals, 29 August 1804.

19. [John Ordway, Journals, 6 to 7 September 1804, Meriwether Lewis, William Clark, and Gary Moulton, ed., *Journals of the Lewis and Clark Expedition* (Lincoln: University of Nebraska Press, 1983)]; Unless otherwise specified, subsequent Ordway journal citations are from this source.

20. William Ashley, Jedediah Smith, and Harrison Dale, ed., *The Ashley-Smith Explorations and the Discovery of a Central Route to the Pacific, 1822–1829* (Cleveland: Arthur H. Clark Company, 1918), p. 137; George Catlin, *North American Indians* (Edinburgh: John Grant, 1926), vol. 1, p. 31, and vol. 2, p. 206; Edwin Denig and John Ewers, ed., *Five Indian Tribes of the Upper Missouri: Sioux, Arickaras, Assiniboines, Crees, Crows* (Norman: University of Oklahoma Press, 1961), p. 160; John Fahey, *The Flathead Indians* (Norman: University of Oklahoma Press, 1974), p. 20; Warren Ferris, *Life in the Rocky Mountains: A Diary of Wanderings on the Sources of the Rivers Missouri, Columbia, and Colorado, 1830–1835* (Denver: Old West Publishing Company, 1940), p. 43; Charles Larpenteur and Elliott Coues, ed., *Forty Years a Fur Trader on the Upper Missouri* (Minneapolis: Ross and Haines, 1962), p. 21; Thomas Leforge and Thomas Marquis, *Memoirs of a White Crow Indian* (Lincoln: University of Nebraska Press, 1974), p. 156; Zenas Leonard and Milo Quaife, ed., *Narrative of the Adventures of Zenas Leonard* (Chicago: The Lakeside Press, 1934), pp. 9, 49; John Luttig and Stella Drumm, ed., *Journal of a Fur-Trading Expedition on the Upper Missouri, 1812–13* (New York: Argosy-Antiquarian, 1964), p. 35; Alfred Jacob Miller and Marvin Ross, ed., *The West of Alfred Jacob Miller* (Norman: University of Oklahoma Press, 1968), pp. 124, 158; Samuel Parker, *Journal of an Exploring Tour beyond the Rocky Mountains* (Ithaca: Mack, Andrus, & Woodruff, 1842), pp. 61, 199–200, 202, 206, 209; Russell Reid

and Clell Gannon, eds., "Journal of the Atkinson-O'Fallon Expedition," *North Dakota Historical Quarterly* 4 no. 1 (October 1929): 40; Rufus Sage, *Rocky Mountain Life, or, Startling Scenes and Perilous Adventures in the Far West, during an Expedition of Three Years* (Lincoln: University of Nebraska Press, 1982), pp. 55–56, 64, 69, 71, 149–50, 155, 163, 296, 329, 347; Jedediah Smith and Maurice Sullivan, ed., *The Travels of Jedediah Smith* (Lincoln: University of Nebraska Press, 1992), pp. 19, 67, 98; Henry Spalding, "A Letter by Henry H. Spalding from the Rocky Mountains, 1836," New York: *Evangelist*, October 22, 1836, p. 3; William Swagerty, *Indianization of Lewis and Clark*, 2 vols. (Norman: Arthur H. Clark Company, 2012), pp. 324–25, 391; John Townsend, *Narrative of a Journey across the Rocky Mountains* (Philadelphia: Henry Perkins, 1839), pp. 159, 169, 210, 216, 235; Mrs. Frances Fuller Victor, *The River of the West: Life and Adventure in the Rocky Mountains and Oregon* (Hartford: Columbian Book Company, 1871), p. 247; Narcissa Whitman, "A Journey across the Plains in 1836," *Transactions of the Nineteenth Annual Reunion of the Oregon Pioneer Association for 1891* (Portland: A. Anderson, 1893), p. 57; Narcissa Whitman, "Additional Letters," *Transactions of the Twenty-first Annual Reunion of the Oregon Pioneer Association for 1893* (Portland: George Himes and Company, 1894), p. 107; F. A. Wislizenus, *A Journey to the Rocky Mountains in the Year 1839* (St. Louis: Missouri Historical Society, 1912), pp. 51–52; Nathaniel Wyeth and F. G. Young, ed., "The Correspondence and Journals of Captain Nathaniel J. Wyeth, 1831–6," *Sources of the History of Oregon* (Eugene: University of Oregon Press, 1899), pp. 163, 166, 172, 180.

21. Sage, *Rocky Mountain Life*, pp. 306–7; Smith, *The Travels of Jedediah Smith*, p. 97; David Thompson, W. Raymond Wood, and Thomas Thiessen, eds., "David Thompson Journal," 22 January 1798, *Early Fur Trade on the Northern Plains* (Norman: University of Oklahoma Press, 1999); Victor, *The River of the West*, p. 120; Wyeth, "The Correspondence and Journals of Captain Nathaniel J. Wyeth," p. 163.

22. Luttig, *Journal of a Fur-Trading Expedition on the Upper Missouri*, p. 104; Parker, *Journal of an Exploring Tour beyond the Rocky Mountains*, p. 92; Sage, *Rocky Mountain Life*, p. 73; Smith, *The Travels of Jedediah Smith*, p. 7; Swagerty, *Indianization of Lewis and Clark*, p. 351.

23. William Clark, Journals, 18 June 1805.

24. Meriwether Lewis, Journals, 24 August 1805.

25. Meriwether Lewis, Journals, 26 August 1805; John Ordway, Journals, 26 August 1805.

26. William Clark, Journals, 5 July 1806.

27. Meriwether Lewis, Journals, 10 September 1805.

28. William Clark, Journals, 10 September 1805.

29. John Ordway, Journals, 10 September 1805.

30. William Clark, Journals, 24 and 27 September 1805.

31. William Clark, Journals, 13 to 14 November 1805.

32. William Clark, Journals, 7 November 1805.

33. William Clark, Journals, 17 November 1805.

34. William Clark, Journals, 25 August 1804.

35. Meriwether Lewis, Journals, 29 November 1805.

36. William Clark, Journals, 15 to 16 December 1805.

37. John Ordway, Journals, 14 June 1806.

38. William Clark, Journals, 14 June 1806.

39. William Clark, Journals, 19 June 1806; Meriwether Lewis, Journals, 21 August 1805; Irving, *The Adventures of Captain Bonneville*, p. 75; Luttig, *Journal of a Fur-Trading Expedition on the Upper Missouri*, p. 75; Parker, *Journal of an Exploring Tour beyond the Rocky Mountains*, p. 90; Carl Russell, *Firearms, Traps, and Tools of the Mountain Men* (New York: Skyhorse Publishing, 2011), pp. 321–22; Robert Stuart, Wilson Price Hunt, and Philip Rollins, ed., *The Discovery of the Oregon Trail: Robert Stuart's Narratives of His Overland Trip Eastward from Astoria in 1812–13* (Lincoln: University of Nebraska Press, 1995), p. 109; Townsend, *Narrative of a Journey across the Rocky Mountains*, p. 209; Whitman, "A Journey across the Plains in 1836," p. 51; Wyeth, "The Correspondence and Journals of Captain Nathaniel J. Wyeth," p. 169.

40. Meriwether Lewis, Journals, 5 June 1806.

41. John Ordway, Journals, 5 May 1806.

42. Meriwether Lewis, Journals, 18 June 1806; William Clark, Journals, 18 June 1806.

43. Washington Irving, *Astoria, or Enterprise beyond the Rocky Mountains* (London: Richard Bentley, 1839), p. 121.

44. Meriwether Lewis, Journals, 9 August 1806.

45. John Ordway, Journals, 12 August 1806.

46. John Ordway, Journals, 16 April 1805.

47. Meriwether Lewis, Journals, 12 August 1806.

48. Meriwether Lewis, Journals, 12 August 1806.

49. William Clark, Journals, 15 and 16 August 1806.

50. William Clark, Journals, 17 August 1806; John Ordway, Journals, 17 August 1806.

51. James Beckwourth and T. D. Bonner, *The Life and Adventures of James P. Beckwourth, Mountaineer, Scout, Pioneer, and Chief of the Crow Nation of Indians* (Williamstown, MA: Corner House Publishers, 1977), p. 81; Joseph Medicine Crow, *From the Heart of the Crow Country: The Crow Indians' Own Stories* (New York: Orion Books, 1992), p. 2; William Tomkins, *Indian Sign Language* (New York: Dover Publications, 1969).

52. Robert Lowie, *The Crow Indians* (New York: Farrar and Rinehart, 1935), p. 90.

53. Anderson, *The Rocky Mountain Journals of William Marshall Anderson*, p. 75; Beckwourth, *The Life and Adventures of James P. Beckwourth*, pp. 45–46, 112, 229–30; Denig, *Five Indian Tribes of the Upper Missouri*, p. 148; Ferris, *Life in the Rocky Mountains*, pp. 248, 303; François Larocque and L. J. Burpee, ed., *Journal of Larocque from the Assiniboine to the Yellowstone, 1805* (Ottawa: Government Printing Bureau, 1910), pp. 35, 65; Larpenteur, *Forty Years a Fur Trader on the Upper Missouri*, p. 45; Leforge, *Memoirs of a White Crow Indian*, pp. 100–1, 179, 183–85; Alexander Maximilian von Wied, *Travels in the Interior of North America,* in Early Western Travels series (New York: AMS Press, 1966), p. 111; Miller, *The West of Alfred Jacob Miller*, p. 144; Daniel Potts, "To Robert Potts, July 16, 1826," Philadelphia: *Gazette and Daily Advertiser*, November 14, 1826, p. 2; Osborne Russell and Aubrey Haines, ed., *Journal of a Trapper* (Portland: Oregon Historical Society, 1955), p. 143; Sage, *Rocky Mountain Life*, pp. 199, 343; Victor, *The River of the West*, p. 137; John Wyeth, *Oregon; or, A Short History of a Long Journey* (Cambridge: Printed for John B. Wyeth, 1833), p. 54.

54. Ashley and Smith, *The Ashley-Smith Explorations*, pp. 105, 119, 122, 125, 130, 137–38, 146; Beckwourth, *The Life and Adventures of James P. Beckwourth,* pp. 57, 272; Kit Carson and Milo Quaife, ed., *Kit Carson's*

Autobiography (Lincoln: University of Nebraska Press, 1966), pp. 24, 49; Catlin, *North American Indians*, vol. 1, p. 49; Paul Cutright, "Lewis and Clark and Cottonwood," *Bulletin of the Missouri Historical Society* 22 no. 1 (October 1965): 35–44; Irving, *The Adventures of Captain Bonneville*, pp. 226, 296; James Kennerly and Stella Drumm, ed., "Diary of James Kennerly," *Missouri Historical Society Collections* 6 (1928–31): 60; Leonard, *Narrative of the Adventures of Zenas Leonard*, pp. 20, 41; Meriwether Lewis, William Clark, and Gary Moulton, ed., *Herbarium of the Lewis and Clark Expedition* (Lincoln: University of Nebraska Press, 1999); Maximilian, *Travels in the Interior of North America*, p. 94; Miller, *The West of Alfred Jacob Miller*, pp. 21, 188; Sage, *Rocky Mountain Life*, pp. 135, 291; Smith, *The Travels of Jedediah Smith*, p. 10; Townsend, *Narrative of a Journey across the Rocky Mountains*, p. 188; Victor, *The River of the West*, pp. 82–83, 196.

55. Harris, *John Colter*, pp. 53–55.

56. Larocque, *Journal of Larocque from the Assiniboine to the Yellowstone*, pp. 43–46; Leforge, *Memoirs of a White Crow Indian*, pp. 78–79, 88–89, 188–89, 253; Harris, *John Colter*, pp. 83–84; Medicine Crow, *From the Heart of the Crow Country*, p. 84; Russell, *Journal of a Trapper*, p. 50.

57. George Drouillard's map shows a Crow encampment on the *Ap-so-roo-kah* or Absaroka Fork (present-day Rock Creek) of Clark's Fork. Drouillard visited this camp in late 1808. Then he continued up the Clark's Fork, apparently bypassing Clark's Fork Canyon, which does not appear on his map. Instead, he headed for Heart Mountain and the Stinking Water River. William Clark's 1810 map included Drouillard's description of the area. [George Drouillard Map of September 6, 1808, with William Clark inscriptions, A0289 Clark Family Collection 1766–1991, Box 11: William Clark Papers, Folder 18: 1808, Missouri Historical Society, St. Louis, Missouri; William Clark, "Notes on the Chart Obtained from George Drewyard (Drouillard) September 6, 1808," A0289 Clark Family Collection 1766–1991, Box 11: William Clark Papers, Folder 18: 1808, Missouri Historical Society, St. Louis, Missouri; Jeffrey Hanson, "The George Drouillard Maps of 1808," *Archaeology in Montana* 21 no. 1 (January–April 1980): 45–53.]

58. John Ball, *Autobiography of John Ball* (Grand Rapids: Dean-Hicks

Company, 1925), p. 86; Ferris, *Life in the Rocky Mountains*, pp. 248, 254, 303; Larocque, *Journal of Larocque from the Assiniboine to the Yellowstone*, p. 70; Miller, *The West of Alfred Jacob Miller*, pp. 55, 152, 193; Parker, *Journal of an Exploring Tour beyond the Rocky Mountains*, p. 57; Tomkins, *Indian Sign Language*, pp. 63, 93–95.

59. Brackenridge, *Views of Louisiana*, p. 90.

60. Hiram Chittenden, *The American Fur Trade of the Far West*, 2 vols. (Stanford, CA: Academic Reprints, 1954), pp. 65–66; Ferris, *Life in the Rocky Mountains*, p. 1; Leonard, *Narrative of the Adventures of Zenas Leonard*, p. 105; Smith, *The Travels of Jedediah Smith*, p. 26.

61. Chittenden, *The American Fur Trade of the Far West*, p. 54; Miller, *The West of Alfred Jacob Miller*, p. 29; George Ruxton, *Life in the Far West* (New York: Harper and Brothers, 1849), pp. iv–v; Sage, *Rocky Mountain Life*, pp. 33, 297.

62. Anderson, *The Rocky Mountain Journals of William Marshall Anderson*, p. 117; Miller, *The West of Alfred Jacob Miller*, pp. 154, 162.

63. Beckwourth, *The Life and Adventures of James P. Beckwourth*, p. 317; Catlin, *North American Indians*, vol. 1, pp. 73–74; Chittenden, *The American Fur Trade of the Far West*, pp. 65–66; Miller, *The West of Alfred Jacob Miller*, p. 156; Sage, *Rocky Mountain Life*, pp. 38–39; Smith, *The Travels of Jedediah Smith*, pp. 21, 63; Townsend, *Narrative of a Journey across the Rocky Mountains*, pp. 271–72; Wislizenus, *A Journey to the Rocky Mountains*, p. 155.

64. Ferris, *Life in the Rocky Mountains*, pp. 292–94; Irving, *Astoria*, p. 172; Larpenteur, *Forty Years a Fur Trader on the Upper Missouri*, p. 409; Maximilian, *Travels in the Interior of North America*, p. 103; Parker, *Journal of an Exploring Tour beyond the Rocky Mountains*, p. 232; Smith, *The Travels of Jedediah Smith*, pp. 4–5.

65. Harris, *John Colter*, p. 59; Larry Morris, *The Fate of the Corps: What Became of the Lewis and Clark Explorers* (New Haven: Yale University Press, 2004), p. 39.

66. Irving, *Astoria*, pp. 145–46.

67. George Drouillard Map of August 5, 1808 with William Clark inscriptions, G4262 B53 1808 D7, Geography and Map Division, Library of Congress, Washington, DC; Harris, *John Colter*, pp. 69–70.

68. Wyeth, "The Correspondence and Journals of Captain Nathaniel J. Wyeth," p. 210.

69. James, *Three Years among the Indians*, pp. 65–66.

70. George Drouillard Map of September 6, 1808, with William Clark inscriptions.

71. Yale University's excellent digital copy of Clark's 1810 map is accessible online. See Works Cited. Clark's 1810 manuscript map is more accurate than his 1814 published map, but the latter is useful for clarifying the dotted lines marking Colter's route. [Brackenridge, *Views of Louisiana*, pp. 91–92; William Clark Map of 1810, WA MSS 303, Image ID 1053073, Yale Collection of Western Americana, Beinecke Rare Book and Manuscript Library, Yale University, New Haven, CT; William Clark Map of 1814, Meriwether Lewis, William Clark, Nicholas Biddle, and Paul Allen, *History of the Expedition under the Command of Captains Lewis and Clark* (Philadelphia: Bradford and Inskeep, 1814).]

Chapter Two: TRAVELING LIGHT

1. Friedrich Baron von Steuben, *Regulations for the Order and Discipline of the Troops of the United States* (Portsmouth, New Hampshire: Press of J. Melcher, 1804), p. 116.

2. William Ashley and Dale Morgan, ed., "William H. Ashley Diary, March 25–June 27, 1825," *The West of William Ashley* (Denver: Old West Publishing Company, 1964), pp. 112–13; Thomas Beall, "Recollections of William Craig," Lewiston: *Morning Tribune*, March 3, 1918, p. 8; Beckwourth, *The Life and Adventures of James P. Beckwourth*, pp. 39, 196, 437; Miller, *The West of Alfred Jacob Miller*, p. 177; Russell, *Journal of a Trapper*, p. 115; Whitman, "A Journey across the Plains in 1836," p. 50.

3. William Duane, *A Military Dictionary* (Philadelphia: Printed and Published by William Duane, 1810), p. 53.

4. Meriwether Lewis, Journals, 21 August 1805; Joseph Whitehouse, Journals, 2 March 1805, Meriwether Lewis, William Clark, and Gary Moulton, ed., *Journals of the Lewis and Clark Expedition* (Lincoln: University of Nebraska Press, 1983); Larocque, *Journal of Larocque from the Assiniboine to the Yellowstone*, p. 67; Lowie, *The Crow Indians*, p. 82; Robert Moore and Michael Haynes, *Tailor Made, Trail Worn: Army Life, Clothing, and Weapons of the Corps of Discovery* (Helena, Montana: Farcountry Press, 2003), p. 193.

5. Meriwether Lewis, Journals, 19 July 1805.

6. Randolph Marcy, *Prairie Traveler* (New York: Harper and Brothers, 1859), p. 41; Sage, *Rocky Mountain Life*, pp. 154–55.

7. Alfred Jacob Miller said of moccasins: "They are verily the most comfortable covering for the feet that can be fashioned." [Marcy, *Prairie Traveler*, p. 37; Miller, *The West of Alfred Jacob Miller*, p. 174.]

8. [Marcy, *Prairie Traveler*, p. 50; Carson, *Kit Carson's Autobiography*, p. 11; Ferris, *Life in the Rocky Mountains*, p. 61; Reid and Gannon, "Journal of the Atkinson-O'Fallon Expedition," p. 27; Smith, *The Travels of Jedediah Smith*, p. 19; George Neumann, *Collector's Illustrated Encyclopedia of the American Revolution* (Harrisburg, PA: Stackpole Books, 1975)]; Neumann's book offers an excellent look at military equipage of the period. Many items mentioned here are illustrated by Neumann.

9. Marcy, *Prairie Traveler*, p. 47; Sage, *Rocky Mountain Life*, p. 193; Victor, *The River of the West*, p. 157; Russell, *Journal of a Trapper*, p. 35; Stuart, *The Discovery of the Oregon Trail*, pp. 75–76; Townsend, *Narrative of a Journey across the Rocky Mountains*, p. 234.

10. Anderson, *The Rocky Mountain Journals of William Marshall Anderson*, p. 178; Ferris, *Life in the Rocky Mountains*, pp. 245, 339; Russell, *Journal of a Trapper*, pp. 74, 119; Sage, *Rocky Mountain Life*, pp. 140, 316.

11. Lowie, *The Crow Indians*, p. 89.

12. Beall, "Recollections of William Craig," p. 8; Ferris, *Life in the Rocky Mountains*, pp. 213–214; Russell, *Journal of a Trapper*, p. 36; Wyeth, "The Correspondence and Journals of Captain Nathaniel J. Wyeth," pp. 168, 248.

13. Catlin, *North American Indians*, vol. 1, p. 26; James Clyman and Charles Camp, ed., *James Clyman, Frontiersman: The Adventures of a Trapper and Covered-Wagon Emigrant as Told in His Own Reminiscences and Diaries* (Portland: Champoeg Press, 1960), p. 21; Ross Cox, *Adventures on the Columbia River, including the Narrative of a Residence of Six Years on the Western Side of the Rocky Mountains* (New York: J. & J. Harper, 1832), p. 121; Ferris, *Life in the Rocky Mountains*, pp. 294, 301; Irving, *The Adventures of Captain Bonneville*, p. 310; Leforge, *Memoirs of a White Crow Indian*, pp. 84, 87; Maximilian, *Travels in the Interior of North America*, p. 110; Miller, *The West of Alfred Jacob Miller*, pp. 22, 159, 194; Parker, *Jour-*

nal of an Exploring Tour beyond the Rocky Mountains, p. 68; Thompson, "David Thompson Journal," 9 January 1798.

14. Ferris, *Life in the Rocky Mountains,* p. 293; Irving, *Astoria,* p. 338; Leforge, *Memoirs of a White Crow Indian,* p. 88; Parker, *Journal of an Exploring Tour beyond the Rocky Mountains,* p. 241.

15. Cox, *Adventures on the Columbia River,* p. 122; Larocque, *Journal of Larocque from the Assiniboine to the Yellowstone,* p. 68; Parker, *Journal of an Exploring Tour beyond the Rocky Mountains,* p. 106; Sage, *Rocky Mountain Life,* p. 196.

16. Baron von Steuben, *Regulations for the Order and Discipline of the Troops of the United States,* p. 128.

17. Baron von Steuben, *Regulations for the Order and Discipline of the Troops of the United States,* pp. 123–124.

18. Anderson, *The Rocky Mountain Journals of William Marshall Anderson,* p. 209; Robert Campbell and Drew Holloway, ed., *A Narrative of Colonel Robert Campbell's Experiences in the Rocky Mountain Fur Trade from 1825 to 1835* (Fairfield, Washington: Ye Galleon Press, 1991), p. 23; Miller, *The West of Alfred Jacob Miller,* pp. 26, 52; Smith, *The Travels of Jedediah Smith,* p. 31; Victor, *The River of the West,* p. 82; Alphonso Wetmore, "The Missouri Trapper," James Hall, *Letters from the West* (London: Henry Colburn, 1828), p. 304.

19. Russell, *Firearms, Traps, and Tools of the Mountain Men,* p. 174.

20. Beckwourth, *The Life and Adventures of James P. Beckwourth,* p. 39; Charles Camp, "The Chronicles of George C. Yount," *California Historical Society Quarterly* 2 no. 1 (April 1923): 30; Irving, *The Adventures of Captain Bonneville,* pp. 480–81; Leonard, *Narrative of the Adventures of Zenas Leonard,* p. 64; Wislizenus, *A Journey to the Rocky Mountains,* p. 122.

21. Anderson, *The Rocky Mountain Journals of William Marshall Anderson,* p. 83; Miller, *The West of Alfred Jacob Miller,* p. 106; Russell, *Firearms, Traps, and Tools of the Mountain Men,* pp. 37–39, 53, 90; Sage, *Rocky Mountain Life,* p. 74.

22. Nelson Miles witnessed bison hunts on foot in deep snow and on horseback at other times of the year. He illustrated both in his book. [Nelson Miles, *Personal Recollections* (Chicago: Werner Company, 1896), pp. 124, 128.]

23. Anderson, *The Rocky Mountain Journals of William Marshall Anderson*, p. 135; Beckwourth, *The Life and Adventures of James P. Beckwourth*, p. 55; Catlin, *North American Indians*, vol. 1, p. 28; Fahey, *The Flathead Indians*, p. 9; Irving, *The Adventures of Captain Bonneville*, p. 469; Luttig, *Journal of a Fur-Trading Expedition on the Upper Missouri*, p. 112; Miller, *The West of Alfred Jacob Miller*, pp. 84, 106; Asahel Munger and Eliza Munger, "Diary of Asahel Munger and Wife," *Quarterly of the Oregon Historical Society* 8 no. 4 (December 1907): 391; Parker, *Journal of an Exploring Tour beyond the Rocky Mountains*, pp. 53, 210; Potts, "To Robert Potts, July 16, 1826," p. 2; Reid and Gannon, "Journal of the Atkinson-O'Fallon Expedition," p. 26; Townsend, *Narrative of a Journey across the Rocky Mountains*, pp. 160–1, 217.

24. Beckwourth, *The Life and Adventures of James P. Beckwourth*, pp. 55, 289; Leonard, *Narrative of the Adventures of Zenas Leonard*, pp. 235–6; Miller, *The West of Alfred Jacob Miller*, p. 200.

25. Sage, *Rocky Mountain Life*, p. 73; Townsend, *Narrative of a Journey across the Rocky Mountains*, pp. 217–18; Wislizenus, *A Journey to the Rocky Mountains*, pp. 49–50.

26. Fahey, *The Flathead Indians*, pp. 19–20; Miller, *The West of Alfred Jacob Miller*, pp. 4, 50, 85, 173; Sage, *Rocky Mountain Life*, pp. 66, 69; Townsend, *Narrative of a Journey across the Rocky Mountains*, pp. 166, 170, 213; Wislizenus, *A Journey to the Rocky Mountains*, p. 51.

27. Anderson, *The Rocky Mountain Journals of William Marshall Anderson*, p. 81; Ball, *Autobiography of John Ball*, p. 85; Beckwourth, *The Life and Adventures of James P. Beckwourth*, p. 96; Cox, *Adventures on the Columbia River*, pp. 211, 213; Miller, *The West of Alfred Jacob Miller*, p. 140; Parker, *Journal of an Exploring Tour beyond the Rocky Mountains*, pp. 61, 122; Sage, *Rocky Mountain Life*, pp. 56, 163; Smith, *The Travels of Jedediah Smith*, p. 85; Townsend, *Narrative of a Journey across the Rocky Mountains*, pp. 159, 194.

28. Beckwourth, *The Life and Adventures of James P. Beckwourth*, p. 50; Ferris, *Life in the Rocky Mountains*, p. 339; Lewis, Clark, and Jackson, *Letters of the Lewis and Clark Expedition*, p. 70; Luttig, *Journal of a Fur-Trading Expedition on the Upper Missouri*, p. 120; Meriwether Lewis, Journals, 1 February 1806.

29. Duane, *A Military Dictionary*, p. 544.

30. Marcy, *Prairie Traveler*, p. 157.

31. Ashley, "William H. Ashley Diary," p. 104; Ashley and Smith, *The Ashley-Smith Explorations*, p. 133; Ferris, *Life in the Rocky Mountains*, p. 75; Irving, *The Adventures of Captain Bonneville*, p. 305; Munger and Munger, "Diary of Asahel Munger and Wife," p. 389; Sage, *Rocky Mountain Life*, pp. 71, 162; Stuart, *The Discovery of the Oregon Trail*, p. 286 (the journal of Wilson Price Hunt appears in this publication on pp. 281–308); Wislizenus, *A Journey to the Rocky Mountains*, p. 72.

32. Anderson, *The Rocky Mountain Journals of William Marshall Anderson*, p. 115; Ball, *Autobiography of John Ball*, p. 89; Denig, *Five Indian Tribes of the Upper Missouri*, p. 157; Fahey, *The Flathead Indians*, pp. 15, 21; Parker, *Journal of an Exploring Tour beyond the Rocky Mountains*, p. 73.

33. Ashley and Smith, *The Ashley-Smith Explorations*, p. 120; Irving, *The Adventures of Captain Bonneville*, p. 332; Miller, *The West of Alfred Jacob Miller*, p. 4; Munger and Munger, "Diary of Asahel Munger and Wife," p. 391; Parker, *Journal of an Exploring Tour beyond the Rocky Mountains*, p. 60; Daniel Potts, "To Dr. Lukens, July 8, 1827," Philadelphia: *Gazette and Daily Advertiser*, October 19, 1827, p. 2; Sage, *Rocky Mountain Life*, p. 71; Spalding, "A Letter by Henry H. Spalding from the Rocky Mountains," p. 3; Victor, *The River of the West*, p. 137; Whitman, "Additional Letters," p. 104; Wislizenus, *A Journey to the Rocky Mountains*, pp. 43–44.

34. Fahey, *The Flathead Indians*, p. 13; Miller, *The West of Alfred Jacob Miller*, p. 4; Sage, *Rocky Mountain Life*, p. 71; Tomkins, *Indian Sign Language;* Wislizenus, *A Journey to the Rocky Mountains*, p. 51.

35. Moore and Haynes illustrate the typical clothing and accoutrements of a Kentucky frontiersman of the period. [Moore and Haynes, *Tailor Made, Trail Worn*, p. 198.]

36. Duane, *A Military Dictionary*, p. 314.

37. Meriwether Lewis, Journals, 20 August 1805.

38. Anderson, *The Rocky Mountain Journals of William Marshall Anderson*, p. 159; Cox, *Adventures on the Columbia River*, p. 122; P. J. De Smet, *Letters and Sketches, with a Narrative of a Year's Residence among the Indian Tribes of the Rocky Mountains,* in Early Western Travels series (New York: AMS Press, 1966), p. 172; Ferris, *Life in the Rocky Mountains*, pp. 131–32;

Irving, *The Adventures of Captain Bonneville*, pp. 104, 365; Leforge, *Memoirs of a White Crow Indian*, pp. 154–55; Maximilian, *Travels in the Interior of North America*, pp. 102–3; Miller, *The West of Alfred Jacob Miller*, p. 147; Sage, *Rocky Mountain Life*, p. 84; Tomkins, *Indian Sign Language*, p. 63.

39. Beckwourth, *The Life and Adventures of James P. Beckwourth*, pp. 261–62; Catlin, *North American Indians*, vol. 1, p. 52; Leonard, *Narrative of the Adventures of Zenas Leonard*, p. 253; Sage, *Rocky Mountain Life*, p. 348; Victor, *The River of the West*, p. 55; Wislizenus, *A Journey to the Rocky Mountains*, pp. 52–53.

40. Ashley, "William H. Ashley Diary," p. 111; Ball, *Autobiography of John Ball*, p. 76; Beckwourth, *The Life and Adventures of James P. Beckwourth*, p. 434; Fahey, *The Flathead Indians*, p. 20; Ferris, *Life in the Rocky Mountains*, pp. 61, 148; Victor, *The River of the West*, p. 82.

41. Catlin, *North American Indians*, vol. 2, p. 243; Harold Tichenor, *The Blanket: An Illustrated History of the Hudson's Bay Blanket* (Toronto: Madison Press, 2002).

42. Harris, *John Colter*, p. 6.

43. Marcy, *Prairie Traveler*, pp. 134–35.

44. Anderson, *The Rocky Mountain Journals of William Marshall Anderson*, p. 199; Beckwourth, *The Life and Adventures of James P. Beckwourth*, p. 63; William Henry Jackson, "Jackson Photo of Shoshone Indians," 1871 (Yellowstone National Park Photo Collection, National Park Service Photo 14826); Larpenteur, *Forty Years a Fur Trader on the Upper Missouri*, p. 52; Lowie, *The Crow Indians*, p. 89; Miller, *The West of Alfred Jacob Miller*, pp. 62, 110; Sage, *Rocky Mountain Life*, pp. 43, 291; Townsend, *Narrative of a Journey across the Rocky Mountains*, pp. 247, 257; Whitman, "A Journey across the Plains in 1836," p. 54; Wislizenus, *A Journey to the Rocky Mountains*, p. 40; Wyeth, "The Correspondence and Journals of Captain Nathaniel J. Wyeth," pp. 187, 246.

45. Patrick Gass, Journals, 15 May 1806, Meriwether Lewis, William Clark, and Gary Moulton, ed., *Journals of the Lewis and Clark Expedition* (Lincoln: University of Nebraska Press, 1983).

46. Baron von Steuben, *Regulations for the Order and Discipline of the Troops of the United States*, p. 119; Duane, *A Military Dictionary*, p. 682.

47. Lowie, *The Crow Indians*, p. 89; Baron von Steuben, *Regulations for*

the Order and Discipline of the Troops of the United States, p. 119; Duane, *A Military Dictionary*, p. 123; Beckwourth, *The Life and Adventures of James P. Beckwourth,* p. 39; Ferris, *Life in the Rocky Mountains*, pp. 173, 241; Leforge, *Memoirs of a White Crow Indian*, p. 115; Russell, *Journal of a Trapper*, pp. 73–74; Sage, *Rocky Mountain Life*, pp. 37, 44.

48. Marcy, *Prairie Traveler*, p. 48.

49. Marcy, *Prairie Traveler*, pp. 40, 138; Philip Cooke, *Scenes and Adventures in the Army* (Philadelphia: Lindsay and Blakiston, 1857), p. 148; Irving, *The Adventures of Captain Bonneville*, p. 449.

50. Frontiersmen normally bundled their possessions in a bison hide, elk skin, wool blanket, or oil cloth, then slung it over their backs. The sling could be made of single strips of rawhide or braided rawhide, bison hair, hemp, bark, or other plant matter. [Irving, *Astoria*, p. 202; Sage, *Rocky Mountain Life*, p. 197; Swagerty, *Indianization of Lewis and Clark*, pp. 531–32.]

51. The total estimated weight of gunpowder that Colter likely carried in his powder horn and pack was one and one-half pounds. His total weight of lead and rifle balls carried in his hunting bag and pack was about three pounds. This estimate comes from the amounts used by the Corps of Discovery, in particular the hunters, over a twenty-eight-month period. It also comes from the record of Colter selling Thomas James one and one-half pounds of powder for the 1809–10 hunting and trapping season. [James, *Three Years among the Indians*, pp. 29–30.]

52. Marcy, *Prairie Traveler*, p. 33; Anderson, *The Rocky Mountain Journals of William Marshall Anderson*, p. 193; Fahey, *The Flathead Indians*, p. 20; Leforge, *Memoirs of a White Crow Indian*, p. 156; Miller, *The West of Alfred Jacob Miller*, p. 129; Munger and Munger, "Diary of Asahel Munger and Wife," p. 398; Sage, *Rocky Mountain Life*, p. 81; Townsend, *Narrative of a Journey across the Rocky Mountains*, pp. 213–14, 216; Wislizenus, *A Journey to the Rocky Mountains*, p. 52.

53. Campbell, *A Narrative of Colonel Robert Campbell's Experiences in the Rocky Mountain Fur Trade*, p. 28; Robert Campbell and George Brooks, ed., "The Private Journal of Robert Campbell," *Bulletin of the Missouri Historical Society* 20 (October 1963 to July 1964): 11, 18; Carson, *Kit Carson's Autobiography*, p. 46; Cox, *Adventures on the Columbia River*, p. 100; Fahey,

The Flathead Indians, pp. 12–13; Larpenteur, *Forty Years a Fur Trader on the Upper Missouri*, p. 54; Leforge, *Memoirs of a White Crow Indian*, p. 160; Lewis, Clark, and Moulton, *Herbarium of the Lewis and Clark Expedition*; Parker, *Journal of an Exploring Tour beyond the Rocky Mountains*, pp. 127, 221; Russell, *Journal of a Trapper*, p. 48; Sage, *Rocky Mountain Life*, pp. 76, 110, 147, 171, 177; Stuart, *The Discovery of the Oregon Trail*, p. 83; Swagerty, *Indianization of Lewis and Clark*, p. 401; Thompson, "David Thompson Journal"; Townsend, *Narrative of a Journey across the Rocky Mountains*, pp. 199, 247, 268; Victor, *The River of the West*, p. 176; Whitman, "A Journey across the Plains in 1836," pp. 54–55; Wislizenus, *A Journey to the Rocky Mountains*, p. 61.

54. The Crow and Blackfoot were not fish eaters. But fish was important to the Shoshone diet, and they gladly traded for fishing line and metal hooks. [Ashley, "William H. Ashley Diary," p. 114; Larocque, *Journal of Larocque from the Assiniboine to the Yellowstone*, p. 60; Lowie, *The Crow Indians*, p. 72.]

55. Catlin, *North American Indians*, vol. 1, p. 58; Larpenteur, *Forty Years a Fur Trader on the Upper Missouri*, pp. 396–97; Tomkins, *Indian Sign Language*.

56. Beckwourth, *The Life and Adventures of James P. Beckwourth*, p. 265; Maximilian, *Travels in the Interior of North America*, p. 101; Sage, *Rocky Mountain Life*, p. 182.

57. Beckwourth, *The Life and Adventures of James P. Beckwourth*, pp. 203, 434; Ferris, *Life in the Rocky Mountains*, p. 167.

58. Lewis, Clark, and Jackson, *Letters of the Lewis and Clark Expedition*, pp. 72–99.

59. Meriwether Lewis, Journals, 13 August 1805; Miller, *The West of Alfred Jacob Miller*, pp. 143, 175; Parker, *Journal of an Exploring Tour beyond the Rocky Mountains*, p. 56.

60. De Smet, *Letters and Sketches*, p. 306; Townsend, *Narrative of a Journey across the Rocky Mountains*, p. 254.

61. Lewis, Clark, and Moulton, *Herbarium of the Lewis and Clark Expedition*; Leforge, *Memoirs of a White Crow Indian*, p. 161; Swagerty, *Indianization of Lewis and Clark*, p. 570; Townsend, *Narrative of a Journey across the Rocky Mountains*, p. 146; George West, *Tobacco, Pipes, and Smoking*

Customs of the American Indians (Two Parks, Milwaukee: Board of the Public Museum of the City of Milwaukee, 1934), pp. 63–64, 107–9, 112.

62. Anderson, *The Rocky Mountain Journals of William Marshall Anderson*, p. 85; Ashley, "William H. Ashley Diary," pp. 112–13; Ashley and Smith, *The Ashley-Smith Explorations*, p. 197; Campbell, "The Private Journal of Robert Campbell," pp. 18, 22; Carson, *Kit Carson's Autobiography*, p. 169; Larocque, *Journal of Larocque from the Assiniboine to the Yellowstone*, p. 23; Miller, *The West of Alfred Jacob Miller*, p. 1; Sage, *Rocky Mountain Life*, p. 232; Smith, *The Travels of Jedediah Smith*, p. 15; Townsend, *Narrative of a Journey across the Rocky Mountains*, pp. 137, 255, 261; Wyeth, "The Correspondence and Journals of Captain Nathaniel J. Wyeth," p. 168.

63. In summary, a reconstruction of Colter's pack includes: a seven-by-eight-foot piece of heavy water-repellent cloth (seven pounds); a four-point Hudson's Bay blanket (six pounds); lead bars (two pounds); gunpowder (one pound); a bullet mold, rifle cleaning and repair parts, and tools (one pound); food and salt (four pounds); utensils, fish hooks, gigs, sewing supplies, and trade samples (one and one-half pounds); tobacco (two pounds); extra clothing or cloth (two pounds); snowshoes (three pounds); and leather straps for tying the pack and forming a sling (half a pound). Total weight is thirty pounds.

Chapter Three: GOING NATIVE

1. Thomas James mentioned Colter's knowledge of the language. [James, *Three Years among the Indians*, p. 59.]

2. Irving, *The Adventures of Captain Bonneville*, p. 103.

3. De Smet, *Letters and Sketches*, pp. 303–4; Ferris, *Life in the Rocky Mountains*, p. 302; Miller, *The West of Alfred Jacob Miller*, pp. 1, 156; Wislizenus, *A Journey to the Rocky Mountains*, p. 155.

4. Ball, *Autobiography of John Ball*, pp. 68, 80; De Smet, *Letters and Sketches*, p. 400; Munger and Munger, "Diary of Asahel Munger and Wife," p. 394; Sage, *Rocky Mountain Life*, p. 349; Whitman, "Additional Letters," p. 106.

5. Beckwourth, *The Life and Adventures of James P. Beckwourth*, pp. 277, 317; Wyeth, "The Correspondence and Journals of Captain Nathaniel J. Wyeth," p. 194.

6. Lowie, *The Crow Indians*, p. 84.

7. Anderson, *The Rocky Mountain Journals of William Marshall Anderson*, pp. 192–93; Catlin, *North American Indians*, vol. 1, pp. 49, 51; Miller, *The West of Alfred Jacob Miller*, p. 66; Sage, *Rocky Mountain Life*, pp. 87, 103.

8. Anderson, *The Rocky Mountain Journals of William Marshall Anderson*, p. 138; Denig, *Five Indian Tribes of the Upper Missouri*, p. 159; Fahey, *The Flathead Indians*, p. 17; Ferris, *Life in the Rocky Mountains*, p. 301; Irving, *Astoria*, pp. 212–13; Larocque, *Journal of Larocque from the Assiniboine to the Yellowstone*, p. 64; Leforge, *Memoirs of a White Crow Indian*, p. 173; Miller, *The West of Alfred Jacob Miller*, pp. 79–80, 167; Parker, *Journal of an Exploring Tour beyond the Rocky Mountains*, pp. 98, 234; Sage, *Rocky Mountain Life*, p. 182; Stuart, *The Discovery of the Oregon Trail*, pp. 284–85; Victor, *The River of the West*, p. 127.

9. William Clark, Journals, 23 July 1806; Beckwourth, *The Life and Adventures of James P. Beckwourth*, pp. 142, 171, 183, 267; Paul Carlson, *The Plains Indians* (College Station: Texas A&M University Press, 1998), p. 44; Denig, *Five Indian Tribes of the Upper Missouri*, pp. 144–45, 147; Larocque, *Journal of Larocque from the Assiniboine to the Yellowstone*, p. 64; Leforge, *Memoirs of a White Crow Indian*, p. 173; Wislizenus, *A Journey to the Rocky Mountains*, p. 154.

10. Carlson, *The Plains Indians*, pp. 51–52, 72.

11. William Clark, Journals, 14 November 1805.

12. Meriwether Lewis, Journals, 9 April 1806.

13. Bradbury, *Travels in the Interior of America*, p. 26 note.

14. Leforge, *Memoirs of a White Crow Indian*, p. 175.

15. Campbell, *A Narrative of Colonel Robert Campbell's Experiences in the Rocky Mountain Fur Trade*, p. 34; Denig, *Five Indian Tribes of the Upper Missouri*, p. 149; Ferris, *Life in the Rocky Mountains*, p. 259; Victor, *The River of the West*, p. 106.

16. Ferris, *Life in the Rocky Mountains*, p. 92; Larocque, *Journal of Larocque from the Assiniboine to the Yellowstone*, pp. 42, 46, 66; Leforge, *Memoirs of a White Crow Indian*, p. 198.

17. James, *Three Years among the Indians*, p. 251.

18. James, *Three Years among the Indians*, p. 94; Anderson, *The Rocky*

Mountain Journals of William Marshall Anderson, pp. 159, 161, 199; De Smet, *Letters and Sketches;* Sage, *Rocky Mountain Life*, p. 87; Tomkins, *Indian Sign Language*, p. 9; Wyeth, "The Correspondence and Journals of Captain Nathaniel J. Wyeth," p. 168.

19. Beckwourth, *The Life and Adventures of James P. Beckwourth,* pp. 290, 379–80; Larpenteur, *Forty Years a Fur Trader on the Upper Missouri*, p. 45; Sage, *Rocky Mountain Life*, p. 122.

20. Beckwourth, *The Life and Adventures of James P. Beckwourth,* pp. 37, 160–61, 175; Ferris, *Life in the Rocky Mountains*, pp. 248, 299; Larocque, *Journal of Larocque from the Assiniboine to the Yellowstone*, p. 62; Larpenteur, *Forty Years a Fur Trader on the Upper Missouri*, p. 408; Leonard, *Narrative of the Adventures of Zenas Leonard*, p. 248; Parker, *Journal of an Exploring Tour beyond the Rocky Mountains,* pp. 194, 235; Sage, *Rocky Mountain Life*, pp. 87–88, 102, 115, 130–31, 360; Townsend, *Narrative of a Journey across the Rocky Mountains*, p. 227; Wyeth, "The Correspondence and Journals of Captain Nathaniel J. Wyeth," pp. 192, 200.

21. James, *Three Years among the Indians*, pp. 96–97.

22. Ferris, *Life in the Rocky Mountains*, p. 283; Leonard, *Narrative of the Adventures of Zenas Leonard*, pp. 50, 58; Miller, *The West of Alfred Jacob Miller*, pp. 156, 160, 182; Sage, *Rocky Mountain Life*, pp. 58, 139, 331; Tomkins, *Indian Sign Language*.

23. De Smet, *Letters and Sketches*, p. 304; Larocque, *Journal of Larocque from the Assiniboine to the Yellowstone*, p. 35; James Ronda, "A Chart in His Way: Indian Cartography and the Lewis and Clark Expedition," *Great Plains Quarterly* 4 no. 1 (Winter 1984): 43–48.

24. Chittenden, *The American Fur Trade of the Far West*, pp. 714–15.

25. Wayne Replogle, *Yellowstone's Bannock Indian Trails* (Yellowstone Park, WY: Yellowstone National Park, 1956); reprinted in Peter Nabokov and Lawrence Loendorf, *American Indians and Yellowstone National Park* (Yellowstone National Park, WY: National Park Service, 2002); Anderson, *The Rocky Mountain Journals of William Marshall Anderson*, p. 138.

26. Anderson, *The Rocky Mountain Journals of William Marshall Anderson*, pp. 82, 96, 178, 186, 188, 190, 192, 200–4; Beckwourth, *The Life and Adventures of James P. Beckwourth,* pp. 38–39; Carson, *Kit Carson's Autobiography*, pp. 30, 138; Irving, *Astoria*, pp. 243, 313; Irving, *The Adven-*

tures of Captain Bonneville, p. 80; Larocque, *Journal of Larocque from the Assiniboine to the Yellowstone*, pp. 48, 51; Russell, *Journal of a Trapper*, pp. 4–5, 102–8; Sage, *Rocky Mountain Life*, pp. 179–80, 208; M. O. Skarsten, *George Drouillard: Hunter and Interpreter for Lewis and Clark, and Fur Trader* (Lincoln: University of Nebraska Press, 2005), pp. 266, 269; Smith, *The Travels of Jedediah Smith*, p. 3; Stuart, *The Discovery of the Oregon Trail*, pp. 129, 292, 294; Townsend, *Narrative of a Journey across the Rocky Mountains*, pp. 212–213; Wislizenus, *A Journey to the Rocky Mountains*, pp. 103, 118; Wyeth, "The Correspondence and Journals of Captain Nathaniel J. Wyeth," pp. 155–58, 170, 172.

27. Ball, *Autobiography of John Ball*, p. 66; De Smet, *Letters and Sketches*, p. 304; Denig, *Five Indian Tribes of the Upper Missouri*, p. 159; Irving, *The Adventures of Captain Bonneville*, p. 80; Larocque, *Journal of Larocque from the Assiniboine to the Yellowstone*, p. 34; Leforge, *Memoirs of a White Crow Indian*, p. 105; Spalding, "A Letter by Henry H. Spalding from the Rocky Mountains," p. 3; Whitman, "Additional Letters," p. 105; Wislizenus, *A Journey to the Rocky Mountains*, pp. 70, 73; Wyeth, *Oregon*, p. 27.

28. Ashley, "William H. Ashley Diary," p. 110; Cox, *Adventures on the Columbia River*, p. 86; John Gale and Roger Nichols, ed., *The Missouri Expedition: 1818–1820* (Norman: University of Oklahoma Press, 1969), p. 46; Irving, *The Adventures of Captain Bonneville*, pp. 277, 299; Leonard, *Narrative of the Adventures of Zenas Leonard*, p. 128; Parker, *Journal of an Exploring Tour beyond the Rocky Mountains,* p. 57; Smith, *The Travels of Jedediah Smith*, pp. 58, 75, 85; Wislizenus, *A Journey to the Rocky Mountains*, p. 29; Wyeth, "The Correspondence and Journals of Captain Nathaniel J. Wyeth," p. 188.

29. Ashley and Smith, *The Ashley-Smith Explorations*, p. 124; Ferris, *Life in the Rocky Mountains*, pp. 76, 194; Irving, *The Adventures of Captain Bonneville*, pp. 169, 372; Leonard, *Narrative of the Adventures of Zenas Leonard*, pp. 23, 40, 124–25; Robert Newell and Dorothy Johansen, ed., *Memoranda: Travles in the Teritory of Missourie* (Portland: Champoeg Press, 1959), pp. 35–36; Alexander Ross and T. C. Elliott, ed., "Journal of Alexander Ross: Snake Country Expedition, 1824," *Quarterly of the Oregon Historical Society* 14 no. 4 (December 1913): 374–78; Sage, *Rocky Mountain Life*, p. 139; Victor, *The River of the West*, p. 223.

30. James, *Three Years among the Indians*, pp. 47–49; Leonard, *Narrative of*

the Adventures of Zenas Leonard, p. 125; Wyeth, "The Correspondence and Journals of Captain Nathaniel J. Wyeth," p. 245.

31. Snowshoes proved essential in deep snow, especially for journeys of great distance. They were standard equipment for natives and frontiersmen in the western plains and mountains. With the use of snowshoes, a good depth of snow actually made paths through the woods easier because it covered rocks and underbrush. Sleighs were used in the same manner to haul equipment. [Campbell, *A Narrative of Colonel Robert Campbell's Experiences in the Rocky Mountain Fur Trade*, pp. 31–33; Carson, *Kit Carson's Autobiography*, p. 40; Harris, *John Colter*, p. 107; Luttig, *Journal of a Fur-Trading Expedition on the Upper Missouri*, p. 104; Russell, *Journal of a Trapper*, p. 68; Smith, *The Travels of Jedediah Smith*, p. 139; Thompson, "David Thompson Journal"; Victor, *The River of the West*, pp. 81, 102.]

32. George Drouillard Map of August 5, 1808, with William Clark inscriptions.

33. George Drouillard Map of September 6, 1808, with William Clark inscriptions.

34. Sage, *Rocky Mountain Life*, pp. 210–11.

35. Denig, *Five Indian Tribes of the Upper Missouri*, p. 139; Irving, *The Adventures of Captain Bonneville*, pp. 225–27; Victor, *The River of the West*, p. 85.

36. George Drouillard Map of August 5, 1808, with William Clark inscriptions.

37. Brackenridge, *Views of Louisiana*, pp. 91–92; George Drouillard Map of August 5, 1808, with William Clark inscriptions; George Drouillard Map of September 6, 1808, with William Clark inscriptions.

Chapter Four: A WINTER TREK AND A RACE FOR LIFE

1. The names that William Clark assigned to landmarks along this stretch of the Yellowstone are visible on his maps from the expedition. [William Clark Maps of 1806, Meriwether Lewis, William Clark, and Reuben Thwaites, *Original Journals of the Lewis and Clark Expedition, 1804–1806*, vol. 8, map numbers 50, 51 (New York: Dodd, Mead and Company, 1904–1905).]

2. The sites traversed by Colter are mentioned in the text by the names used during his time. For modern names, see the Appendix.

3. The child's name was Jean Baptiste Charbonneau, but William Clark fondly nicknamed him Pompey.

4. Bradbury, *Travels in the Interior of America*, pp. 169, 182, 198–99; Carson, *Kit Carson's Autobiography*, p. 65; Chittenden, *The American Fur Trade of the Far West*, pp. 65–66; Irving, *Astoria*, p. 140; Irving, *The Adventures of Captain Bonneville*, pp. 493–94; Larpenteur, *Forty Years a Fur Trader on the Upper Missouri*, pp. 401, 404; Leonard, *Narrative of the Adventures of Zenas Leonard*, p. 263; Luttig, *Journal of a Fur-Trading Expedition on the Upper Missouri*, pp. 144–45; Parker, *Journal of an Exploring Tour beyond the Rocky Mountains,* p. 105; Potts, "To Robert Potts, July 16, 1826," p. 2; Smith, *The Travels of Jedediah Smith*, p. 63.

5. Sam Houston, and Walter Douglas, ed., "Documents: Captain Nathaniel Pryor," *American Historical Review* 24 no. 2 (January 1919): 262.

6. Colter followed the preferred Crow route from the Yellowstone River, up Pryor's Fork, through Pryor Gap, to the upper Clark's Fork. Later trappers made use of the same thoroughfare. [Newell, *Memoranda*, p. 31.]

7. Drouillard noted the presence of Indian camps here. [George Drouillard Map of September 6, 1808, with William Clark inscriptions.]

8. Beckwourth, *The Life and Adventures of James P. Beckwourth,* p. 353; Ferris, *Life in the Rocky Mountains*, p. 145; Larocque, *Journal of Larocque from the Assiniboine to the Yellowstone*, pp. 40, 51; Larpenteur, *Forty Years a Fur Trader on the Upper Missouri*, p. 48; Leforge, *Memoirs of a White Crow Indian*, pp. 85–86; Leonard, *Narrative of the Adventures of Zenas Leonard*, p. 52; Miller, *The West of Alfred Jacob Miller*, pp. 5, 18; Sage, *Rocky Mountain Life*, p. 210; Wislizenus, *A Journey to the Rocky Mountains*, p. 134; Wyeth, *Oregon*, p. 65; Wyeth, "The Correspondence and Journals of Captain Nathaniel J. Wyeth," p. 208.

9. Replogle, *Yellowstone's Bannock Indian Trails*, pp. 307–309.

10. The Crow recognized the seasons of green grass (spring), yellow grass (summer), leaf falling (autumn), and snow falling (winter). [Beckwourth, *The Life and Adventures of James P. Beckwourth,* p. 225; Tomkins, *Indian Sign Language.*]

11. George Drouillard indicated on his map the presence of snow in these mountains. The author has seen patches of snow on the slopes of the Pryor

Mountains in the first few days of October. [George Drouillard Map of September 6, 1808, with William Clark inscriptions.]

12. Drouillard's map indicates that he visited Indian villages in the vicinity of Red Cliffs. [George Drouillard Map of September 6, 1808, with William Clark inscriptions.]

13. William Clark Map of 1810.

14. The George Drouillard Map of September 6, 1808, and the William Clark Map of 1810 correctly located Heart Mountain, but it is incorrectly located on Clark's 1814 map. [William Clark Map of 1814.]

15. George Drouillard Map of September 6, 1808, with William Clark inscriptions; Meriwether Lewis, Journals, 13 August 1805; Fahey, *The Flathead Indians*, p. 21; Ferris, *Life in the Rocky Mountains*, p. 171; Larocque, *Journal of Larocque from the Assiniboine to the Yellowstone*, p. 72; Leforge, *Memoirs of a White Crow Indian*, p. 162; Willis Nelson, "White Mountain, Northwestern Wyoming: A Pseudo-Volcanic Neck," *Geology of the Beartooth Uplift and Adjacent Basins: Montana Geological Society and Yellowstone Bighorn Research Association Joint Field Conference and Symposium* (Billings, Montana: Montana Geological Society, 1986); Parker, *Journal of an Exploring Tour beyond the Rocky Mountains,* p. 74; George Reed, "Dictionary of the Crow Language" (M.A. thesis, Massachusetts Institute of Technology, 1975), pp. 84, 88; West, *Tobacco, Pipes, and Smoking Customs of the American Indians*, pp. 131, 360, 506–7.

16. This mountain crossing from Clark's Fork Canyon, along Dead Indian Creek to Blue Bead Mountain and down Valley River, became misinterpreted on Clark's maps as the crossing of a range. In fact, at this point along the route Colter only ascended and descended a portion of the eastern slope of the massive Absaroka Range. [William Clark Map of 1810; William Clark Map of 1814.]

17. Washington Irving claimed that the area was "held in superstitious awe by the Indians." [William Clark, "Notes on the Chart Obtained from George Drewyard (Drouillard) September 6, 1808"; Meriwether Lewis, William Clark, and Reuben Thwaites, "Miscellaneous Memoranda," *Original Journals of the Lewis and Clark Expedition, 1804–1806*, vol. 6 (New

York: Dodd, Mead and Company, 1904–5), p. 267; Irving, *The Adventures of Captain Bonneville*, p. 236.]

18. Irving, *The Adventures of Captain Bonneville*, pp. 236–37.

19. Later observers provided similar descriptions of Indian bands fording rivers with bison skin floats. [James, *Three Years among the Indians*, p. 90.]

20. Bradbury, *Travels in the Interior of America*, p. 25; Marcy, *Prairie Traveler*, p. 85.

21. Beckwourth, *The Life and Adventures of James P. Beckwourth*, p. 142; Ferris, *Life in the Rocky Mountains*, p. 252; Smith, *The Travels of Jedediah Smith*, p. 24; Whitman, "A Journey across the Plains in 1836," p. 52; Verne Huser, *On the River with Lewis and Clark* (College Station: Texas A&M University Press, 2004), pp. 67–68, 70, 73.

22. Ashley, "William H. Ashley Diary," p. 107; Ball, *Autobiography of John Ball*, p. 79; Irving, *Astoria*, pp. 165–66; Smith, *The Travels of Jedediah Smith*, p. 63; Victor, *The River of the West*, p. 87; Wislizenus, *A Journey to the Rocky Mountains*, p. 59; Wyeth, *Oregon*, pp. 33–34.

23. Campbell, "The Private Journal of Robert Campbell," p. 117; Denig, *Five Indian Tribes of the Upper Missouri*, p. 201; Luttig, *Journal of a Fur-Trading Expedition on the Upper Missouri*, p. 33; Sage, *Rocky Mountain Life*, p. 144; Wyeth, "The Correspondence and Journals of Captain Nathaniel J. Wyeth," pp. 208–9, 217–18; Wyeth, *Oregon*, pp. 25–26.

24. Fahey, *The Flathead Indians*, p. 4.

25. Harris, *John Colter*, p. 95; Irving, *The Adventures of Captain Bonneville*, p. 236; Leonard, *Narrative of the Adventures of Zenas Leonard*, p. 225; Sage, *Rocky Mountain Life*, p. 220.

26. George Drouillard Map of September 6, 1808, with William Clark inscriptions.

27. Castle Rock on the Salt Fork (present-day South Fork of the Shoshone River) should not be confused with Castle Rocks in Pryor Gap.

28. William Clark Map of 1810.

29. Clyman, *James Clyman, Frontiersman*, pp. 20–21; Irving, *The Adventures of Captain Bonneville*, p. 227; Leonard, *Narrative of the Adventures of Zenas Leonard*, p. 255.

30. Irving, *Astoria*, p. 218; Stuart, *The Discovery of the Oregon Trail*,

pp. 286–88; Gary Wright, *A Preliminary Report on the Archaeology of the Jackson Hole Country, Wyoming* (Moose, Wyoming: Grand Teton National Park, 1975), p. 5.

31. In all fairness, those who support the Brooks Lake theory might be doing so in an attempt to explain why Clark drew Lake Biddle as a source of the Bighorn River. But a more likely explanation for this cartographic error is discussed below. Readers are encouraged to make the above-mentioned comparisons between Clark's 1810 manuscript map and modern maps. Yale University's digital copy is accessible online. See Works Cited.

32. Irving, *Astoria*, pp. 221, 225–26; Parker, *Journal of an Exploring Tour beyond the Rocky Mountains,* p. 90; Stuart, *The Discovery of the Oregon Trail,* p. 289; Victor, *The River of the West*, p. 84; John Daugherty, *A Place Called Jackson Hole* (Moose, Wyoming: Grand Teton National Park, 1999), pp. 36–37; Charles Love, "Archaeological Survey of the Jackson Hole Region, Wyoming" (M.A. thesis, University of Wyoming, 1972), p. 29.

33. William Clark, Journals, 5 July 1806; Ferris, *Life in the Rocky Mountains*, pp. 157, 224; Stuart, *The Discovery of the Oregon Trail,* p. 153; Whitman, *A Journey across the Plains in 1836,* p. 51.

34. Daugherty, *A Place Called Jackson Hole*, pp. 26, 33, 37–38.

35. Ferris, *Life in the Rocky Mountains*, p. 204; Irving, *Astoria*, p. 227; Love, "Archaeological Survey of the Jackson Hole Region, Wyoming," p. 31; Stuart, *The Discovery of the Oregon Trail,* pp. 153, 289; Wright, *Archaeology of the Jackson Hole Country,* p. 7; Wyeth, "The Correspondence and Journals of Captain Nathaniel J. Wyeth", p. 158.

36. Russell, *Journal of a Trapper*, p. 15 (see this source for literal transcript); Campbell, *A Narrative of Colonel Robert Campbell's Experiences in the Rocky Mountain Fur Trade*, pp. 29–30; Ferris, *Life in the Rocky Mountains*, pp. 213–14; Irving, *Astoria*, p. 338; Ross, "Journal of Alexander Ross," p. 381; Stuart, *The Discovery of the Oregon Trail,* pp. 152–53, 289; Victor, *The River of the West*, p. 214.

37. Zebulon Pike and Elliott Coues, *The Expeditions of Zebulon Montgomery Pike*, vol. 2 (New York: Francis P. Harper, 1895), p. 574.

38. William Clark, Journals, 3 August 1806.

39. Lewis, Clark, and Thwaites, "Miscellaneous Memoranda," *Original Journals*, vol. 6, p. 267.

40. Fahey, *The Flathead Indians*, p. 21; Larocque, *Journal of Larocque from the Assiniboine to the Yellowstone*, pp. 42, 45, 68, 72; Maximilian, *Travels in the Interior of North America*, p. 96; Richard Oglesby, *Manuel Lisa and the Opening of the Missouri Fur Trade* (Norman: University of Oklahoma Press, 1963), p. 60; Stuart, *The Discovery of the Oregon Trail*, p. 286; Pike, *The Expeditions of Zebulon Montgomery Pike*, p. 524.

41. [Doctor Thomas, "Journal of a Voyage from St. Louis, Louisianna, to the Mandan Village," St. Louis: *Louisiana Gazette* (also known as *Missouri Gazette)*, part 1, November 30, 1809, p. 2]; Doctor Thomas' first name does not appear in the original newspaper accounts of 1809 and 1810. Nor had Donald Jackson discovered the name by 1964, although he speculated that it could have been one of several individuals with the last name Thomas who resided on the frontier at the time. Their first names were Stephen, Peyton, and Thomas. In recent years the name William is sometimes affixed. But the mystery of Dr. Thomas' first name remains unsolved. [Doctor Thomas and Donald Jackson, ed., "Journey to the Mandans, 1809; The Lost Narrative of Dr. Thomas," *Bulletin of the Missouri Historical Society* 20 (April 1964): 182.]

42. Manuel Lisa, "To the Spaniards of New Mexico," September 8, 1812, trans. Herbert Bolton, *Southwestern Historical Quarterly* 17 (July 1913 to April 1914): 63–64.

43. Ferris, *Life in the Rocky Mountains*, pp. 156, 199; Stuart, *The Discovery of the Oregon Trail*, pp. 136–37.

44. William Clark made a cartographic error by confusing the watersheds that drain Pierre's Hole. He accurately showed Crooks River flowing west and south, as Wilson Price Hunt had described. But he drew the Henry's Fork and Snake (Lewis) River flowing west and northwestward, incorrectly. Hunt's party had traveled overland across a divide from Crooks River northwest to Henry's Fort on Henry's Fork. There, Hunt specified that the fort stood "on a tributary of the Columbia." One might assume from this that Crooks River and Henry's River existed in separate watersheds. As such, Clark assigned Crooks River to the next watershed southward, which he incorrectly assumed to be the Rio Grande. As a result, Colter's River also was wrongly assigned to the Rio Grande watershed. [Stuart, *The Discovery of the Oregon Trail*, pp. 152–53.]

45. Carson, *Kit Carson's Autobiography*, p. 24; Irving, *The Adventures of Cap-*

tain Bonneville, p. 469; Sage, *Rocky Mountain Life*, pp. 290–91, 348–49; Victor, *The River of the West*, p. 83.

46. F. M. Fryxell, letter to Arno Cammerer, May 8, 1934, Collections Accession File 63, "The Colter Stone," Grand Teton National Park.

47. [Harris, *John Colter*, pp. 13, 163; Vinton, *John Colter*, p. 29; Aubrey Haines, "John Colter," *The Mountain Men and the Fur Trade of the Far West* (Glendale, CA: Arthur H. Clark Company, 1971), p. 73]; Colter's signature is visible on several documents signed at Three Forks and after his return to St. Louis. Illustrations of these appear in the following source: [L. R. Colter-Frick, *Courageous Colter and Companions* (Washington, MO: By the author, 1997), pp. 99, 113, 123, 136, 143, 144.]

48. Anderson, *The Rocky Mountain Journals of William Marshall Anderson*, p. 210; Russell, *Journal of a Trapper*, pp. 109, 171–72; Sage, *Rocky Mountain Life*, p. 180; Victor, *The River of the West*, pp. 84, 196.

49. Anderson, *The Rocky Mountain Journals of William Marshall Anderson*, pp. 121, 184–85; Cox, *Adventures on the Columbia River*, p. 106; William Clark, Journals, 18 November 1805.

50. Warren Ferris wrote, "Early in April wild geese began to make their appearance—a happy omen to the mountain hunter. The ice soon disappeared from the river, and the days became generally warm and pleasant, though the nights were still extremely cold." [Ferris, *Life in the Rocky Mountains*, p. 74.]

51. Daugherty, *A Place Called Jackson Hole*, pp. 35, 38.

52. Love, *Archaeological Survey of the Jackson Hole Region,* pp. 29, 33, 120; Deward Walker, "An Assessment of American Indian Occupation and Uses of the Cultural and Natural Resources of Grand Teton National Park" (Boulder, CO: Walker Research Group, 2007), pp. 91–92; Wright, *Archaeology of the Jackson Hole Country,* pp. 3–4, 50, 56–59; Daugherty, *A Place Called Jackson Hole*, pp. 26, 36–37; Grand Teton Quadrangle, 1899, Wyoming Historical Topographic Maps, Perry-Castaneda Library, University of Texas Libraries, Austin, Texas.

53. James, *Three Years among the Indians*, p. 62.

54. [Vinton, *John Colter*, pp. 57–58]; William Clark's 1810 map provides the primary evidence for Colter's winter route of 1807–8. Colter conveyed information that allowed Clark to mark the path sufficiently well so that it

can be reconstructed on a modern map. Still, Clark's map presents several difficulties. He began drawing it in 1806 as a composite sketch of firsthand observations with the Corps of Discovery. For the next several years he added information acquired from others, some valid, some exaggerated. As he received new information, he often forced it to fit the map's preexisting composition, causing distortions. Because of this, the eastern portion of the map covered by Colter's route appears oversized and the western portion undersized. On the western portion, Teton Pass, Lake Jackson, Lake Yellowstone, and the Bannock Trail Crossing at Hot Spring Brimstone closely match modern maps in distance and orientation. But there is variation in cardinal directions. This may be attributed to increased magnetic variation in the western United States that affected compass readings. To add to the confusion, Clark's 1810 map contains certain stylistic features that do not conform to geographic reality, such as mountain ranges depicted in uniformly narrow widths. Clark misrepresented the Absaroka Mountains as a single, narrow chain ranging from southeast to northwest. The Absaroka is actually a broad range dissected by several major valleys. But considering the paucity of information available to Clark and the fact that he never saw the land south of the Yellowstone River, his depictions are surprisingly accurate. As a river man, he was most interested in documenting arteries for transportation and trade. The accurate depiction of mountain ranges was of secondary importance to him. Drouillard's earlier map of September 6, 1808, offers a rather accurate supplement to the eastern portion of Clark's 1810 map.

55. Harris, *John Colter*, p. 81.

56. Daugherty, *A Place Called Jackson Hole*, pp. 36–37; Aubrey Haines, *Yellowstone National Park: Its Exploration and Establishment* (Washington: US Department of the Interior, National Park Service, 1974), p. 5.

57. Gustavus Doane, Orrin Bonney, and Lorraine Bonney, *Battle Drums and Geysers: The Life and Journals of Lt. Gustavus Cheyney Doane* (Chicago: Swallow Press, 1970), pp. 247–49.

58. Aubrey Haines, who worked for the National Park Service out of Bozeman, Montana, provided a similar description in 1971: "There are manifestations of volcanism at the ford—a group of tepid springs near the mouth of Tower Creek, on the west bank, and an odiferous area of fumeroles known

locally as 'the sulphur beds,' on the east bank. This feature, which extends several hundred yards above and below the crossing, has no counterpart at any other ford on the Yellowstone River. It is the best evidence we have that John Colter did pass through what is now Yellowstone National Park and should be known as its discoverer." [Haines, *John Colter,* p. 80; Harris, *John Colter,* p. 112; Henry Heasler, letter to David Marshall, 30 August 2012.]

59. Haines, *Yellowstone National Park,* pp. 4–5.

60. Replogle, *Yellowstone's Bannock Indian Trails,* p. 310.

61. Russell, *Journal of a Trapper,* pp. 26–27.

62. The Soda Butte geothermal formation, from which the Soda Butte River gets its name, was not yet formed at the time Colter passed this way.

63. Replogle, *Yellowstone's Bannock Indian Trails,* p. 311.

64. [William Clark, "Notes on the Chart Obtained from George Drewyard (Drouillard) September 6, 1808"]; The George Drouillard Map of September 6, 1808, correctly shows Gap Creek flowing into the Stinking Water River upstream from the Stinking Water's juncture with the Bighorn River. Drouillard followed this route to visit the Ap-sha-roo-kee villages, and Colter most likely did the same. The William Clark Map of 1810 differs from Drouillard's map at this point. Clark erroneously shows Gap Creek flowing into the Bighorn River and Colter's route ascending Gap Creek from there. He was probably confused by Colter's account of descending the Stinking Water to reach the Bighorn, then returning upstream to ascend Gap Creek. It appears that Clark simply misunderstood and omitted the return up the Stinking Water to the mouth of Gap Creek.

65. Chittenden, *The American Fur Trade of the Far West,* p. 717.

66. Denig, *Five Indian Tribes of the Upper Missouri,* p. 144; John C. Calhoun, "To Thomas Smith, March 16, 1818," reprinted in John Gale and Roger Nichols, ed., *The Missouri Expedition: 1818–1820* (Norman: University of Oklahoma Press, 1969), p. 90; John C. Calhoun, "To Henry Atkinson, March 27, 1819," reprinted in Gale and Nichols, *The Missouri Expedition: 1818–1820,* p. 96; Andrew Jackson, "To Henry Atkinson, May 15, 1819," reprinted in Gale and Nichols, *The Missouri Expedition: 1818–1820,* p. 96.

67. Beckwourth, *The Life and Adventures of James P. Beckwourth,* pp. 93, 310; Carson, *Kit Carson's Autobiography,* p. 98; Catlin, *North Ameri-*

can Indians, vol. 1, p. 48; Irving, *The Adventures of Captain Bonneville*, pp. 244–45, 420; Maximilian, *Travels in the Interior of North America*, p. 96; Pierre Menard, "Letter to Pierre Chouteau from Three Forks of the Missouri, April 21, 1810," reprinted in Hiram Chittenden, *The American Fur Trade of the Far West* (Stanford, CA: Academic Reprints, 1954), vol. 2, p. 897; Miller, *The West of Alfred Jacob Miller*, p. 148; Sage, *Rocky Mountain Life*, p. 210; Townsend, *Narrative of a Journey across the Rocky Mountains*, p. 214.

68. [James, *Three Years among the Indians*, pp. 52–54]; Thomas James indicated that the site was within a day's march of Three Forks; Henry Brackenridge later recounted the event when he said that upon Colter's return from the long winter trek, "A party of Indians in whose company he happened to be, was attacked, and he was lamed by a severe wound in the leg." [Brackenridge, *Views of Louisiana*, p. 92]; Frontiersmen were almost always complimentary toward the Flatheads and Nez Perces and held them in high esteem for their valor and ethical values. William Anderson called them "remarkable for their . . . honesty, veracity, and every moral virtue." They "despise and discountenance lying, stealing and begging." In particular, the Flatheads had a reputation for courage, kindness, and a sense of justice. Moreover, they seemed to be happy people who "enjoyed jokes and laughter." [Anderson, *The Rocky Mountain Journals of William Marshall Anderson*, p. 132; Fahey, *The Flathead Indians*, p. 16; Wyeth, *Oregon*, pp. 53–54; Wyeth, "The Correspondence and Journals of Captain Nathaniel J. Wyeth," pp. 192–93, 201.]

69. Stallo Vinton established that Colter departed for Three Forks with John Potts sometime after July 7, 1808. [Vinton, *John Colter*, p. 80.]

70. Beckwourth, *The Life and Adventures of James P. Beckwourth,* p. 129; Campbell, *A Narrative of Colonel Robert Campbell's Experiences in the Rocky Mountain Fur Trade*, pp. 22–23.

71. John Potts had similar interests in trapping and trading. Drouillard's September 6, 1808, map shows a site on the Yellowstone River midway between the Bighorn River and Pompey's Tower labeled "Potts' Establishment." This was probably a small post erected by John Potts upriver from Manuel's Fort. Like Colter, Potts was a free trapper and trader. As such, he was free to operate independently of Manuel Lisa's venture. The establish-

ment probably did not exist when Colter passed through at the beginning of his trek in October 1807, but was likely there upon his return the following spring. Clark's 1810 map shows a simple mark that appears to represent the post.

72. Meriwether Lewis, Journals, 22 April 1806.

73. William Clark, Journals, 13 July 1806; John Ordway, Journals, 26 July 1806.

74. Thomas James provided the most accurate account of Colter's Run. He is the only chronicler who received an on-site description of the event from Colter, and his narrative matches the topography of the site perfectly. [James, *Three Years among the Indians*, pp. 56–63.]

75. Colter and Potts perhaps assumed that the Blackfoot bands had migrated north. Or they might have considered it unlikely that they would cross paths in the vast landscape. After all, the Corps of Discovery had crossed and recrossed the Three Forks previously without seeing any sign of them. Even so, according to John Bradbury, they remained cautious. Bradbury, in recounting the event, said, "Aware of the hostility of the Blackfeet Indians, one of whom had been killed by [Meriwether] Lewis, they set their traps at night, and took them up early in the morning, remaining concealed during the day. They were examining their traps early one morning" when a war party appeared. [John Bradbury, *Travels in the Interior of America* (London: Sherwood, Neely, and Jones, 1819), pp. 25–29.]

76. In this account, Colter only anticipated robbery, whereas John Bradbury's account suggests that the Blackfoot held a lasting enmity for white Americans because Meriwether Lewis and Reubin Field had killed two of their warriors two years earlier. Some historians claim that Colter caused the animosity when he was escorting Flatheads to Manuel's Fort a few months earlier and resisted a fierce Blackfoot attack. But Blackfoot hostility is better explained by the tribe's warlike nature, the British encouragement of Blackfoot aggression, and Blackfoot resentment toward American traders who supplied weapons to their traditional enemies—the Crow, Shoshone, Flathead, and Nez Perce. [Campbell, *A Narrative of Colonel Robert Campbell's Experiences in the Rocky Mountain Fur Trade*, p. 25; Dale Morgan, ed., *The West of William Ashley* (Denver: Old West Publishing Company, 1964), p. xxxv.]

77. In 1808, the Blackfoot could have been armed with either guns or arrows. The natives of the northern plains and mountains had a substantial number of guns by the time Colter arrived among them. In 1805, François Larocque had observed the weaponry of 645 warriors of the Rocky Mountain tribes and determined that they owned a total of 204 guns. The Blackfoot would have been much better armed with rifles due to their long-established trade with the British. [Larocque, *Journal of Larocque from the Assiniboine to the Yellowstone*, pp. 22, 27]; John Bradbury said the Blackfoot shot Potts with arrows: "He was instantly pierced with arrows so numerous, that, to use the language of Colter, 'he was made a riddle of.'"

78. Butchering a person and throwing the internal organs into the face of their surviving friends was an act of derision practiced by Plains Indians toward their enemies. [Leonard, *Narrative of the Adventures of Zenas Leonard*, pp. 245–46.]

79. The Blackfoot prided themselves on being fast runners. They were known to chase down bison on foot in the springtime when bison hooves sank into the prairie mud, causing the beasts to founder. Twenty-six years after Colter's run, Joe Meek was chased by a Blackfoot band on foot and reportedly said, "Them Blackfeet are powerful runners—no better than us mountain-men, though." [Irving, *The Adventures of Captain Bonneville*, p. 482; Victor, *The River of the West*, p. 172.]

80. John Bradbury reported that Colter "was considered by the hunters as remarkably swift."

81. John Bradbury noted that Colter had to "traverse a plain six miles in breadth, abounding with the prickly pear, on which he was every instant treading with his naked feet." Prickly pear still abounds in the area.

82. Doctor Thomas claimed that "he hid in a beaver dam." John Bradbury, on the other hand, said, "There was an island, against the upper point of which a raft of drift timber had lodged. He dived under the raft, and after several efforts, got his head above water amongst the trunks of trees, covered over with smaller wood to the depth of several feet. Scarcely had he secured himself, when the Indians arrived on the river, screeching and yelling, as Colter expressed it, 'like so many devils.'" Whether a beaver lodge, dam, or drift timber, all agree that Colter found refuge under a pile of brush in the river. [Doctor Thomas, "Journal of a Voyage from St. Louis, Louisi-

anna, to the Mandan Village," Pittsburgh: *Pittsburgh Gazette*, part 2, July 13, 1810, p. 2.]

83. Thomas James clearly stated that Colter, after leaving his hideout, "hastened towards the mountain gap or ravine, about thirty miles above on the river." This could only be Bozeman Gap thirty miles up the Gallatin River east fork. He then climbed the mountain "four miles below the gap and hastened on the open plain towards Manuel's fort on the Big Horn, about three hundred miles ahead in the northeast." This description fits the topography of the open plains along the Yellowstone River and, at about three hundred miles, provides the shortest and easiest route to reach the fort. In his condition, Colter certainly would take this route, Blackfoot country or not. Besides, the Blackfoot threat did not easily deter him, as he demonstrated by returning a couple months later and again the following year. However, a recent study claims that, although naked, limping, and starving, he opted for a more circuitous and rugged route, wandering as far south as Tower Falls and Dead Indian Pass, crossing the Gallatin Range and the entire breadth of the massive Absaroka Range, then returning to Manuel's Fort along a route that would have required about four hundred miles. This theory does not match Thomas James' account.

84. Doctor Thomas said Colter made his journey "without even mowkasons to protect him from the prickly pear, which covered the country, subsisting on such berries as providence threw in his way." John Bradbury specified that he "subsisted on a root much esteemed by the Indians of the Missouri, now known by naturalists as *Psoralea esculenta.*" This plant, commonly known as prairie turnip, was a staple of the Plains Indians.

85. Washington Irving said that, despite being crippled by thorns and exhausted by starvation, "he pushed resolutely forward." Dogged determination was one of Colter's defining characteristics. [Irving, *Astoria*, p. 121.]

86. By 1830 the story of Colter's Run had been published several times and had already emerged as a western American classic.

87. [James, *Three Years among the Indians*, pp. 63–64]; Thomas James' description suggests that Colter camped on the north bank of the Gallatin River east fork near Bozeman Gap.

88. When Colter left the Crow and traveled downriver to the village of the Hidatsa (Gros Ventre of the Missouri River), he was simply moving from

one branch of family to another. The Crow and Hidatsa had once been one nation, and kinship loyalties remained. [Beckwourth, *The Life and Adventures of James P. Beckwourth*, p. 245.]

89. Thomas, "Journal of a Voyage from St. Louis," part 1, p. 2.

90. John Bradbury and Henry Brackenridge, "From Mr. Bradbury and Mr. Brackenridge, lately arrived from the Mandan villages," St. Louis: *Louisiana Gazette* [also known as *Missouri Gazette*], August 8, 1811, p. 3.

91. James, *Three Years among the Indians*, pp. 29–30.

Chapter Five: A BEAUTIFUL, HOSTILE LAND

1. Meriwether Lewis, Journals, 17 September 1804.

2. Meriwether Lewis, Journals, 31 May 1805.

3. Meriwether Lewis, Journals, 13 and 14 June 1805.

4. William Clark, Journals, 12 July 1804.

5. William Clark, Journals, 7 May 1806.

6. James, *Three Years among the Indians*, pp. 67–68.

7. Russell, *Journal of a Trapper*, pp. 27–28, 63, 118; Anderson, *The Rocky Mountain Journals of William Marshall Anderson*, pp. 129, 205; Ball, *Autobiography of John Ball*, pp. 75, 92; Beckwourth, *The Life and Adventures of James P. Beckwourth*, pp. 47, 60; Leonard, *Narrative of the Adventures of Zenas Leonard*, p. 5; Miller, *The West of Alfred Jacob Miller*, pp. 81, 172; Victor, *The River of the West*, p. 136.

8. [Anderson, *The Rocky Mountain Journals of William Marshall Anderson*, p. 176; Fahey, *The Flathead Indians*, pp. 3-4; Sage, *Rocky Mountain Life*, pp. 72, 79–80, 332; Townsend, *Narrative of a Journey across the Rocky Mountains*, pp. 218, 244; Wislizenus, *A Journey to the Rocky Mountains*, p. 74; Wyeth, "The Correspondence and Journals of Captain Nathaniel J. Wyeth," pp. 163, 244]; The feist and dachshund were both small hunting dogs—one on the American frontier and one in Germany. These dogs offered the best comparisons that Clark and Wislizenus could make to describe the coyote.

9. James, *Three Years among the Indians*, pp. 38–39.

10. [James, *Three Years among the Indians*, pp. 76–77, 84–86]; The grizzly bear was known by various names in the early nineteenth century. The

men of the Corps of Discovery and later western travelers often referred to grizzlies as white bears. Perhaps this was a simple means of distinguishing them from the better-known black bears. Or maybe the name came from the white or light gray tips of hair that often appear on their backs, or from the blond fur that is quite common among them. As late as 1857, Philip Cooke referred to the bruin as "the white, or more properly, the gray or grizzly bear."

11. Clyman, *James Clyman, Frontiersman*, p. 18.

12. This account of Hugh Glass' grizzly bear encounter is a composite of the records left by George Yount (as dictated to Orange Clark), Philip Cooke, and Alphonso Wetmore. The preferred primary account is that of Yount. Warren Ferris also provided a lively story of Hugh Glass. [Camp, "The Chronicles of George C. Yount," pp. 26–28, 30–32; Cooke, *Scenes and Adventures in the Army*, p. 141; Ferris, *Life in the Rocky Mountains*, pp. 315–17; Wetmore, *The Missouri Trapper,* pp. 297–300.]

13. Anderson, *The Rocky Mountain Journals of William Marshall Anderson*, pp. 181–82; Carson, *Kit Carson's Autobiography*, p. 38; Cooke, *Scenes and Adventures in the Army*, p. 136; Cox, *Adventures on the Columbia River*, p. 213; Sage, *Rocky Mountain Life*, p. 156; Victor, *The River of the West*, pp. 91–92, 220.

14. Ferris, *Life in the Rocky Mountains*, p. 315; Miller, *The West of Alfred Jacob Miller*, p. 107; Smith, *The Travels of Jedediah Smith*, pp. 68, 76; Townsend, *Narrative of a Journey across the Rocky Mountains*, p. 185.

15. Catlin, *North American Indians*, vol. 1, p. 30; Cox, *Adventures on the Columbia River*, p. 82; Leonard, *Narrative of the Adventures of Zenas Leonard*, p. 224; Sage, *Rocky Mountain Life*, pp. 114, 132.

16. Ross, "Journal of Alexander Ross," p. 372; Sage, *Rocky Mountain Life*, pp. 135, 144; Townsend, *Narrative of a Journey across the Rocky Mountains*, pp. 238–39; Whitman, "A Journey across the Plains in 1836," p. 40; Wyeth, "The Correspondence and Journals of Captain Nathaniel J. Wyeth," pp. 189, 205.

17. Anderson, *The Rocky Mountain Journals of William Marshall Anderson*, p. 77; Catlin, *North American Indians*, vol. 1, p. 51; Irving, *The Adventures of Captain Bonneville*, p. 249; Maximilian, *Travels in the Interior of North America*, p. 104; Miller, *The West of Alfred Jacob Miller*, p. 128; Munger

and Munger, *Diary of Asahel Munger and Wife*, pp. 390, 394; Sage, *Rocky Mountain Life*, pp. 135–36; Tomkins, *Indian Sign Language*; Victor, *The River of the West*, pp. 190, 210; Wislizenus, *A Journey to the Rocky Mountains*, p. 140.

18. Anderson, *The Rocky Mountain Journals of William Marshall Anderson*, p. 206; Cox, *Adventures on the Columbia River*, p. 82; Luttig, *Journal of a Fur-Trading Expedition on the Upper Missouri*, p. 48; Parker, *Journal of an Exploring Tour beyond the Rocky Mountains*, p. 62; Sage, *Rocky Mountain Life*, p. 356; Townsend, *Narrative of a Journey across the Rocky Mountains*, p. 174; Victor, *The River of the West*, p. 137.

19. Irving, *Astoria*, p. 117.

20. Brackenridge, *Views of Louisiana*, p. 92.

21. James, *Three Years among the Indians*, pp. 41, 64; Ball, *Autobiography of John Ball*, pp. 73, 83; Miller, *The West of Alfred Jacob Miller*, pp. 119, 156; Munger and Munger, *Diary of Asahel Munger and Wife*, p. 397; Wislizenus, *A Journey to the Rocky Mountains*, p. 123.

22. Beckwourth, *The Life and Adventures of James P. Beckwourth*, p. 256; Carson, *Kit Carson's Autobiography*, p. 26; Parker, *Journal of an Exploring Tour beyond the Rocky Mountains*, p. 77; Wislizenus, *A Journey to the Rocky Mountains*, p. 87.

23. Despite his three escapes through the pass and the terrible blizzard he encountered there, Colter favored the gap as a worthy route to the rich valley of the Three Forks. He recommended it to Henry Brackenridge as a potential wagon road. Brackenridge wrote, "The course of the Rocky mountains, is . . . about the same length with the Allegheny mountain, but much higher, and more resembling the Alps, or Andes. . . . At the head of the Gallatin Fork . . . it is found less difficult to cross than the Allegheny mountains; Coulter [sic], a celebrated hunter and woodsman, informed me, that a loaded waggon [sic] would find no obstruction in passing." Interstate 90 now follows the route. [Henry Brackenridge, "Sketches of the Territory of Louisiana," St. Louis: *Louisiana Gazette* (also known as *Missouri Gazette*), April 18, 1811, p. 2.]

24. Upon his arrival at Three Forks, Pierre Menard recognized the immense number of beavers and the need to enlist the Blackfoot as trade partners. To this end, he planned to capture some Blackfoot prisoners, treat them

well, and release them in the hope of establishing goodwill and commerce with the Blackfoot nation. [Menard, "Letter to Pierre Chouteau from Three Forks of the Missouri," vol. 2, pp. 897–98]; Lt. James Bradley visited the site of Henry's Fort in 1870 and reported, "The outlines of the fort were still intact . . . enclosing an area of about 300 feet square, situated upon the tongue of land (at that point a half mile wide) between the Jefferson and Madison Rivers about two miles above their confluence, upon the south bank of a channel now called Jefferson Slough." [James, *Three Years among the Indians*, p. 55.]

25. James, *Three Years among the Indians*, pp. 54–55, 69–70, 72–73, 75.

26. James, *Three Years among the Indians*, pp. 82–83.

Epilogue: HOME TO THE SHADY BLUFF

1. Vinton, *John Colter*, pp. 100–1; Carson, *Kit Carson's Autobiography*, pp. 40, 62; Victor, *The River of the West*, p. 88.

2. By 1828, of the thirty-two members of the Corps of Discovery, seven had been killed, including at least three—Potts, Drouillard, and Collins—at the hands of the Blackfoot and Arikara. In addition, Colter had barely escaped the Blackfoot, and Pryor and Shannon had almost lost their lives to the Arikara. Shannon was wounded by them and had a leg amputated. Pryor later had close brushes with the Sauk and Winnebago, and lost substantial property to the Winnebago and Cherokee. Besides the seven members killed, ten others had died of various causes by 1828. These included Meriwether Lewis, John Ordway, and Sacagawea. The whereabouts of five members were unknown. Of the remaining ten, five lived on the extreme frontier west of the Mississippi River, and at least four of the other five lived on the Ohio River Valley frontier. There is much debate over Sacagawea's date of death. John Luttig, while visiting the Mandan villages, recorded in his journal entry of December 20, 1812: "This evening the wife of Charbonneau, a Snake squaw, died of a putrid fever. She was a good and the best woman in the fort, aged about twenty-five years. She left a fine infant girl." William Clark listed her as *Dead* in his report dated c. 1825–28. [Luttig, *Journal of a Fur-Trading Expedition on the Upper Missouri*, pp. 106, 133–

34; Lewis, Clark, and Jackson, *Letters of the Lewis and Clark Expedition*, p. 638.]

3. Anderson, *The Rocky Mountain Journals of William Marshall Anderson*, p. 217; Brackenridge, *Views of Louisiana*, p. 205; Irving, *The Adventures of Captain Bonneville*, pp. 420, 430; Wyeth, "The Correspondence and Journals of Captain Nathaniel J. Wyeth," pp. 215, 218.

4. Bradbury, *Travels in the Interior of America*, p. 24.

5. William Clark specifically stated on the August 5, 1808, map that Drouillard made the sketch. Clark's "Notes on the Chart" suggested that Drouillard also drew the second map and presented it to him on September 6, 1808. Clark, however, added the inscriptions on both maps and wrote the attached notes for the second map. They appear in his handwriting. [George Drouillard Map of August 5, 1808, with William Clark inscriptions; George Drouillard Map of September 6, 1808, with William Clark inscriptions; William Clark, "Notes on the Chart Obtained from George Drewyard (Drouillard) September 6, 1808."]

6. [William Clark Map of 1810; William Clark Map of 1814]; William Clark's map of 1814 is most useful for clarifying information on the 1810 map that is difficult to see. In particular, it can be used to distinguish the dotted line representing Colter's route from that marking the trail of Wilson Price Hunt in Jackson and Pierre's Hole. A high-resolution copy of the map may be viewed online. See Works Cited.

7. Chittenden, *The American Fur Trade of the Far West*, p. 722.

8. Henry Brackenridge traveled upriver soon after John Bradbury. Brackenridge was with Manuel Lisa's 1811 expedition, which was hurrying to catch up with the larger Wilson Price Hunt expedition for the sake of protection from the Indians. Brackenridge and Bradbury later met at the Mandan villages and descended the river together. After his return to St. Louis, Bradbury relocated to New Madrid, Missouri, where he witnessed the massive New Madrid earthquake on December 16, 1811. [Henry Brackenridge, "To Mr. Joseph Charless," St. Louis: *Louisiana Gazette* (also known as *Missouri Gazette*), August 8, 1811, p. 3.]

9. [Bradbury, *Travels in the Interior of America*, pp. 24–28]; Historians have reasonably established that Colter married a lady named Sarah Loucy (maiden name unknown), who went by the name Sally. The marriage date

is unknown, but occurred just before Bradbury's visit in March 1811. Colter also had a son named Hiram, who later applied for the land warrant his father had received for service in the Corps of Discovery. [Colter-Frick, *Courageous Colter*.]

10. Colter, a neighbor of Nathan Boone, enlisted with Boone's Mounted Rangers on March 3, 1812, for the purpose of building defensive forts to protect against Indian attacks. He died two months later, on May 7. L. R. Colter-Frick recently verified that printed military records which appear in Carter's *The Territorial Papers of the United States* under the name John Cotter are actually those of John Colter. She determined this by searching the original handwritten service records from which the printed records were copied. Despite Colter's death in May 1812, the settlement of his estate did not begin until November 1813, which has caused several historians to surmise a date of death in that month and year. A notice regarding the settlement of Colter's estate was dated November 26, 1813, and appeared in the *Missouri Gazette* on December 11, 1813. [James, *Three Years among the Indians*, p. 65; Clarence Carter, ed., *The Territorial Papers of the United States*, vol. 14 (Washington: United States Government Printing Office, 1949), pp. 560–61; Colter-Frick, *Courageous Colter*, p. 137; Daniel Richardson, "Notice," St. Louis: *Missouri Gazette*, December 11, 1813, p. 1.]

11. Vinton, *John Colter*, p. 26.

ACKNOWLEDGMENTS

My sincere thanks to friends and colleagues who offered editorial assistance, and to Texas Tech University for providing generous research opportunities. I am indebted to the Amon Carter Museum of American Art in Fort Worth for the use of reproductions from its excellent collection of early nineteenth century frontier paintings.

A special thanks to Alan Bean and Jonathan Jarvis for their encouraging words. Captain Bean was an Apollo 12 and Skylab II astronaut, and is one of only twelve individuals who share the distinction of standing on the moon. Beyond this, Alan is one of the nicest people you could meet—a real "down to Earth" person who is quick to laugh and share a story. Jonathan Jarvis was Director of the National Park Service from his 2009 Presidential appointment and Senate confirmation until his retirement in 2017. He is an avid outdoorsman who has wandered many trails in the manner of Colter.

Above all, I am grateful for the love and support of my wife and best friend, Vicki, in whose memory this book is dedicated. Always patient and undaunted, she remained my constant companion throughout the West and around the world in pursuit of research and adventure.

INDEX